BASEBALL HEAVEN

BASEBALL HEAVEN

Up Close and Personal,
What It Was Really Like in the Major Leagues

PETER GOLENBOCK

ROWMAN & LITTLEFIELD
Lanham • Boulder • New York • London

Published by Rowman & Littlefield
An imprint of The Rowman & Littlefield Publishing Group, Inc.
4501 Forbes Boulevard, Suite 200, Lanham, Maryland 20706
www.rowman.com

86-90 Paul Street, London EC2A 4NE, United Kingdom

Distributed by NATIONAL BOOK NETWORK

British Library Cataloguing in Publication Information Available

Library of Congress Cataloging-in-Publication Data Available

ISBN 978-1-5381-8182-9 (cloth : alk. paper) | ISBN 978-1-5381-8183-6 (ebook)

♾™ The paper used in this publication meets the minimum requirements of
American National Standard for Information Sciences—Permanence of Paper for
Printed Library Materials, ANSI/NISO Z39.48-1992.

When I first started in this business in 1972, I was aided by two of the finest writers in the game, Roger Kahn and Bob Lipsyte. We met in the New York Yankees PR office while I was doing my initial research for *Dynasty*. They provided advice and inspiration. Roger is gone now, and I never had the chance to properly thank him. Bob, who wrote the foreword to this book, continues to be an inspiration. In his own quiet, modest way, he has been the finest sports journalist for the past fifty years. For all they have done for me, I dedicate this book to them.

CONTENTS

FOREWORD

To really love baseball, you need to really love baseball players and you can't really do that if they are your gambling chips or the people—nice guys, screwballs, assholes, doesn't matter—who get credit for loving, hating, jaking, in a personal relationship with the game that has grown out of childhood catches with Dad or a craftsman's quest for the perfect cutter or a coldhearted mercenary's pursuit of major bank.

But you're never going to find out who they really are from those ESPN transactional reporters or those bland broadcasters who work for the franchise or your own projections about your dreamboys. The true story hinted at on the back of the bubblegum cards needs to come from their own words, especially those teased out by the sympathetic knack of Peter Golenbock to draw pathos, hilarity, classified info, and so many surprises from the outfield corners of their psyche.

Here is Dock Ellis, famous for pitching a no-hitter while floating on LSD, years later terrified as a Senior League starter that his skills would desert him now that he was sober. Here are tales of Leo Durocher, all-star criminal and henchman of actor George Raft, who stole money and a watch from roommate Babe Ruth. And the baseball commissioner Happy Chandler, a former governor of Kentucky who has often been characterized as a buffoon when he was actually a hero, run out of baseball as payback for his courage standing up to the owners' 15–1 vote to keep Jackie Robinson out of the major leagues.

All of this and way more lies ahead in this wonderful mosaic of the game. Golenbock has been astonishing and delighting us—and himself, I'm sure—for many seasons now, ever since after a cup of coffee at the law trade he wrote *Dynasty*, the seminal book about the Yankee glory years and the best-selling *The Bronx Zoo*, the amazing tale of the Bombers in disarray.

Golenbock has successfully strayed into football and car racing and national politics, but he owns the soul of baseball, from his wildly original (and viciously attacked) novel of Mickey Mantle in heaven (my fave) to his equally unexpected interview of underhand Red Sox pitcher Elden Auker, who leads off this book. Elden who?

Well, there is Golenbock's genius at work, first digging up the obscure submarine baller and then getting him to talk so freely about his roommate, the Babe, as well as Ruth's ex-roommate, Durocher the thief. How does he do it? Go talk to Golenbock yourself. You'll tell him everything. One can only imagine the old pitcher eager to please the wide-eyed enthusiast as has hundreds of other ballplayers to our everlasting joy.

Not to quibble, but if only Golenbock had been able to talk to the Babe . . .

—Robert Lipsyte

INTRODUCTION

I have loved the game since I was a child. I grew up in Stamford, Connecticut, a forty-five-minute train ride and then a subway ride on the Lex to Yankee Stadium. Beginning when I was three years old, the Yankees won the pennant almost every year until I was eighteen and in college.

When I was thirteen, I went to the Stamford library where I came upon a book in the sports section by Frank Graham titled *The New York Yankees*. It was written in 1947 and in it were conversations with Babe Ruth, Lou Gehrig, and Joe DiMaggio. I learned about managers Miller Huggins and Joe McCarthy, and I was overwhelmed by how much the book meant to me because what it told me more than anything else was what *really* was going on behind the scenes. It was factual gossip, and I was hooked and glued to the pages.

After I graduated from St. Luke's School in New Canaan, Connecticut, where headmaster Dr. Joseph R. Kidd made me religiously memorize *The Century Handbook of Writing*, which still sits behind my desk, I went to Dartmouth College, where I became the sports editor of the *Dartmouth*, the daily newspaper. As a freshman I wrote varsity football, and I had a weekly column, Dartmouth Sports Today, in which mostly I lionized our athletes.

Former star Yankee third baseman Red Rolfe was Dartmouth's athletic director, and I idolized him. I would go into his office, and he would tell me stories about his teammates including Joe DiMaggio and Bill Dickey. He was in uniform on the field the day a dying Lou Gehrig proclaimed he was "the luckiest man on the face of the earth." I wish I had taped those conversations.

My choice was either to go to Vietnam or to New York University Law School, and I chose law school, and while there I worked a deal with my friend Bob Kennedy, son of J. Walter Kennedy, the NBA commissioner.

Bob was the sports editor of the *Stamford Advocate*. If he would give me press credentials, I said, I would write him articles on the weekends for free. He agreed.

I then had access to all the professional New York teams: the Yankees, Mets, Giants, Jets, Knicks, Rangers, Islanders, and Cosmos with Pele. I interviewed the likes of OJ Simpson, Joe Namath, and Andy Bathgate. The Knicks' Phil Jackson and I became close friends.

After I somehow graduated from law school, I took a job working for a law firm in Manhattan. I was handed a tall pile of tort cases and told to go through them. I discovered that in a dozen cases, mostly trip and fall and minor injury cases, the ten-year statute of limitations had run out. In other words, because of the firm's lack of interest, their clients were no longer legally allowed to sue.

I asked one of the partners what I should do.

"Call them up and tell them why they don't have a case," he said.

"I quit," I said.

I went home and opened the *New York Times* want ads section for employment. One said: "WANTED: A lawyer and a writer for our publication." At the end was a 201 area code and a telephone number. New Jersey.

I lived in a tiny apartment in the Roger Williams Hotel in Manhattan. I figured I could drive there.

I called. The woman who answered said I was calling Prentice-Hall, located in Englewood Cliffs. They were looking for an associate editor for a new monthly publication about President Richard Nixon's wage and price controls. Was I interested?

I drove to Englewood Cliffs and was hired. The job paid $7,500 a year.

Beginning in July 1972, I pondered the new regulations relating to wages and prices. My job was to translate them into English for the weekly Prentice-Hall publication that went to banks and to interested corporations.

I discovered rather quickly that when any union or group of employees wanted to raise their wages, they were turned down. At the same time when a company wanted to hike prices, the Wage and Control Board approved their action.

Something is really wrong about this, I thought.

After six weeks, I was ready for something new.

Before lunch one day, I happened to run across a catalog of Prentice-Hall's trade books. One was *Ah-One, Ah-Two,* by Lawrence Welk. Another was *Where the Money Is,* by the infamous bank robber Willie Sutton. There was another nice book by New York Giants lineman Steve Wright titled *I'd Rather Be Wright.*

This might be my chance to write the sequel to Frank Graham's New York Yankees, I mulled. I walked downstairs to the white-walled offices of the trade book division and knocked on the door of the head honcho, Nick D'Incecco. There were no secretaries I had to go through to see him.

"Come in," Nick said, and I did, and I walked over to where he was seated at his desk and introduced myself. I told him I worked upstairs.

"I have a book idea," I said. "Beginning in 1949, the Yankees won the pennant in 1949, 1950, 1951, 1952, 1953, 1955, 1956, 1957, 1958, 1960, 1961, 1962, 1963, and 1964. In sixteen years, they won fourteen pennants and nine World Series. I want to write a book about that."

In what amounted to one of the most important moments of my life, D'Incecco smiled at the idea. He said he too was a Yankee fan. He asked about my background in writing.

I told him about being the sports editor of the *Dartmouth* and about writing for the *Stamford Advocate.*

"Would you write me a four-page proposal?" he asked.

"I'd be glad to."

I had no idea what I was doing, but in my proposal I cited the many millions of die-hard Yankee fans in attendance for those sixteen years.

"If five percent of Yankee fans buy the book," I said, "We'll have a best seller."

He gave me a contract with a conservative advance of $2,500.

I quit my law job at Prentice-Hall and immediately drove to Yankee Stadium to begin research in the voluminous files housed in the Yankees PR office. It was the fall of 1972, and Marty Appel, the assistant sports information director for the Yankees, said I could hang with him in his office and go through the thousands of old clippings at my leisure.

CBS had bought the Yankees from longtime owners Dan Topping and Del Webb, and it was now run by Mike Burke, a renaissance man who invited poets and musicians to throw out the first ball at Yankee games. There were days when I went along with Marty and his crew for lunch at Joe DiMaggio's favorite mob restaurant in the Bronx. The older men at the next table always wore pinky rings. For a terrific steak sandwich, we were charged $2.

A couple of times, Yankee slugger Ron Blomberg came to me and asked if I would shag balls for him while he took batting practice. Teammate Hal Lanier pitched to him. I thought I was a pretty good outfielder and so when Ron batted, I stood about fifty feet in front of the right-field wall of Yankee Stadium.

The first thirty balls went way over my head. I was in awe. I finally stood with my back smack up against the right-field wall, and I started catching a few of his blasts.

I got to see Fritz Peterson drive to the stadium in Mike Kekich's station wagon with Mike's wife and kids. I did a double take, but it didn't take long for the world to discover that Fritz and Mike had traded wives and families. Fritz and Mrs. Kekich are married to this day. Mike wasn't so lucky.

I spent three months going through the scrupulously kept files. Meanwhile in January 1973, CBS sold Mike Burke the Yankees and Yankee Stadium for $10 million. Burke couldn't do it alone, but without checking into the checkered history of his new partner, he brought to the Yankees as his equal partner a young, flamboyant, egomaniacal Cleveland shipping magnate by the name of George Steinbrenner.

Steinbrenner, a young man with a dictatorial persona, brought with him from Cleveland a veteran baseball expert by the name of Gabe Paul. Steinbrenner very quickly let Burke know who was going to be in charge. He began giving Mike Burke incredible grief. Whatever Burke wanted to do, Steinbrenner said no.

Paul, meanwhile, fired most of Burke's hires, and many of the rest, including general manager Lee MacPhail, quit. After two long months of aggravation, Mike Burke sold his share of the Yankees and left for his farm in Ireland. With George now in charge, things at the Yankees quickly got pretty ugly.

Meanwhile, very cleverly I discovered that you can't write a book based on newspaper clippings. I asked Marty Appel if he would help me get in touch with his legion of retired Yankees. I was given names, addresses, and telephone numbers, and Mike Burke wrote a beautiful letter to his former players on his personal stationery asking them to cooperate with me.

I called Nick D'Incecco and told him my plans to travel the country and visit all these former players. Would he advance me another $2,500?

He didn't flinch. And he agreed to give me $2,500 a third time and a fourth. In two years, I traveled thirty-three thousand miles, interviewing former Yankees from Massachusetts to California, from Wisconsin to Florida. For almost every player, I had a story to tell.

My first book, *Dynasty: The New York Yankees 1949–1964*, was a big hit, and with it on my resume, I was hired by the *Bergen Record* to be a journalist covering four towns in Bergen County, New Jersey. My salary: $7,500 a year.

I covered the four towns for a year. In one of the high schools I covered, one of their teachers was named Teacher of the Year for the state of New Jersey. The teacher was in charge of both the school newspaper and the literary magazine. I interviewed David Remnick, the editor of the school newspaper, and Rhonda Sonnenberg, the editor of the school literary magazine. David went on the become the distinguished editor of the *New Yorker* magazine, and I would go on to marry Rhonda Sonnenberg. Our marriage would last for thirty years. I also discovered that the teacher, a woman, was having an affair with one of the male students, but I didn't write that in my article.

I was asked to work on the copy desk, a job I loved, and then I was made the assistant night news editor, a job I loved even more. I was doing what I was born to do, work—it wasn't work—perform on a daily newspaper. I knew it wouldn't be long before I ended up on the *New York Times*.

All that changed with one phone call.

It was from a man by the name of Doug Newton. He said he was Billy Martin's business manager.

"Peter," he said, "Billy would like you to write his book. Are you interested?"

I had interviewed Billy while he was the manager of the Texas Rangers. We had sat in the stands during spring training, and we talked at length about his career. Later I would find out that there was one sentence that I had written in *Dynasty* that convinced Billy I was the coauthor for him. Here's what I said:

Billy Martin was as important to the Yankees as Mickey Mantle and Whitey Ford.

It was early February 1978. A week later Doug Newton called me again.

"Billy can't do it right now," he said, "but I have another client, Sparky Lyle, and he'd like to write a book."

Sparky Lyle was the left-handed relief ace of the Yankees. He had won the Cy Young Award for being the best pitcher in the American League in 1977.

"What does Sparky have to say?" I asked. "Why would anyone care about his life?"

For all the years Sparky was on the Yankees, he had kept mostly quiet while George Steinbrenner, Billy Martin, and Reggie Jackson made the headlines.

"I'll tell you what you should do," Newton said. "We're down here in Fort Lauderdale for spring training. Come on down and meet Sparky and see."

Doug Newton was a smart man.

I booked a Saturday flight to the Sunshine State.

I met Sparky in the Yankee clubhouse in Fort Lauderdale. It wasn't hard to notice that standing among us were the likes of Billy Martin, Reggie Jackson, Graig Nettles, Catfish Hunter, Thurman Munson, Chris Chambliss, Lou Piniella, and Mickey Rivers. And hovering above all of them was the specter of George Steinbrenner.

"Sparky," I said, "if you would work with me to keep a diary of this season, I do believe we could have something special."

Sparky agreed.

I lived in Englewood, New Jersey, and conveniently Sparky lived just two towns over in Cresskill, a short ten-minute drive. The Yankees started the season on the road. Sparky said he'd bring a tape recorder with him and talk into it.

When he returned, he was crestfallen.

"I didn't know what to say. I guess we can't do this," he said.

I told him a better way would be if I came over to his house every day during homestands and questioned him about what was going on inside Yankee world.

He agreed, and once we got underway, I knew this book would be something special. Sparky was a great reporter, and he had a tremendous cast of characters to discuss. For someone who loved to hear gossip, as I did, and for someone who loved the Yankees, as I did, I immediately knew this was a once-in-a-lifetime opportunity.

A number of the Yankee players had grievances, and Sparky was one of them. What I didn't know was that Sparky was angry about his contract and about his status on the team. In 1977 Sparky won the Cy Young Award for best pitcher of the year in the American League. He was making a salary of $140,000, which wasn't bad money, but at the end of the year Steinbrenner signed free agent closer Goose Gossage. He gave Gossage $2 million.

Sparky saw he was making peanuts compared with Gossage, but even worse, he intuited that Goose would take over his closer's role.

And that's the way it turned out. In the final Yankees–Red Sox playoff game with left-hander Carl Yastrzemski at bat, the textbook move would have been to bring in the left-handed pitcher Lyle. Manager Bob Lemon stuck with the right-handed Gossage who got Yaz to pop out to third to end the game and put the Yankees in the World Series while Sparky sat stewing in the bullpen.

Sparky had no trouble talking about Steinbrenner's narcissism, the way he bullied his managers, the way he mistreated his players. Before Sparky, everyone was too afraid of Steinbrenner to talk about him, because they knew how vindictive he could be.

Sparky had no trouble letting the world know exactly the sort of person Steinbrenner was and what sort of person Reggie Jackson was. Reggie had come to the Yankees with his rich free agent contract and immediately drew the enmity of everyone by announcing that he was "the straw that stirred the drink."

He then dissed Thurman Munson, the captain of the team, saying that if Munson stirred the drink, "he could only stir it bad." Sparky and many of the other Yankees despised Jackson, no matter how great a home run hitter he was. Sparky was happy to tell the world about how he felt, and when we were done, *The Bronx Zoo* sold 220,000 copies in hardback, and Sparky and I each took home $100,000.

That year, 1978, Steinbrenner had fired Billy Martin in the middle of the season after Steinbrenner took Reggie Jackson's side in Jackson's feud with Billy. In the airport in Kansas City, Billy spoke how he felt about Jackson and Steinbrenner when he told the press, "One's a born liar and the other's convicted."

George had been convicted of illegally contributing to Richard Nixon's reelection campaign. George, being the narcissist that he was, couldn't abide any criticism. He fired Billy the next day, and a few days later realized his mistake and hired him back for two seasons hence. Talk about insanity!

Doug Newton, Billy's agent, wanted to know if I was ready to write Billy's book. I had asked for a split of two-thirds for Billy and one-third for me. Newton had agreed. We wrote a proposal and were given a $250,000 advance.

On the day Newton and I met to sign the collaboration agreement, I sat down alone and looked at the contract. It read: Nine-tenths for Billy. One-tenth for me.

"Take it or leave it," Newton said.

It would not be the last time I'd be blindsided like this, but for this experience I wasn't going to back away. I signed the collaboration agreement and also the contract, and I'm glad I did. I worked closely with Billy, Casey Stengel's protégé. I would argue Billy Martin was among the best baseball minds in managerial history. Billy was always one step ahead of the opposition. Every team he managed he made better.

Billy lived in an apartment in New Jersey about a half an hour from me. We met at some of his favorite bars, but he never drank an alcoholic drink. It was always soda water with a twist of lime. He had once again gotten in trouble for punching someone, and he knew he needed to control himself better. Not drinking was the way to do it.

Fired by Steinbrenner, Billy, like Sparky, had no problem telling the truth about George Steinbrenner, and our book, *Number 1*, was an immediate best seller. Billy had a problem, though. He should have been the manager of Oakland when the book came out, but when George told Billy to get himself fired and come back to the Yankees, he did just that. He busted up his office and called one of the Oakland owners an anti-Semitic slur. When *Number 1* came out, he was the manager of the Yankees.

In the book Billy accused George of bugging his phones, among other things, and George was threatening to fire him *again* if he didn't take out four accusations.

Billy's and Doug Newton's problem was that they needed my approval to take them out. I had been paid an advance of $25,000 rather than the $83,000 I should have gotten. *Sport* magazine was offering us $25,000 for excerpts from Billy's book.

"If you let us take out the four things," Newton said to me, "we'll give you the $25,000."

I didn't want to see Billy get fired again over something we had written in our book.

"Okay," I said. "Take them out."

More than anything, Steinbrenner had wanted the four accusations taken out so he could say that Billy was a liar and couldn't be trusted, and therefore no one should buy his book. It worked to a certain extent, but *Number 1* still sold 140,000 copies in hardcover.

Somehow, some way, I had hit the baseball writer's jackpot. And because of it I would have a career that has lasted more than fifty years.

I would go on to write *Balls* with Graig Nettles, *Guidry* with Ron Guidry, *Bats* with New York Mets manager Davey Johnson, *They Called Me God* with umpire Doug Harvey, *House of Nails* with the criminal mind of Lenny Dykstra, and *Valentine's Way* with Bobby Valentine.

I also wrote a series of oral team histories. After *Dynasty*, I wrote *Bums* about the Brooklyn Dodgers, *Fenway* about the Red Sox, *Wrigleyville* about the Chicago Cubs, *The Spirit of St. Louis*, which was an oral history of the Cardinals and the Browns, and *Amazin'*, my last team history written in 2002. I also wrote an oral history of the Dallas Cowboys football team called *Cowboys Have Always Been My Heroes*.

I had been able to get good contracts to write these oral histories because of the proliferation of independent bookstores, which would order as many as fifty of my books at a time.

Then came the chains. Borders and Barnes & Noble many times set up shop opposite these independent bookstores in an effort to force them out of business. The chains sold you books cheaper than the independents, and when they first opened up, they sold them especially cheap.

My problem was that a Barnes & Noble store would only order two copies of my book at a time. After they sold the two copies, they ordered two more copies. It was no longer financially feasible to write a book about a team in one city. There weren't enough chain stores in any one city to make it possible to sell more than a handful of books. In the future I would have to find books with national interest. The world of books was changing, and to survive, I had to change with the times.

It's 2023 and I'm still at it. My last book, *Whispers of the Gods*, sold well, and now my publisher wants a sequel. What I thought I'd do this time is choose particularly riveting interviews from baseball figures I interviewed over the past fifty years. They are an interesting group, not just a cross section of thoughtful, insightful ballplayers, but men such as team owner Del Webb of the Yankees and Albert Happy Chandler, who arguably made the most important decision in the history of the game, allowing Jackie Robinson to play for the Brooklyn Dodgers.

Each one of these people tells us something we don't know but wish we had known. These are the ones who are letting us know what was *actually going on* behind the scenes with star players and during important moments in baseball history such as when Jackie Robinson joined the Dodgers, the days leading up to the Shot Heard round the World during the 1951 playoffs, the first year of the Mets, and the Mets' miraculous win over the Red Sox in the 1986 World Series.

These are the ones who remind us all *why* we love the game of baseball so much.

CHAPTER ONE

ELDEN AUKER

"I'd Like to See You Throw Directly Underhand"

W*hat I loved most going to the homes of these former players and interviewing them about their lives was that most of the time I was interviewing a blank check. I had no idea what they were going to say and knew almost nothing about what they had experienced.*

Almost always, I was filled with awe about what I learned.

In the year 2000 I was awarded a contract to write a book about the St. Louis Cardinals, which before long I decided would encompass both the Cardinals and the St. Louis Browns, because the Cardinals always were a very serious organization with very button-down players while the Browns had such outstanding personalities as gadfly owner Bill Veeck and such wild personalities as pitcher Sig Jakucki, who helped lead the Browns to the 1944 World Series and who in 1945 tortured one-armed outfielder Pete Gray because he felt Gray was there mostly as a fan draw. When Jakucki was thrown off the team for his drunken behavior, the Browns lost the 1945 pennant.

One of the Browns I wanted to interview was pitcher Elden Auker, who played with the team in 1941, 1942, and 1943. Using Jack Smalling's Baseball Address List, *a book of addresses used mostly by autograph seekers, I found that Auker lived at 15 Sailfish Road in Vero Beach, Florida. I visited him at his beautiful home where on the wall of his study was hung a large, majestic photo of Babe Ruth swinging a bat. The photo was signed by the Babe to Auker, who had started his career pitching in the American League for the Detroit Tigers from 1933 to 1938. Auker had pitched in both the 1934 World Series against the Gas House Gang of the St. Louis Cardinals and the 1935 World Series against the Detroit Tigers.*

Though I was interviewing Auker for my Cardinals/Browns book, I was also incredibly curious about his days with both the Tigers and the Boston Red Sox. Of course, I also wanted to know how he ended up playing major-league baseball.

Among the things that I learned was that Auker was also a college football star who was named to Grantland Rice's All-America football team. The Chicago Bears, in the person of Bronko Nagurski, even offered him a contract to play with them. Auker was also offered a contract by Brooklyn Dodger manager Casey Stengel to sign with the Dodgers before he signed with the Tigers.

The man ended up living quite a life in and out of baseball.

Elden Auker

Where did you grow up?

I grew up in Norcatur, Kansas, a little town in the northwest corner of the state of Kansas, about 300 people. My dad was a rural route carrier for the federal government. He started in the early 1900s on horseback, and then got a motorcycle and later rode automobiles. When I was six weeks old, my mother got on the back of that motorcycle, and my father and mother took me on his route to introduce me to his patrons. There were about 19 or 20 of them in the 25-mile route that he had to deliver mail. That was a long ways out in Kansas. They were old dirt roads, no paved highways.

Where did you find kids with whom to play baseball?

In the fall the kids played football and baseball. We played on an open field, on a pasture sometimes. Wherever we could find an open lot.

Did you have baseball heroes?

No. When I was growing up in the early 1920s, radio was a crystal set. There was no television, no national broadcasting system, no radio. It was strictly a crystal set. I must have been 14 years old, before we had a regular radio.

We had a weekly paper in our hometown, and that was the main source of our communication with the outside world. No sports. All farm business.

We were about 300 miles west of Kansas City, and about 250 miles east of Denver. We were 12 miles from the Nebraska line, and about 90 miles from the Colorado line. We were right on the northwestern corner of the state, right on the wheat belt.

I worked on a farm during the wheat season. I worked the harvest fields. A dollar a day. They had what they called headers. Big equipment.

When did you begin pitching in an organized way?

We didn't have any high school baseball. There was no little league, no nothing. We just played. I played on a town team. Town teams were the most popular in that part of the country. Most of the players on the town teams I played on were grown men. It just happened I could throw a ball pretty hard, and I was the youngest player on the town team. In fact, I was the *only* kid on the town team.

They played their games on Sundays, which my mother wasn't very happy about. She saw I was playing with these rowdy men. She wanted me to go to church, and I went to church in the morning. I played in the afternoon. She thought I was running around with older men who were going to lead me astray.

They were just local businessmen and farm people. They were gentlemen.

My going to college was very, very unusual. If I'm not mistaken, I was the first out of our high school to go to college.

I was playing in a basketball tournament in Norton, Kansas, about 70 miles away, and we were playing a school called Almena, and we won the game 10 to 9, and I scored 9 of the 10 points, and the official of the game was the head basketball and baseball coach at Kansas State University.

After the game he wanted to know if I wanted to come down to Manhattan and come to Kansas State.

I had talked to the coach at Norton, Pete Peterson, and he had graduated from the University of Nebraska, and he had already gotten a job for me at the University of Nebraska. I planned on going there, and then when Charlie Corso, who was the official, wanted me to come down to Manhattan, I felt I should play for Kansas since I had been raised in Kansas. Going to Nebraska was like going to a foreign country. I switched and went to Kansas State.

I had to have a job to go to school. My dad couldn't afford my going to college. He was making $60 a month all the time I was in college, and he had to pay all his own expenses on his automobile and his travel delivering the mail, and I was the only child in the family. The only way I could go to school was if I had a job.

They gave me a job in a drug store. I swept the drug store in the morning and mopped it, and I did that for four years, and I got one dollar a day, and that put me through school. You could buy breakfast in those days for 15 cents, and if you had lunch, it would cost 25 cents, and dinner at night was 35 to 40 cents.

In college I played football, basketball, and baseball. I was all conference in all three sports. Do you remember *College Humor Magazine*? It was a great magazine for all universities, very popular, and I was the first college athlete to be placed on *College Humor*'s All American team in three sports.

Football was really my forte. My last year in school I was on Grantland Rice's second All American team. I was All Western. I had an invitation to go play in the East-West game. Dana Bible, who was the coach at Nebraska, was coaching the West team, and he wanted me to be quarterback for him.

I was captain of basketball, and we had a chance to win the Big Six Conference. Right after Christmas they took the team out to Colorado, and we trained out there for ten days for the high altitude, and we played various colleges around there for about ten days. That went over New Years, which was when the Shrine East-West game was played. I felt as captain of basketball that I should stay with the team, so I turned down the East-West game.

When I graduated, Chicago Bears star fullback Bronko Nagurski came out to see me with the center named Burt Pierson, who was a graduate of Kansas State University. The two of them offered me a contract with the Bears for $500 a game and a 12-game guarantee. Six thousand dollars doesn't sound like much, but in those days when I graduated, a teacher was getting a hundred dollars a month, and that was a very good job.

I was offered the athletic directorship of Country Day School in Kansas City for $2,400 a year, and that was a big job. I turned that down. I turned football down and played baseball.

My college coaches were Bo McMillan in football, and Charlie Corso in basketball and baseball. Charlie was renowned in basketball. He was the coach of an old team called Cook Paints out of Kansas City, and for four or five years in a row they won the National championship in basketball.

The Detroit Tigers then came calling. A fellow by the name of Steve O'Rourke was a scout for the Tigers. He watched me all during college, and in the three years I was there in the Big Six Conference, I lost two games. I lost one to the University of Missouri, 1 to nothing, and lost one to Oklahoma 2 to 1. Buster Mills got the hit off me that beat me, and later I pitched against him in the major leagues.

O'Rourke offered me $450 a month for the time we played. I had an offer, and I had it in writing. A fellow by the name of Casey Stengel was scouting for the Brooklyn Dodgers, and they offered me $500 a month. The reason I took the Tigers was that I saw Steve O'Rourke regularly. He watched practices, and he lived in St. Mary's, Kansas, about 12 miles from the university, and he watched me every game I pitched, and I became a friend of his.

He kept telling me about how the Tigers were building a club on young players. Brooklyn at that time had a bunch of old players. They had a pretty good pitching staff made up of older players. Steve sold me on the idea that Detroit was building a young club, and I'd fit into it. So that's why I took it.

I reported to Detroit thirty minutes after I got my degree. I went to Detroit, and I reported to Mr. Frank Navin, who owned the ballclub. Mr. Navin, a wonderful, wonderful person, was like a father. He knew everyone on the club and did good things for us.

I went directly to his office at the stadium. He was the first person I met in the organization, and he sat down with me, and he told me that he had a good report from Steve O'Rourke, the scout, and he said, "We need good starting pitchers. Steve thinks you have a chance to be a part of our organization." But he said, "We have to give you some experience in professional baseball. Professional baseball is quite different from college baseball, so you're not going to be an asset for us until you can come up here and win ballgames.

"You're going to be an expense to me. I don't have a lot of money. We're going to pay your expenses and send you to Decatur [Illinois]," a farm club in the Three-I League. "We'll send you down there. We have a manager named Bob Coleman, one of the best minor league managers, and if you have the ability, any ability at all, Bob Coleman will do the job for you."

I was in Detroit about eight days. I threw batting practice to the Tigers, and they sent me down, and I reported to Bob. I was throwing sidearm, because, as I told you, I had played football, and I got my shoulder broken twice. I had to wear a steel brace on it for one year in order for me to play. My arm became muscle-bound, and it wasn't free like it was before I got hurt, and so instead of throwing overhead, as I always had, I had to start throwing three-quarters and then sidearm.

I was fast and had a good hardball, a good curveball, but when I reported to Bob Coleman in Decatur, I pitched batting practice a couple days down there, and he said, "Elden, if you're going to pitch in the major leagues, you have to have control. You have to get the ball over the plate. A sidearm pitcher cuts down on that considerably. The plate is only seventeen inches wide, and you're throwing from sixty feet six inches, and the best control is to throw directly overhand, because then all you talk about is your height. Because you're automatically lined up with the plate."

He said, "With your fastball and curveball, I'd like to see you quit throwing sidearm, and I'd like to see you throw directly underhand in order to get lined up with the plate. I think you'll have better control, which is what you need to pitch in the major leagues."

It sounded strange to me, but he said, "There was a very successful pitcher by the name of Carl Mays, who pitched for the Yankees, and he was an underhanded pitcher. With your speed there's no reason why you can't do that. And I'd like you to try it."

I went out and worked on it for about a week, and it was very natural for me, and in fact, I had a little bit more speed that way because I could get my arm higher and more loose.

Quincy. which was leading the Three-I League, was coming to town for a series.

"Elden," Bob said, "Quincy is coming to town, and I want you to start that game. I want you to throw underhand. I don't want you to throw any other way. You're going to be out there for nine innings, and I don't care how many you walk, or what happens. You're going to pitch nine innings underhand."

I did, and I shut them out. I won 1 to nothing and struck out 12, and I've never pitched any other way since then.

I was in the minor leagues about six weeks when the league went broke. It was during the Depression. The minor leagues were having a lot of trouble, because people didn't have enough money to go see the games, although it didn't cost very much. I was being paid by the Tigers, so they kept four of us including Claude Passeau, my roommate. He later came up to the Cubs.

The Tigers sent four of us over to another Tiger farm team, Moline, Illinois, in the Mississippi Valley League. I was there about six weeks to the end of the 1932 season. I had signed with the Tigers in June, and the season ended in the latter part of August.

The next year I reported to Beaumont, in the Texas League. Bob Coleman was again my manager. I was there until the latter part of June, a couple months, and I won a lot of ballgames [he pitched 220 innings, had a 16–10 record, and a 2.50 ERA], and the Tigers called me up in the early part of the 1933 season.

On the team was Schoolboy Rowe, Hank Greenberg, Pete Fox, Gerald Walker, and JoJo White, who all came out of the farm system out of the Texas League. We had Charlie Gehringer at second base, Billy Rogell at short, and Marvin Owen at third base.

Charlie was a very quiet person. He was a leader. He led by you following him. He didn't criticize or anything like that. His work ethic and the way he played the game, he was a master. He was a great hitter and one of the greatest second basemen we ever had, and he was so admired by the entire ballclub.

When I came up, I was 22 years old. Hank Greenberg was about the same age. Schoolboy Rowe was a little younger. We were all just young kids.

I had never seen a major league ballpark until I went to see Mr. Navin at Navin Field. To me it was the biggest ballpark I ever saw in my life. Of course, it was one of the smaller parks in the league. Because they only had the two-tiered stadium in right field and left field behind third base. And then they had bleachers in right field, and in left field was a wall. Cherry Street, they called it, a wall that was completely enclosed. Then later on, when Walter Briggs came there, he had a lot of money, so he built up and made it for 50,000 people.

When you were a rookie in 1933, one of the clubs that came in were the Yankees, with Babe Ruth and Lou Gehrig. Bill Dickey. Tony Lazzeri. Crosetti. You're a rookie, and you have to face these people. What are your remembrances of having to do that?

I have one very distinct memory. Right after I came up, we were only in Detroit a few days when we started an Eastern road trip. We went directly to New York and opened up against the Yankees. I had never been to New York in my life. The first day in New York I was in uniform, and [manager] Bucky Harris put me in the bullpen. We had a pitcher by the name of Carl Fisher, and in the third inning he got in trouble. The bases were loaded. Bucky called me in from the bullpen, and I made the long walk from left field, and the first hitter I pitched to, the guy who was waiting to hit, was Babe Ruth.

I threw four pitches and struck him out.

Later on I played golf with Babe and Dizzy Dean. My wife and I became very friendly with Claire, Babe's wife. In the wintertime Babe lived in St. Pete, and we lived in Lakeland, and we had a group that used to play golf together. A sideline of that, which is humorous now, but at that particular time it wasn't really humorous—the Yankees had a coach by the name of Art Fletcher. Art Fletcher was notorious for being what we called a jockey. He was a real jockey, and as a youngster when you walked on that pitcher's mound out there, this guy was really on you. He would do everything in the world to distract you, and call you bush. You could hear him because he was only a few feet away. And he was in your ear all the time.

So I struck Ruth out, and I got out of that inning, and I went out to start the next inning. And Fletcher starts on me. He started yelling at me. "Hey bush. Bush. Bush." He knew I wouldn't look at him, but he knew I could hear him. He said, "Bush, you have the Bam all upset. He just made a statement on the bench when he came in. He said he had been struck out a lot of times, but this was the first time a goddamn woman ever struck him out."

Babe Ruth

Of course, being rather sensitive as I was, it upset me a little bit, and I could have killed him. He really insulted me.

Later on, Art and I became close friends. I told him, "If I had only two minutes to spare, at that moment, I'd have come over there, and we'd have had a fight in the coach's box."

I also became very close friends with Lou Gehrig. He was a very, very nice guy. We had a little thing going. If you ever saw Gehrig bat, he was a left handed hitter, and he'd take his left foot and screw it into the ground. Turn it around and plant that left foot, and he had big, powerful legs. He was a low-ball hitter. You get anything below his belt, and he'd rake you off the mound with it.

Tommy Bridges and Schoolboy Rowe kept the ball above his waist and made him hit fly balls. My strength was low. I had a sinkerball, and I couldn't throw above the belt. I had to work the lower part. Ruth didn't like to hit against me, because I did throw the sinkerball, and he didn't like to hit the low ball. He liked the ball up and away from him. So I kept the ball low, and that's why he had trouble with the sinkerball.

But Gehrig, I was pitching to his strength, and this was my strength, so it was strength against strength. Well, I decided I had to find a way from his getting set in there, so I started throwing at his feet. I'd get a strike on him, and the next pitch I'd throw at his feet and make him get that big foot out of the way. That bothered him a lot, because he kept saying to me, "You so and so, you're throwing at my feet."

"What am I throwing at your feet for?" I said. "I'm just a low-ball pitcher. I'm throwing inside."

"I know you're throwing at my feet," Gehrig said.

One day I'm working the ballgame at Yankees Stadium, and I'm ready to pitch inside to him, and I got him on the toe of his foot and fractured it. It really did. He went down in the pile. Bill McGowan was umpiring. Gehrig had a high voice. He was laying on the ground, and he was holding his foot, and he looked at Bill, and he said, "I told you he was throwing at my feet. God, he broke my toe."

"Oh come on. Get up," Bill said. "If he's gonna hit you, he'd hit you in the head where it wouldn't hurt you."

Lou came out the next day, and he had an aluminum cast on that thing. He had his shoe cut out. In order to keep his streak going [Gehrig would play in 2,140 games in a row], he would play the first inning, and he was out. And he hobbled around on that thing for about ten days. And as a result of that little incident, we became close friends.

I was on the Boston club in 1939, and we opened up against the Yankees, and we had the same runway—the Red Sox and the visiting team had the same runway, and Gehrig was always a guy who would come up and put a hammerlock on your head and wrestle with you. If you put one around him, he'd lift you off the ground.

Lou Gehrig

I had been running in the outfield prior to the game, just before the game started, and Lou was standing on the first step on the floor of the runway when I came out, and he was smoking a cigarette. I came up and grabbed him by the neck, and usually he would just lift you off the ground, but this time he said, "Oh my God, don't do that," and he just crumpled. I had to help him to his feet.

"What the matter with you?" I asked.

"I don't know, Elden. I have something wrong with me. I'm sick. I've had a heck of a time. I don't have any strength. I can hardly walk. I don't know what it is. The doctors are trying to find out what it is."

Well, after that series the Yankees went to Detroit, and that was when he went to the Mayo Brothers, and that's when he found out he had the disease [ALS].

When he died, it was a sad day. I miss him, because he was a nice guy. A wonderful person. And so was Babe, who died a terrible death. He had cancer of the throat. I saw him in Detroit. He couldn't hardly talk. He was in pain all the time.

The American Legion was paying Babe $50,000 a year. Henry Ford personally paid him $50,000 a year to be the honorary head of American Legion baseball. Many of the Ford Motor Company dealers promoted American Legion baseball. Henry Ford hired Babe Ruth when he was out of baseball and no one wanted him, and he paid him $50,000 a year.

When you faced the Philadelphia A's, you had to face Jimmie Foxx and Mickey Cochrane.

Right. In fact, when I went to Boston in 1939, Jimmie Foxx was my roommate. My son is named after Jimmie Foxx. James Emory Auker. Jimmie was a wonderful person. Jimmie was like a big bear, strong. Boy, he had muscles in his ears. And one of the mildest guys you have ever seen. Mild-tempered.

Everybody loved Jimmie Foxx except the pitchers who pitched against him. But he was the nicest person I've ever known in baseball. One of the nicest—Charley Gehringer and Hank Greenberg were great guys too.

Jimmie had a lot of problems. When I was with him in 1939, he was in the midst of getting a divorce. His wife was going to marry a banker.

She was a society gal, was a social climber in Philadelphia, a Mainliner, and Jimmie wasn't like that at all. They ended up getting a divorce, and during that year in 1939 he was going through this, and Jimmie also had sinus problems. He had hay fever, and in the season when we went into Philadelphia, Washington, St. Louis, where it was real muggy and hot, he had problems.

I remember one time we were in St. Louis, and Jimmie and I had gone to a movie, and we came back and went to bed about 11 o'clock, and we were in St. Louis playing the St. Louis Browns, and Jim woke up about 1:30 and he was coughing and sneezing, and he started to nose bleed, and we couldn't get it stopped. We got ice and we worked on him.

We called the trainer up and we plugged up his nose and did everything trying to get the blood stopped. He must have bled profusely for an hour and a half. I never saw anything like it. He evidently broke a vessel in his nose when he was blowing or sneezing. And he had practically no sleep. I didn't either.

The next morning I got up and went down to breakfast, and Jim said, "I think I'll just stay here. I'll sleep in for a while."

I went on down for breakfast and came back, and we usually went out to the ballpark around 10:30. It was an afternoon game at one o'clock. He was still sleeping, and I said to him, "Look, why don't you just sleep in. We're playing the Browns today. You just take it easy."

"I'll see," he said.

I went on to the ballpark. When we were taking infield practice prior to the game, here comes Jim in a uniform. And he's going to play.

"I don't know how the guy can walk," I told Joe Cronin. "He bled all night."

When Jimmie came out, we all said, "How do you feel?"

"I feel all right," he said.

He went to bat, and I forgot who was pitching, but the first time at bat Jimmie hit a home run into the centerfield bleachers in old Sportsman's Park, four hundred and some feet. He hit a home run in his first at bat!

He was an unbelievable person. He really was.

I understood later on he had financial problems. In those days we didn't make much money, and his wife took about everything he had. He had some financial setbacks, and I understood he got to drinking quite a lot, and he had an untimely death. He choked to death on a piece of meat, as I understood it.

I kept track of him for a while. I was in business when he retired. He was coaching.

And he was drinking too much, and he was fired.
He didn't do that when he was playing.

Tell me about Mickey Cochrane.
Mickey was a .320 hitter [over 13 seasons], and he was tough. He was a hard ballplayer. All those Philadelphia Athletics in 1930 were tough: Al Simmons, Jimmy Dykes, Mule Haas. They didn't have anyone who couldn't hit. Eric McNair was the shortstop. He was just a youngster who came up. Mickey was catching. Al Simmons was in centerfield. Simmons could hit, and so could Mule Haas. He played right field. And Bing Miller, they could all hit. Jimmy Dykes.

They were hard to beat. We had to get more runs than they did.

Bucky Harris quit as manager with only a few games left in the 1933 season.
We were in fifth place.

The Tigers hadn't won since 1909.
That was the last year they won the pennant.

I don't know the reason why Bucky quit. We were all sorry to see Bucky go. But he left for some reason and went to Washington. I think what happened, that was the year Joe Cronin went to Boston, and [Washington owner] Clark Griffith went after Harris, and he and Navin must have talked, because that was part of it. Connie Mack might have been in on that because Connie Mack had to break up that team, and what he needed was money. Though Connie Mack's Philadelphia A's won all those ballgames, nobody would come out and watch them play. The attendance at Shibe Park with such a great team was very poor. That's why Mack broke them up. He sold Foxx to Boston, sold Mickey to Detroit, and Dykes went to Chicago, and he cashed in on it while he was at the top, and then he had to start a rebuilding program.

Navin in Detroit didn't have much money either.

He did not. Frank Navin was a baseball man. As a youngster he started selling shoe-strings. He was a shoestring salesman. He had nothing as a youngster. He liked baseball, and he started working for the old organization in the park and later got into the office.

Frank Navin was a very intelligent guy, and as the years went by, he became an official. He didn't have any money, so for him to buy the team he went to Mr. Kelsey of Kelsey Wheel. Kelsey Wheel was a manufacturer of automobile wheels, and they sold them to Ford, General Motors, Chrysler, Dodge, Chevrolet, and all those.

The wheels are what you put the tires on. Kelsey Hayes was half owner of the organization, and he had a lot of money. Walter Briggs owned the Briggs body company, and they made automobile bodies for the Chrysler corporation. Chrysler made the chassis and the engine. Briggs made a deal with Chrysler that he would supply the bodies. The body is what sets on top of the chassis. Fisher body made the body for General Motors corporation. Later Chrysler bought Briggs, and General Motors bought Fisher. In those days when Henry Ford started out, he didn't make wheels. He bought them from Kelsey. He didn't make mufflers. He had to buy them from Hudie Hershey. Gears from gear companies.

Mr. Briggs was the president and major owner of Briggs body company, and so Mr. Navin went to Mr. Briggs—incidentally Mr. Briggs was a paraplegic. As a young man he had syphilis, and he had a disease called locomotive taxi, and it paralyzed his lower limbs. He was in a wheelchair most of his life. But he was very successful in business. He was a tough businessman. That wheelchair made him tougher cause he was mad at everybody. He had a terrible personality. Boy, he was a mean, tough guy.

But he had money, and Mr. Navin didn't have anything, so Mr. Navin said to Mr. Kelsey and Mr. Briggs, "We can buy the ballclub."

I don't know what the amount was. "But if you two will put up the money, I will run the ballclub, and we'll have a 33 1/3 percent interest each. And we'll have an agreement when the first one dies, the stock will be divided equally between the other two. And when the other one dies, the final one who lives will get all the stock."

That was the deal.

Mr. Kelsey had heart problems, but he was very active. Mr. Navin was the picture of health. Great physical condition. He rode horses. He kept himself in great physical condition. Mr. Briggs was in a wheelchair.

Mr. Kelsey died not long after they made the agreement. Mr. Navin and Mr. Briggs then owned the team equally. Mr. Navin took care of the baseball.

And of all the things that could happen, following the 1935 World Series, about four weeks after—Mr. Navin made a statement to the newspapers after we beat the Cubs in 1935, "We have won the World Championship. Now I'm ready to die."

Four to five weeks later Mr. Navin died from a heart attack. He was out riding his horse with Mrs. Navin, and he fell off his horse, and he was dead when he hit the ground.

Mr. Briggs then owned all the stock. He became the outright owner of the Detroit Tigers.

The deal to buy Mickey Cochrane from the A's was made in January of 1934. Mr. Navin operated on a shoestring, because Briggs was tight with a buck, and he made Navin operate on his own. And it was tough going. But Navin talked Mr. Briggs into buying Cochrane. Mr. Briggs had to supply the money. A lot of money, the most money ever paid for a player. [The Tigers paid $100,000 for Cochrane.]

Did you hear a story that Navin had wanted to hire Babe Ruth to manage the Tigers, but Babe was barnstorming and couldn't make a meeting?

There was some talk about that. I never did know the details of that, but I had heard scuttlebutt about that. The hiring of Mickey Cochrane came out of the clear sky. I think Connie Mack and Mr. Navin and maybe Clark Griffith was in on that. Because Bucky Harris went to Washington, and Cronin went to Boston, and Mickey came to the Tigers. The owners were all very close friends.

Bucky Harris was our manager. He had come over from Washington and had been there for three or four years. Bucky was a great person, a good manager. He was a great second baseman himself. He was a playing manager at Washington. Not for us. A wonderful guy. He proved himself to be an excellent manager.

You became a star that first year under Mickey Cochrane. [In 1934 Auker pitched 205 innings with a 15–10 record, and a 3.42 ERA.]

Well, not a star. I had a good year. We didn't consider that we were stars.

What was Mickey's contribution to that, if any?

It all started in spring training of 1934, and I will never forget it. In fact, I have a picture up here, with Cochrane holding the first meeting of our baseball team in spring training. Mickey called us all together, and he told us, "Look, we have great talent here."

Hank Greenberg was a young first baseman. Charley Gehringer was a great player. Billy Rogell was a good shortstop, about as good a shortstop as there was in the league. Marv Owen was a young third baseman. We had Jo Jo White in centerfield, and Schoolboy Rowe and Tommy Bridges were great pitchers.

And I fit into the picture. We had Fred Marberry, who came over from Washington. Fred had had a great career in Washington. We had a solid pitching staff.

I was the one who was going to make it or not make it onto the pitching staff, because I was the least experienced. Schoolboy was the youngest, but he had been up the year before. He had done pretty well in '33. [In 1933 twenty-three-year-old Rowe had a 7–4 record with a 3.58 ERA in 19 games.]

"We have the nucleus of a great ballclub," Mickey said. "There is no reason why we can't win the pennant. It's all up to us, this group right here, as to whether we can win the American League pennant. I think we can. If you fellas would just believe that you could, forget about being young, forget about your inexperience, just think that what we have to do is go out there every day and win every game. That's all we have to do.

"We're not going to win every game. We'll lose some, but we are going to win most of our games. All we have to do is win the major portion of our ballgames, and we will win the American League pennant."

We had never even thought about that. For some of us, this was the first time we had been in the major leagues. Here we're talking about winning the American League pennant, about being the champion.

The spirit on our ballclub in 1934 and 1935 was just like the spirit we had when I played football for Bo McMillan. Mickey was an inspirational leader. He was the best catcher in baseball. He handled Schoolboy Rowe and Tommy Bridges and myself, and even Fred Marberry like babies. Mickey Cochrane was responsible for 70 percent of my success in 1934, Schoolboy Rowe the same way.

A great catcher gets you to think together. Mickey had a meeting with the pitching staff.

"Look, I'm the manager," he said. "And I'm a catcher. And I'm going to give you signals, what pitch to throw. The reason I give you those signals is to keep you from breaking my fingers. I want to know when you're going to throw the fastball or the curveball. It's easier for me to give you the signals than for you to give me the signals. I'll give the signals.

"But I want you to never throw a pitch that you don't want to throw. If you don't agree with the signal and you don't want to throw that pitch, you shake me off. You tell me what *you* want to throw. If you get the guy out, it's to your credit. If the guy hits the ball out of the ballpark, that's your fault. It's not mine. It's your game to pitch. It's my game to catch. That's all I'm here for, to catch what you throw. But don't you ever throw a pitch to me that you never want to throw."

And that's the way we worked. As we worked with him, our minds were so close together as to how you were pitching this fellow. We pitched to these fellows many times during the season. We knew how to pitch to them. We knew who the high-ball hitters were, who hit this, hit that, pitch inside, pitch outside, or brush 'em away or knock 'em down. Some hitters you never knock down because that woke them up. I never knocked down Babe Ruth or Lou Gehrig or Jimmie Foxx or Ted Williams.

I knocked down Al Simmons, who didn't like it. There were some you brushed back.

Mickey gave us real confidence, and we got to the point where we didn't think anybody could beat us. We went into Yankee Stadium, and we had to go through the Yankee dugout to get to our dugout.

"When we go to Yankee Stadium," Mickey said, "I don't want you to talk to the Yankee players. They are our enemies. And they are going to be our enemies all year long. And that's the way we want to treat them. We're not afraid of them. We're going to beat them."

That first year when he was there, we didn't speak to any Yankees, before the game or after the game. In fact, it went on the whole time he managed. They weren't our friends. The newspapers wanted [Tiger outfielder] Gerald Walker to have his picture taken with Lou Gehrig, because they were similar in build and the kind of people they were, but Gerald refused to have his picture taken with Lou Gehrig.

"He's not my friend, and I don't want him to be my friend," Walker said. "He's my enemy."

And that's the way we were. We were not friends with the Yankees the first couple of years, but as we played [Lefty] Gomez and [Red] Ruffing and those guys, and Gehrig of course, and Babe was only there during the '35 season. I had played golf with Babe in the winter of '34. Babe and Mickey were very good friends. We were friends, but what Cochrane was telling us as young players, *We didn't come in here for a social gathering. We came to beat you.*

That's what he wanted us to feel, and really, we were almost afraid to speak to the Yankees.

Each of our starting infielders drove in 100 runs in 1934. At one time during the season when Schoolboy Rowe was pitching, *nine* players on the Tigers were hitting .300. Schoolboy had a batting average of a little over .300. Rogell was a little over .300 and so was Marvin Owens.

They called that the Infield of Dreams.

I had these people playing behind me. Oh yes. I told Charlie Gehringer and Hank Greenberg and Goose Goslin that if it wasn't for me, they never would have been in the Hall of Fame. If I'd have done my job, I wouldn't have needed them.

They gave you all the confidence in the world. You didn't worry about it after they hit it, unless they hit it in between them.

There was never a finer man in baseball or that God ever put on this earth than Hank Greenberg. Oh yeah. Hank and his parents—I knew his dad and mother and knew his brother Joel and his sister. His family were wonderful people. They were from New York. They'd come out to the Stadium. Hank's dad would come into the clubhouse, and we'd meet his dad and mother and Joel his brother. They came to Detroit to visit him. We knew the whole family.

Hank was a very good friend of mine. Hank wasn't married in those days. Mildred and I would have him out to our apartment for dinner. We were all very, very close, and Hank was a great guy. He was a top gentleman, always a gentleman. Hank Greenberg never did anything that wasn't done in a gentlemanly way. He was a high-class guy. First-class, and a great ballplayer. He was a better fielder than people gave him credit for. He was a great fielder. He was a big target at first base, six foot five, long arms, covered a lot of territory.

Bill Rogell, our shortstop, was rough and tumble. I don't know whether Billy got out of high school or not. He got into professional baseball pretty young. He started in the minor leagues and worked his way up, and he was a great hustler. He was a switch hitter, which was a great thing for him, and he was a pretty good hitter both ways. [His lifetime batting average was .267.] He was a good fielder with an excellent arm, and he and Charlie Gehringer became the best double play combination in baseball.

Marvin Owen at third base was a tall slender guy, and he had a great set of hands. He was a wonderful fielder and had a very strong arm. Owen and Rogell covered that left side of the field in great shape. Anything on the ground, one of them usually had a hold of it. Marvin was a tall, slender guy. He came out of San Jose University. He was a scholarly person. In fact, I think he went back and did teaching after he got out of ball. Marvin was not in real good health. He always had stomach trouble and he had to eat certain foods, and he drank a lot of milk, and during the game his stomach bothered him.

The second year you were in Detroit, 1935, the Tigers traded with Washington and got Goose Goslin, a Hall of Famer who was one of the least written about great players.

That's right. Goose was a very quiet guy. If you want to be well known, all you have to do is be something different. You gotta be like Leo the Lip, you gotta have a Dizzy Dean personality, you gotta have fellas who are outgoing and do things that are different. Yogi Berra was different. They are not only good at the game but different.

Sportswriters are always looking for stories. To get a story out of Charlie Gehringer was a very difficult problem. Charlie didn't talk much. He just did his job. He went out there and hit .340 every year and was a flawless infielder. He went home after the game. He wasn't married. He took care of his mother until she died. He was a solid citizen. He did all the good things for the kids, signed autographs.

A newspaper guy came around and would say, "Charlie, do you have anything new?" And Charlie would say, "No." That was it. But Dizzy Trout or Dizzy Dean, they have a story. Dizzy Trout rode a motorcycle when he came to spring training. He rode it around the infield. That was a great story.

But Goose Goslin was like Charlie Gehringer. Hank Greenberg was that way. Hank wasn't a colorful person. Hank being Jewish made good stories in New York, but there was nothing to write about Hank being flamboyant. He was a quiet, retiring person, and just a great individual. Nothing colorful about him. There was nothing colorful about Goslin except his name, Leon, and they called him Goose. That was colorful. He was never a showboat. He did his job. He was a great fielder with a great arm and a good outfielder. But the newspapers never gave him any credit for it. As a result, he never got much press. As did Gehringer and Greenberg.

Tommy Bridges won 22 games in '34. What type of pitcher was he? What did he throw?

The best curveball that has probably ever been in the major leagues. He was right-handed, had good speed, and one of the best curveballs in baseball. Tommy came out of Tennessee. He only weighed about 160 pounds, but he was a real competitor and a hell of a pitcher. And in 1934 with our ballclub, if we got him runs, he would win. He was a great pitcher.

Tommy was quiet. He was married to a little Southern gal, and they had a daughter, and he was my roommate for six years, the whole time I was there. Tommy was very quiet. We'd pitch a ballgame and maybe go to a show or have dinner and read books. When we were home, we were with our families. We lived in the same apartment building. Our families were very close.

And Schoolboy Rowe?

He was also a righthander. Schoolboy also was very quiet. He came out of Elderberry, Arkansas. He was just a big kid. He got publicity when he got married. That came about when he said, "How am I doing, Edna?"

She was a high school sweetheart. Her name was Edna.

We were on the Walter Winchell program in New York after we played the Yankees. Radio was the only thing then. Schoolboy and I were on that program because we had just beaten the Yankees in a doubleheader. At the end of the interview Schoolboy said, "How am I doing, Edna?" That was before they were married, and a couple weeks later they were married during the season. He lived with "How am I doing, Edna?" for the rest of his life.

That was written up all over New York and Detroit and every place.

The highlights of that 1934 season.

The highlight was when we finally won the pennant. I don't think there was a special highlight except for winning. We were in a state of mind that that was what we were supposed to do, and we got to the point of where, if we did lose a game, that's history and we'll win tomorrow. We didn't look behind. We only looked at what was ahead of us. And we took it for granted.

We didn't look at the newspapers much. I never paid much attention to newspapers, what they would say. We were doing our job, what we were supposed to do, and they printed it, and that was it.

They didn't write much that was controversial.

There wasn't too much to write about us being controversial because we were successful. And we were kind of a wonder team in the eyes of many people, because Detroit hadn't had a winner. Here we were on top of the league, beating the Yankees, and that was something that wasn't done. We were beating the Red Sox. We were beating Cleveland. We were beating everybody.

How did that galvanize the city of Detroit?

Well, we were given credit for bringing them out of the Depression. Detroit changed completely in 1934. When I went to Detroit in 1933, there were soup lines. People were unemployed. Business was no good. The automobile factories were working only part time, and people were earning 35 cents an hour.

In 1934 Mr. Ford paid five dollars a day, and people thought he had lost his mind. But when we started winning, the whole atmosphere in Detroit changed. They got their mind off the sad times. People came to the ballpark. If they could rake up 35 cents to sit in the bleachers, they did. A box seat was two dollars and a half. The Ford family had a box right next to our dugout. Mr. Henry Ford wouldn't miss a ballgame. We all knew Mr. Henry Ford. The old man. Edsel Ford was his son. He was a youngster growing up. And Mr. Ford had Henry II, and little Billy Ford hadn't even been born. And they had a little girl.

To Edsel Ford and Mrs. Ford, Charlie Gehringer was almost like their son. They had him out to dinner. They were crazy over Charlie. There's a story back of that. Edsel Ford was the reason for Charlie Gehringer's huge success in business.

But Detroit changed completely that year. It became a dynamic city. Business picked up. The automobile business picked up. People went to work. The whole attitude of Detroit changed. And that carried over into 1935. When we won it again and then won the World Championship, that year the Red Wings won the National Hockey League championship and the Detroit Lions won the National Football League championship, Joe Louis won the World Heavyweight Championship, and we won the World Series.

We had a dinner at the Masonic temple that held about 2,500 people, called the Breakfast of Champions. All of us were there. The city of Detroit paid tribute to all of us. Detroit was on top of the world.

Let me ask you about the day you clinched the pennant in 1934.

I pitched the ballgame that clinched the pennant, and that was on my birthday, the 21st of September.

Everyone thought the Tigers would be playing the New York Giants in the 1934 World Series.

That was the biggest disappointment of our whole life. We had won the pennant ten days before the season was over, and the Giants were leading the National League by three games. All they needed was to win one game out of three against the Dodgers to win the pennant. The girls had all their bags packed to go to New York to go shopping. We were to play in the Polo Grounds, which had a lot of box seats. We were going to have a good paycheck when it was all over. We were looking forward to playing against Hubbell and Schumacher and those guys, and we were ready for them. And the Giants went to Brooklyn, and they lost four games in a row, and the Cardinals won, and the Cardinals won the pennant by one game on the last day of the season.

CHAPTER TWO

ELDEN AUKER

Ole Diz, Mickey Cochrane, and Hammering Hank

In 1934 you played the Gas House Gang in the World Series. And they have come down in history.

We should have won the 1934 series.

But the team that's remembered is the Cardinals.

That's because of the newspapers, because they had Dizzy Dean, Leo the Lip, Pepper Martin, guys who were colorful people, and they got a lot of publicity as a result of that. The Dean brothers got more publicity for themselves in the [1934] World Series than our entire Tiger team got. Paul was very quiet, but me and Paul got a lot of publicity. In fact, they made more money outside selling sweatshirts and advertising—Dizzy Dean made five times more money outside of baseball than he did in baseball. The Cardinals didn't pay much money. If Dizzy was making $15,000, he was making a lot of money. I doubt he made that much. On the outside I know that Dizzy made over $80,000 in 1934 because he told me that. That was *money*.

Now we have to go to St. Louis to play in that Sportsman's Park, a ballpark that seated about 27,000 people. If we'd been at the Polo Grounds, it would have been 50,000 people. And then we ended up losing the Series to the Cardinals.

We were upset. We thought we should be playing the Giants. We were ready for the Giants, but we weren't ready for the Cardinals. We were upset because we didn't play the Giants. That cost us money.

In 1931 when Mickey Cochrane was with the A's, the A's played the Cardinals in the World Series. The Cardinals stole on him a lot.

Pepper Martin went crazy.

Dizzy Dean with Frankie Frisch

Did Mickey ever talk about that?

He talked about it. He just said they couldn't contain Martin. They were running on the pitchers. The runners usually run on the pitchers, not the catchers. Mickey didn't talk much about that. He wasn't happy about it. Mickey wasn't happy any time he lost.

He couldn't have been too happy about having to play the Cardinals in the 1934 World Series.

No, he wasn't. He really wasn't.

Dizzy Dean was the Cardinals star. Tell me what you remember about Dizzy.

First, he was a great pitcher. There is no doubt about that. He could pitch. He had a hard sinker, a good curveball, good control, and he knew how to pitch. And he was tough to hit. He played the game hard. Paul, his brother, was so-so. He had a couple of good years, but that's about all. But Diz was a strong pitcher.

As an individual Diz was two different personalities. Dizzy and his wife Pat have been in our home in Lakeland during the winter, and we've been in their home in Bradenton. They both love to play bridge. We both love to play bridge. Dizzy was as good a bridge player as you've ever seen. Pat would not allow liquor in the house. You go to the Dean house, and you had Coca-colas. You didn't have any beer or any drinks at all. And Diz did not drink.

It was very quiet around the Dean house. She'd say, "Jerome, now . . ." At home he was that kind of a guy. A homebody. He was just a good old country boy. He talked excellent English. He had a great sense of humor, joked and laughed all the time.

What about Dizzy's funny language on the radio? "I thunk it."

That was Dizzy Dean, the public figure. He put all of that on. With interviews and newspaper people, that's the way he talked. He wanted to be the Arkansas hillbilly. That's the way he was on the outside, but in his home he was completely different. He was just a good old boy at home. A good family man, and a nice guy to know. He laughed all the time. He loved to eat, play cards, play bridge. Just a good guy.

And in public he was a big jokester, and he always loved to tell stories. He was very cagey, very wise. I'll never forget an interview in 1935 in spring training. We played the Cardinals in an exhibition game, and the Tigers had a young fellow come up by the name of Dizzy Trout. He didn't stay, but he came up for spring training. He called himself Dizzy Trout, so the radio people had an interview with him in our clubhouse and made a tape that they played in Detroit.

The interviewer was [former Tiger outfielder] Harry Heilman. He interviewed Dizzy Trout and Dizzy Dean together. Both were trying to outdo themselves, and finally the question was asked of Dizzy Dean, "What do you think of young Dizzy?"

His reply was this, which I thought was pretty good:

"Well," he said, "I like him as a person. Of course, this is the first time we have ever met. But I would say there was one major difference between the young Dizzy and the old Dizzy. If you notice, when the old Dizzy talks, he talks about the things that he has done. And the young Dizzy talks about what he thinks he's going to accomplish. That's the major difference."

That was the true Dean that came out. Dizzy Dean was no hillbilly. He was two kinds of people. He was plenty savvy, and it was his wife who was savvy about money. She was a business gal. She owned a couple of beauty parlors in Bradenton. She gave Dizzy an allowance. That's what he had to spend on the road trips. That was it. She took care of the finances, and Dizzy did the talking when he was away from home. At home *she* did the talking. They were great people.

You pitched in Game 4 of the 1934 World Series against Tex Carlton. Do you recall how you were going to pitch some of those fellows?

Oh yes. One in particular. The first pitch of every game was to Leo Durocher, and the first pitch was to put him in the dirt. To knock him down. That was our opening pitch for all of us to do that. I don't know why. Cochrane didn't like Leo in the first place. Leo was a mouthy individual, and Mickey wanted to let him know we were in the ballgame with him.

Tell me about your first pitch that fourth game.

That was right at Leo Durocher. First pitch.

Did Leo say anything?

No. No. He didn't say anything I could hear, or Mickey either. I think he expected it. Do you know the story of Leo Durocher?

Tell me.

Well, Leo Durocher came up with the Yankees as a youngster. Ed Barrow was the manager, and we always had roommates. Well, they had trouble finding a roommate for Ruth, because Ruth was always prowling around and keeping his roommate awake and doing things where the guys couldn't get to rest. On one road trip if a young guy went with him, at the end of the trip he would be about worn out, because he couldn't keep up. And Babe kept going all the time.

Durocher came into the organization, and they roomed Durocher with Ruth, and Leo was very happy. Not a complaint. They made a couple road trips, and everything was fine until they began to miss things in the clubhouse. Various things were stolen out of lockers. And Ruth, as the story goes, saw Leo was spending a little more money on the trips than he was used to spending, and then one time a gold watch that had been presented to Babe turned up missing on a trip.

The Yankees were in Detroit at the Detroit Leland Hotel, and Ruth had marked some money that he had. They were in the hotel, and Ruth came in at one in the morning. He'd been out, and Durocher was asleep, and so Ruth began to search around to see what he could find, and he found his gold watch and five hundred dollars that he had marked in Durocher's travel bag.

Ruth jerked Durocher out of bed and almost beat him to death. He was tearing the place apart with Durocher. He about killed him. They had to get the manager to get the door open, so they could get Leo out of there. Durocher was gone the next day. He never played another game with the Yankees. And he never played in the American League again.

They found out later some of the things Leo had been stealing from the players. That was a no no in baseball.

The first day I was in the major leagues in the clubhouse I could have put a thousand dollars down in my locker, and it would have been there the last day I left. You didn't do something like that in the clubhouse.

Leo was traded to the Cardinals.

Leo went to St. Louis because the old man, Branch Rickey, was a great guy for the underdog. He picked Leo up and brought him over. Durocher couldn't hit, but he was a good fielder, had a good arm, and he was the kind of player the old man liked. Rickey was a great glove man. He liked hustle, and Durocher fit into that. That's how he got to the Cardinals, and Leo was a spark plug for them.

But Durocher was a bad man. He was a bad person. He did a lot of things in his life. He was suspended from baseball for setting up a gambling deal along with George Raft in New York [see chapter 5]. That's when Hap Chandler kicked him out of baseball for a year. He was part of a gambling operation in the New Yorker Hotel. He and George Raft had a suite of rooms, and they had marked cards and crooked dice, and they'd get the ballplayers from the visiting team over there and take their money away from them. Oh sure, they were running this crooked thing.

Of course, George Raft was the lowest of the lowest, and he and Durocher were great friends, and Raft was as crooked as a dog's hind leg. Oh yeah, he was no good, and Durocher and he were great buddies. They had this gambling joint going, this suite of rooms over there at the New Yorker Hotel. That's how Durocher was kicked out of baseball. He was in on that thing. With Raft. They were bleeding the ballplayers.

And then of course Durocher went to Brooklyn, and along with that Durocher married his first wife, she was a seamstress for the old man—she was Mr. Rickey's seamstress—and so when he came over there Rickey introduced the two of them. She was about ten years older than he was, and they got married. And they were very close with the Rickeys when they were there. Rickey went to Brooklyn, and Rickey brought Durocher to Brooklyn, made him manager, and he was a huge success, became a hit in New York. He dumped her, got a divorce from her, and married [the actress] Laraine Day, and she was married to Durocher's best friend in Hollywood. And he went out there and stayed out there during the wintertime for two years at their house, and he ended up taking his best friend's wife.

Rickey had no part in Durocher's affairs. He was strictly baseball. But without Rickey, I don't think Durocher would have even been in baseball. Rickey was a great guy for the underdog. Do you know Rickey never went to a baseball game on Sunday in his entire life? He was a lay minister and one of the greatest speakers I ever heard. I knew him in St. Louis very well. Man, he could talk. And he preached on Sundays in church. A very righteous man.

Tell me about this ballgame that you pitched. This was also the game when Joe Medwick slid into third and cut Mickey Owens, and the fans went crazy.

I didn't think I had very good stuff. We got a lot of runs. It was an easy game for me to pitch, because I was ahead most of the time. When you're ahead you're pitching a different ballgame than when you're tied, so it was a rather easy game. When you're out in front, you don't pitch to the hitters' weaknesses too much. You take a chance because you can. You can afford it. But if there are men in scoring position then you pitch to their weaknesses. You're pitching then. And that was an easy game for me. I didn't feel I was overpowering.

When I warmed up, I felt great. Mickey felt I had it too. And when I started, I really felt good. But as it ended up, they got me out of there in about the third inning. Frisch got a hit with two men out and the bases loaded. I had three and two on him, and he fouled off about half a dozen pitches, and then he hit a soft liner into left field. Hank Greenberg got his glove on it. The ball fell short of Pete Fox in rightfield and it rolled over into the drainage along with seats, and Pete ran down there to get the ball, and he caught his foot in the drainage ditch, and he kicked the ball before he could pick it up, and kicked it down in the dugout, and Cochrane ended up with the ball. By this time three runs scored, and Frisch ended up on second base.

A three and two pitch. He was a left-hand hitter and he pulled it into right, and it hit Hank's glove. And that broke the game open. Schoolboy came in and two other pitchers, and they scored seven runs in that inning.

Later on, incidentally, Diz and I were playing bridge in the wintertime, and we got talking about that game, and Diz said, "You know, the game you pitched against us in St. Louis, the guys said they didn't know how they even got four runs. All of them said, 'That guy is tough.'" And he added, "The first time they batted against me in the first two innings, each of them came into the dugout and said, 'He doesn't have it today.'"

I didn't have it when I thought I had it, but I had it when I didn't have it. And that's something a pitcher never knows. You may think you know, but you don't. The catcher sometimes knows. But that was the big play of the day that broke it open, and they had the fight at third base, and they threw Medwick out of the game, and Kennesaw Mountain Landis came on the field. Medwick was just a hustler, and he ran in and was running. He didn't try to cut Owens. Joe was a good guy, and a good hitter. He ran hard and fast. Hard-nosed baseball is all it was.

What happened was, when Medwick went into third base, he was out, and he went in with his right spike high, he slid in, and he caught Marvin—Marvin went down to tag him, and his foot came in high, and he caught Marvin on the shoulder and cut him up a little bit, tore through his shirt, and Marvin thought he did it on purpose, and Marvin took the ball and tried to run his neck, and everything blew up.

Marvin Owen was like a preacher. For him to fight was something terrible. No one ever saw that kind of reaction from Marvin until that incident. And they thought that was intentional. It wasn't a fight. It was a scuffle. And when they got up, they went after each other, and the umpire broke it up, but the people wouldn't let up on it.

The people were mad because we were behind. And then the Cards scored seven runs. The people came out the night before, and they brought their breakfast with them and lunched, and they started throwing bottles out on the field at Medwick. They were disgusted. They were mad at Medwick, and then Judge Landis had to come out and take him out of the ball game. And they wouldn't stop. They asked them over the speakers not to do it. But they just kept it up. They were upset.

I understand Dizzy was clowning around at the end of that game.
He was laughing and joking. Of course, he was ahead 11 to nothing. He was having a good time. We were all upset. I left the ballpark at the end of the fourth inning. I listened to it on the radio. I didn't even stay. I got out of there. The game was over, the season was over.

There is one thing that happened in Game 4 that I forgot to mention, which was really a stupid thing on the part of [Cards manager] Frankie Frisch. Why Frisch would do this I don't know. Someone got on base, and it was long about the sixth or seventh inning, but someone pinch hit and got a hit with a man on first, and Frisch put Dean in to run.

On the next play, Diz was on first, and a double play ball was hit to Charlie Gehringer. Rogell came across for the throw to make the double play and Diz came in standing up. He didn't slide, and Rogell touched the bag and was throwing to first base thinking Diz would get out of the way. Rogell threw the ball, and he hit Dean right between the eyes, right in the forehead with the ball. The ball hit the bill of his cap square. It took the power out of the throw and knocked Diz flat. He was out. They had to get a stretcher to take him off the field. They took him to the hospital, and the headline the next day was, "Dean's Head Is X-rayed; They Found Nothing."

That was a joke for years around there. Diz really could have been hurt.

You had a 3 game to 2 lead, and you only had to win one of the last two games in the 1934 series.
That's right. There was a play at third base in that 6th game. Mickey Cochrane slid into third base, and he was the winning run. He slid in there with one out in the 8th inning, and there is a picture of that on record, and it shows where Mickey is into the base with his knees folded up. Pepper Martin has the ball in his hand outstretched, and the ball is

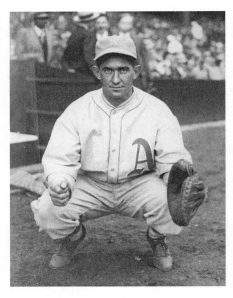

Mickey Cochrane

this far from his glove, and Brick Owens the umpire has his thumb up in the air and called him out. That cost us the series. No doubt about it.

Mickey blamed him for losing the series. Brick Owens shouldn't have even been umpiring. Brick Owens was an old umpire. He was not a good umpire, and he just blew that call. He wasn't even in position to see the play. And he had his thumb up in the air before Martin ever caught the ball.

Cochrane made it into the bag folded up. He was safe. He beat the ball by quite some distance. And he was the winning run. We never would have gone to the 7th game.

In 1935 Babe Ruth was gone from the American League.
That was his last year. He went to the Boston Braves.

Did the league miss him?
Yeah. Oh yeah. The fans missed him. The pitchers didn't miss him. But he could still hit. He was overweight and his legs were failing him. He couldn't run as fast. He couldn't run in the outfield. He had small legs and a big, heavy torso. He had a big stomach by this time, and he was heavy. In the winter he retired. His legs failed him, and he could not do the fielding, but he could still hit.

The Yankees took an early lead in 1935. They were in first place until July.
We lost the first nine ballgames of the season. Look up the record. We lost nine straight games to open up the 1935 season. And the last game we lost was in Cleveland, and I pitched the ballgame against Mel Harder,

and they beat me 2 to 1, and they beat me in the 9th inning when Sammy Hale hit a home run over the short right field fence in League Park. It was 200 and some feet—there was a screen up there, and he hit a pop fly over that thing. Beat us 2 to 1. I was leading 1 to nothing. That was it.

After that Cochrane came in, and he said, "You guys go out and get drunk or do something, and get this thing out of your system. We're too tight. We just can't go through this. Do something. Do anything you want to tonight. Come in any hour of the night you want. Whatever you want to do."

That loosened us up. We came in the next day and the clubhouse had a completely different atmosphere. We were laughing and joking. And we went out and won 12 games in a row, and we lost a game and then won 15 games in a row and were in first place, and we were never out of first place the rest of the season.

We went into Yankee Stadium, and we beat them four in a row. Schoolboy won the first game. Bridges won the second game. I won the third game. I beat Gomez 2 to nothing. I pitched a two-hit ballgame. Schoolboy came back and pitched the fourth game and won that. He beat them two games in one series.

You faced the Chicago Cubs in the 1935 World Series. What were your expectations prior to that series?

We had scouting reports, who was a low-ball hitter, who was a high-ball hitter. Who could run, who couldn't run. Where was the power? When they hit, how the outfielders played them. We had all those reports.

The pitchers' main concern was how to pitch to them. They had some good hitters on that ballclub. Gabby Hartnett was a baseball player. They had Stan Hack, Charlie Grimm, Frank Demaree. We knew they had a good ballclub and a good pitching staff with Warneke, Root, and a couple other hard-throwing guys.

We couldn't hit Lon Warneke. We didn't get a run off that guy in all the time he pitched in the series. He pitched 27 innings against us, and we never got a run against him. We couldn't hit him. He was a master out there, one of the best pitchers we'd seen in a long time. You look up his record. He shut us out twice, then he relieved, and we didn't get any runs off him then.

I started the second game and pitched the first seven innings. I pitched against Bill Lee, and we were tied up 2 and 2 when I left, and we got a guy on first, and Gerald Walker went in to pinch hit for me. He hadn't hit into a double play for I don't know how long. We thought we were going to do something, but darned if he didn't hit into a double play and stop the inning.

An interesting side, about 1960 I was on the Board of Directors of the National Association of Manufacturers, a representative of NAM, the political arm of the industry. Every year we held our annual meeting in New York at the Waldorf in the Starlight Room, and we always had a well-known speaker. We had Presidents Eisenhower and Kennedy, and this year we had Ronald Reagan, the governor of California.

It was customary to have a reception for the guest speaker, so we had this reception. Our board was made up of 50 men, representatives from each state, and I represented the state of Massachusetts.

At this reception Nancy and the governor were there. We were introduced individually. Well, I'm never the first guy in line, and we didn't go through the line until the light flashed. When it was about time to leave, Mildred said to me, "I want to meet Nancy. I've heard a lot about her."

Governor Reagan had met 40 of our members. We got in line to meet him, when our chairman said, "I'd like to present Elden and Mildred Auker."

The governor stuck his hand out and said, "Elden Auker. My god, I will never forget you. You probably don't remember me."

"Wait a minute," I said. "We have this in reverse, don't we?"

"No no no," Reagan said. "In 1935 you pitched the opening game for the Detroit Tigers against the Cubs in Chicago. You went to the seventh inning, and you won the game in the 12th inning. That right?"

"That's right," I said.

He said, "You remember talking to a sports announcer prior to warming up for the game?"

"No. Not any special one," I said.

He said, "And you don't remember talking to the announcer after the game either, do you?"

"I guess not," I said.

"I told you, you didn't remember me, because I'm the guy who interviewed you prior to your warming up and after the game," Reagan said. "I was selected as the official sports announcer for the Chicago Cubs for that World Series. I was announcer over in Des Moines, Iowa, for WHO, and I broadcast all the Cubs game over telegraph."

He said, "The Cubs came over and asked if I would broadcast the games from Chicago. I was the official announcer. That was the first break I had in the entertainment business. I'll never forget that game as long as I live. It was the first break I ever had, and you were the pitcher."

In Game 2 Hank Greenberg got hurt.

He hurt his arm. A guy ran into him. The ball was on this side, and his shoulder was on the inside, and he caught it and the guy hit him and threw his arm out and fractured his wrist. They put Marv Owen on first base and Flea Clinton on third. It was a hell of an accident for us. It was a real blow.

I read that the Cubs had ridden Hank Greenberg rather brutally.

I heard that claim before. I never saw it. The only time I ever heard about anything in this area we were playing the White Sox in Detroit one day. I was working the ballgame, and Hank flew out or grounded out, and he was walking back past the visitor's dugout, which was on the first base side, and Hank came on back, didn't say anything.

Tommy Bridges' locker was next to my locker, and I was next to Hank's for six years. Hank came in after the game, never said anything, but he was upset about something. We didn't know what it was.

We won the ballgame. He didn't say anything. He took off his outside shirt, took his spikes off, and he slipped on his shower slippers, and he walked out.

The visiting clubhouse was right across the hall from us. We had a common ramp to the dugouts, ours to the left, the visitors to the right. Hank walked out of our clubhouse and into the White Sox clubhouse. He opened up the door and walked in, and he stood in front of all of them and he said, "I want the guy who called me a Yellow Jew Son of a Bitch to stand up."

Nobody moved. Hank went around to every one of them, looked at every one of them, and not one guy said one word. He turned around and walked out and came back to our locker like nothing had ever happened.

I didn't know where he went. He told me the story. It's a good thing the guy didn't stand up, because Hank would have killed him. That's the only time I ever heard an incident like that, and I played with Hank for six years. I never heard another player call him a Jew, or ever refer to him in a negative way.

Maybe Hank heard it, but I never heard it. We never thought about anything like that. He was like a brother. If something had been heard, we'd have known about it, and we'd have been ready to fight with him. Hank was our brother. It's hard for me to believe it, because if you knew Hank Greenberg, you'd better be hiding if you said anything like that to him. He'd take you apart. Hank was tough.

We had an incident happen in spring training. We played the Cardinals in an exhibition game over in Bradenton, and Hank had a headache. He had to leave the game about the fourth or fifth inning. He went on the bus and sat down to go to sleep. He didn't feel well.

When the game was over we started back home. Rip Sewell and some of the other guys in the back were cutting up, and Hank was asleep. Sewell, who was kind of a smart ass, reached over and hit him on the top of the head.

"Wake up," Rip said.

"Rip, don't do that again," Hank said. "I have a headache."

Pretty soon Sewell reached over and did it again. Hank never said a word. When we got off the bus in front of the Lakeland Tennis Hotel, Sewell was in the back, and Hank was in front of him. Hank got up. We all got off.

When Sewell stepped off the bus, Hank grabbed him right by the collar. He took him around the side of the hotel, and he slapped his face hard.

"I told you," he said. "Don't you ever do that to me again. Don't you ever lay a hand on me again."

Sewell got out of there like a beat child, and that was the end of it.

When General Crowder won Game 4 of the 1935 World Series, once again the Tigers only had to win one of the two next games to win the series. Talk about the final game.

Tommy Bridges pitched that game at home in Detroit. I can tell you one thing about that game that I well remember: I was sitting on the steps, and I was supposed to pitch the game the next day if it went to the seventh game. I'm sitting on the steps, and Goose Goslin came up to me in the 9th inning. The game was tied up. Bridges had just gotten out of the inning. Goose was the fourth hitter. Jo Jo White led off, and Cochrane got on base.

Before that inning started Goose leaned over to me, and he said, "I have a hunch. I'm going to be on base with the winning run, and we're going to win the series. And I'm going to be the guy who drives the run in."

"I hope so," I said.

And that's exactly what happened. White popped out. Cochrane got on first. They got him over to second base, and there were two men out when Goslin came to bat, and he got the hit over the second baseman's head, and Mickey scored, and we won. Goose came running back from first base. I was waiting on him, and he said, "What did I tell you? What did I tell you? What did I tell you?"

It was Detroit's first World Championship ever, and Detroit went absolutely crazy. They upset street cars. They celebrated all night. The businesses let the people off the next day. Businesses shut down the next day to celebrate.

That night we didn't dare go out anyplace. A friend of mine, Harvey Fruehauf, of Fruehauf trailers, and his wife were friends. We met in Detroit. After the game Harvey called me and said, "What are you doing this evening?"

"We're going to stay home. It's a madhouse out there," I said.

"Why don't you come down to the Detroit Athletic Club, and the four of us will have dinner there?"

I said, "Okay."

We got dressed and snuck out of the apartment and drove down to the Athletic Club and came in the back way. If the fans had seen me in a car, they'd have stopped the car, maybe taken me out of the car. People were crazy. And that's where we spent the evening.

Two months later Frank Navin died. He was 64 years old.

We stayed in Detroit about a month. I attended banquets, went to schools, gave talks, Rotary Clubs, all over the state. We did that because the people wanted to see us, and then we drove out to my hometown to be there for Thanksgiving. We had just arrived that night, when there was a telegram waiting for us. Frank Navin had dropped dead. We turned right around and drove back to Detroit. I never even stayed all night with my folks. We drove 25 straight hours back to Detroit for the funeral. He was a great guy. He was like a father.

I had won three or four games in the first couple months of 1934, and Mr. Navin called me up to the office.

"Here's a little bonus for you," he said.

He gave me $2,500. At that time I was making $450 a month, same salary I had when they signed me.

Later on I got another bonus of $2,500, and we got into the World Series, and I got $3,400 from that. It doesn't sound like much money, but in those days, it was a lot of money. *A lot* of money.

When Navin died, Walter Briggs took over the ballclub. Were there any im-mediate changes that you noticed?

I had a good season in 1935. I led the league in winning percentage that year. We had won the World Series. I was making $7,500 for that year. Mr. Navin gave it to me.

When contract time came, I was in Lakeland, Florida, and they sent me three contracts. The first one was for $10,000. I sent it back unsigned.

"I need to make more money," I said.

They sent another for $11,000. I didn't sign that one.

They sent me another one for $11,500. I was still unhappy, and I sent it back.

I received a call one day from Joel Shevlin, Mr. Briggs' private secre-tary. Mr. Briggs had no women secretaries. Mr. Briggs had a big home on Collins Avenue in Miami. I was in Lakeland.

Joe said, "The old man would like to see you about your contract. Can you come to Miami?"

I drove into the compound, and Briggs' son Walter Junior, who we called Spike, said, "Boy, you got here at a bad time. We have a strike on."

There was a strike at the Mack Avenue Plant in Detroit.

"They are throwing cushions out of the fourth story of the building up there," Spike said. "They are setting it on fire. The Old Man has been up all night long."

He had fought the unions like crazy, you know. Boy, Mr. Briggs was in a foul mood. And he was mean and tough.

Even Mrs. Briggs had to call Joel Shevlin to make an appointment to see him. They had lived together as man and wife for years. They stayed together to raise the kids. She wanted to see the old man. They lived separately in the house. She had to call Joel if she wanted to talk to him.

I waited around for a half hour, then three quarters of an hour, and finally Joel came out and led me to Mr. Briggs' office.

Mr. Briggs had a great big desk, and he had his wheelchair. There were piles of papers, some here, some there, and he wheeled between these. Automobile business in one pile, baseball business in the other, I guess. It was the largest desk I ever saw. They made it for him. It must have been 20-feet long, a beautiful desk.

I went in there, and he said, "Auker, why haven't you signed those contracts?"

"Well, sir, it wasn't enough money," I said.

"How much money do you want to sign a contract?"

"I'd like to get $15,000," I said.

"Fifteen thousand dollars!"

"Yes. I think I'm worth that. I think I'm worth more, but I'd like to have $15,000."

"Jesus Christ," he said. Then he swore.

"Fifteen thousand dollars?" he said. "What am I going to pay the rest of the players? Jesus Christ, I can't afford $15,000."

"$15,000 is what I'd like to have," I said.

He ranted and raved.

I got up.

"Where are you going?" he said.

"If you're mad at me, I'll leave. I don't want you to be mad at me."

"Sit down," he said.

He pushed a button and Joel came in.

"Give him a contract for $15,000," Mr. Briggs said.

I signed it, and that was it. Good day. See you later.

I wasn't in there ten minutes, and I didn't want to be there five minutes longer either. I thought he was going to hit me. Mr. Briggs was really tough.

If he had said, "I'm not going to give it to you," I'd have had no choice.

Charlie Gehringer had hit .370, led the league, and Mr. Briggs had said to him, "I'm going to give you $25,000 this year. I don't give a damn if you hit .500 next year. That's all the money you'll ever get out of me. You're the highest paid player on the ballclub, and I'll never give you another dime more."

Later after Charlie finished playing baseball, the Tigers called and asked him if he would be a consultant.

"I don't know," Charlie said.

"We'll give you $75,000 to be a consultant," they said.

In 1936 Mickey Cochrane got hit in the head with a pitch.

It happened in New York in Yankee Stadium. Bump Hadley hit him. Schoolboy Rowe and I helped him on a stretcher to carry him upstairs to the locker room. I thought he was dead.

Mickey was hitting, and Bump was pitching, and Bump had a good slider, a fast curveball. Mickey was a left-handed hitter, and Bump was a right hand pitcher. Mickey saw the pitch was high, and he just turned his head, and the ball sailed into him and hit him right in the temple. He went down like that. He had seven fractures in his head. It fractured his skull. I thought he was dead. He dropped like someone had shot him. He layed there on the ground kicking. Scared the hell out of everybody. We took him to the hospital.

It took him a while to recover, but his vision was never good after that. He came back and tried to play, but he couldn't see well. He gave it up. He tried to manage, but the old man was on him a lot, trying to run the ballclub and be president of the ballclub. He had Spike in there trying to run things, and Cochrane wouldn't put up with him. They got into a fight, and the old man fired him. He may have been president of the club, but Spike didn't know where third base was. But he was representing the old man. Spike was a figurehead. He didn't have anything to say.

We'd go on road trips, and Spike would go with us, and the old man would send detectives along to see what Spike was doing and report back to him. If Spike had a chance, he'd go out and drink and carouse around. He liked the girls, and the old man knew it.

The old man killed Spike. Spike ended up an alcoholic. Spike had no self-respect really. And he was a pretty good guy.

After Mickey was beaned, your third base coach, Del Baker, took over as manager for a few weeks. Did the players miss Mickey?

Very much. The pitchers missed him. We lost the greatest catcher in the business, and the ballclub missed him with his hitting. He was a .300 hitter and our leader. Baker was not a leader. He was a coach. He had been a catcher who played a few games in the organization. They picked him up, and he had managed the year before in Beaumont, Texas. We needed a third base coach, and they brought Baker up because he knew the boys. Bing Miller was more of a hitters' coach.

In 1937 you once again had a good year. Your catchers were Rudy York and Birdie Tebbetts.

I pitched the first game Birdie ever caught in the big leagues. George Tebbetts came out of Nashua, New Hampshire, went to Providence College, and we were in New York playing a series, and Art Wishaken, our traveling secretary, came to me. Tommy Bridges had been sent back to Detroit because he was going to open up our series. Tommy was my roommate, and Art said, "We have a young fellow we're bringing up from Providence College. Birdie Tebbetts is going to be with us tonight. You mind if I put him in the room with you?"

So he brought him up and introduced me to him, and he was my roommate that night. A little red-headed guy. He was going to work out with us the next day on Sunday before the game. This was on a Saturday.

I was pitching the ballgame the next day against Lefty Gomez. This kid came in, a nice clean-cut kid. I had dinner with him at the New Yorker Hotel. We go to bed, and I had focused on the paper I was reading, getting ready for bed about 9:30, and he wouldn't turn the lights off. He kept fooling around.

"What's the matter?" I said. "Aren't you going to go to bed?"

In a very bashful way he said, "Mr. Auker, would you mind if I said my prayers? I've never gone to bed without ever saying my prayers."

He was a very good Catholic boy.

I said, "No. I'll get down with you. Kneel down and say your prayers. That's great."

I crawled out of bed, got on my knees, hand on the bed, and he said his prayers and went to bed. He worked out the next day, and I never saw him again until the next spring training.

In 1938 Hank Greenberg's 58 home runs came within two of tying Babe Ruth's single season home run record.

I remember it very well. I hit two home runs in one day against the St. Louis Browns. The first home run I hit, I said to Hank, "Here's one for you." Well, we were just pulling like the devil for him to break it. I don't ever remember a pitcher trying to pitch around him. It just went on as a regular game. He could do it. He could hit the ball hard.

Why didn't he do it? He still had a couple of weeks to go.

He just couldn't break it. He just couldn't get it out of the ballpark. There was pressure, but I don't think it bothered Hank. He just didn't hit it.

Oh, he could hit that ball as far as anyone could. Oh, he had a lot of power. He was tall, and he'd swing that bat and Christ, almost like Ruth, when he got through swinging there wasn't any air left in the ballpark to breathe. He could hit most anything, and he could hit to left field and right field.

In August of 1938 Briggs fired Mickey Cochrane. Mickey had fought with Briggs' son Spike. Did Mickey talk about it?

No. But we knew what was going on. Spike was caught in between. The old man was trying to get him into the game. He couldn't participate, and he wanted Spike to take over as president. Spike was the heir apparent. When Spike got in there, this was his chance to be somebody. And he tried to be somebody. The players liked Spike very much. I liked Spike and his wife Laura. I went to their home for dinner. Nice people. Spike was a nice guy, and Laura was a beautiful girl.

Hank Greenberg

When he got put in this position, Mickey was running the ballclub. When Mickey managed, *he* ran the ballclub. *Nobody* told him who was going to play where or what, not Briggs or nobody else. If you're going to do that, get somebody else, and that's what happened. He put Spike in there, and if the old man wanted something, he'd tell Spike, "This is what I want."

Spike would try to tell Mickey, and Mickey would say, "The hell with you. I'm not doing this."

Old man Briggs was telling Spike to tell Mickey where to play people?

Yes, and Spike was caught in between. At one time Mickey and Spike were close friends. Both of them were good guys. But the old man put him in an intolerable position for Spike. And Mickey too.

What was the reaction of the ballclub when Mickey was fired?

We were upset about it, naturally, but there wasn't much you could do about it, because we were just part of the club, and that was a club decision, and that was it. Del Baker was acceptable to us because he had been with us. Of course, he couldn't replace Mickey, but we accepted him and went ahead.

Was there anything between you and Del, because in 1939 you were traded.
In 1938 Marv Owen retired from the Tigers, and that's why I went to Boston. Because when Marvin retired, the Tigers needed a third baseman, and they didn't have anyone in the minor leagues, and so Pinky Higgins was playing third base for the Red Sox, and the Sox had a fellow by the name of Jim Tabor, who was in the minor leagues, and he had a great season in Louisville, and so they were bringing Jim Tabor up at third base, and the Tigers needed a third baseman, and the Red Sox wanted pitching, so they traded me for Pinky Higgins. One reason was that Joe Cronin couldn't hit me with a handful of sand.

That's how I went to Boston. I wasn't happy about going to Boston, because I didn't want to leave Detroit.

Anyway, that was the deal.

CHAPTER THREE

ELDEN AUKER

Joe Cronin Drives Him Crazy

When you were traded over to Boston, you got to witness Ted Williams' rookie season in 1939.

That's right. Ted was a kid. And *all* he had on his mind was hitting. In the clubhouse we had mirrors. Every time he went in the clubhouse he'd pick up a bat and stand in front of the mirror and swing. All he wanted to do was swing that bat, and in spring training he drove everybody crazy by asking them what kind of a pitcher was Red Ruffing, Lefty Gomez, Ted Lyons, and all the rest of them, and every time we went into whatever town we were going into, he wanted to know how this guy pitched.

Ted just bled everybody to death talking to you about how a guy pitched. He studied them. Ted Williams and Hank Greenberg were two of the real students of the game. Hank was not a natural ballplayer. When Hank came to the major leagues, he couldn't catch a pop fly. He would get Del Baker out there at nine o'clock in the morning, hitting him pop flies to where Hank could catch them in his jockstrap. Hank was big. He wasn't fast. He was an awkward guy, and he made himself into a ballplayer. He was a student of the game.

Ted Williams studied how everybody pitched and how they hit, and where they hit. If it was Charlie Gehringer, Ted knew he hit to left field a lot, and he played him that way and adjusted himself. They didn't think Ted could run very fast, but Ted could run fast. He took long strides. Ted had that ability to get himself in position where many other times it would be a base hit, but he was always there. He played the position properly. He was a student of the game. He never quit thinking about baseball.

Ted was 19 years of age. He liked fried chicken. He never drank. He never smoked. His father was an alcoholic. He had a brother who was an alcoholic. His mother worked for the Salvation Army, and he told me his first year up, he was making $6,500. He said, "The first money I get is going to my mother to get her out of the Salvation Army. I want her to quit working for the Salvation Army."

We always had to wear a coat and tie. With the Tigers we had a fifty-dollar fine with Mickey [Cochrane] if we appeared in public at the ballpark, at home or on the road or in a hotel without a shirt, a tie, and a coat. And in Boston they had the same thing.

Ted wouldn't buy anything for himself. He'd send money home every single month for her. I think that's when he started wearing that open-neck shirt. He wore a sports shirt. He wouldn't spend money for a necktie. He wore the same clothes day after day. He had a jacket. And he was the guy who broke the barrier.

Ted Williams

Tell me about the feud between Ted and the sportswriters.

The sportswriters in Boston were terrible. They had mean guys there. Bill Cunningham was a real rat. He was the guy who got into it with Ted, tried to break him. Ted had broken all records in Minneapolis in the American Association. There was a lot of publicity in the Boston papers about this young kid.

During spring training in 1939 we had just had dinner at night. They had a little putt putt golf course down the street, about three blocks from the hotel. We were staying in the Sarasota Terrace Hotel. Lefty Grove and his wife, Fritz Ostermueller and his wife, Jack Wilson and his wife, Jimmie Foxx by himself, and Ted by himself, were all sitting around in the lobby after we finished dinner. Ted was sitting in this big chair and he had his leg cocked, and we were choosing up sides to go down and have a golf game.

The elevator door opened, and this Bill Cunningham came out of the elevator with his porkpie hat on. He came from Dartmouth. He always had his pork pie hat which he was proud of, smoking a cigar. He always had that in his mouth. He was about half drunk, which he was about half the time.

Cunningham walked right up to our group, went over to Williams, and said, "Okay, kid. Let's go upstairs and get it over with. The people in Boston are waiting with bated breath to talk to the great kid from Minneapolis. Let's go up and get the interview over with."

Ted looked at him and said, "I'm sorry, sir, I never give interviews to sportswriters when they're drinking."

Cunningham was furious. He was insulted. He was the dean of all sportswriters. And to have this kid tell him that. He turned and walked away, and to the day Ted Williams left Boston to the day they took Cunningham off the sports section, he never had an interview with Ted Williams.

We had a clubhouse manager in Boston, Johnny Orlando, and Cunningham'd walk in, and Cronin had a little cage for his office, right inside, and the sportswriters would come in and have meetings, get the story from Joe, and Cunningham would open up that door, and Ted would see him, and Ted would yell out, "Orlando, get that son of a bitch out of this clubhouse."

He cussed him out from one end to the other. Cunningham would write the worst stories he could about Ted Williams. Ted Williams never got one good word out of Cunningham, and he spent his entire writing career trying to break Ted Williams. That's what put Ted Williams in the eyes of the fans in Boston who criticized Ted. Because of Cunningham.

Ted Williams was *not* that kind of a guy. But every time Ted would make a mistake, you'd have those guys out there, and the fans would get on him.

Ted got to the point where he said, *Screw you.* And it hurt Ted.

Harold Kaese wrote good things about Ted. Even Dave Egan was all right with Ted. He didn't spend his entire career going after Ted. Ted had no trouble with the other sportswriters. Cunningham did a lot of damage to Ted's character.

Did you like playing for Joe Cronin?

[I had no idea when I asked this question that it would open this particular can of worms. But Elden's answer said as much about why the Red Sox didn't win pennants in the 1940s as any question I could have asked.]

Well, this is a subject. Joe was a nice guy. I had been in the league for six years. My style of pitching was different from anybody else because I threw underhand. I had my own way of pitching. I knew all the hitters in the league except the youngsters on the club, and I would find out about them. But I pitched my own ballgame.

Mickey Cochrane always had the theory: Don't ever throw the pitch you don't want to throw. When I got to Boston, I got on the pitcher's mound. Johnny Peacock and Gene Desautels were my catchers. I pitched a ballgame, and I kept knocking John's glove off. He wasn't a real good receiver.

Joe Cronin kept running in and out to the pitcher's mound. He was playing shortstop, and he'd come out and say to me, "Throw him a fastball." Or "Throw him a curveball. Keep the ball in on him. Keep it away from him." He'd run in and grab the resin bag and just make the comment. He never stopped the game, but he'd run by and say, "Keep the ball down on this guy."

The first couple of games I didn't pay much attention to him, and then when I settled in after a couple games with the team, if Gene Desautels called for a pitch I didn't want to throw, I'd shake him off. And Gene would come back with the same pitch. I'd shake him off again.

Finally I said, "What the hell's the matter with you? Goddamn, when I shake you off, I don't want to throw that pitch."

"Look, I'm not calling the pitches," he said. "Cronin is giving me the pitches."

"Cronin is calling the pitches from shortstop?" I said.

He said, "Yeah."

"Jesus Christ. I never heard of such a thing."

I said something to Joe about it, and he said, "That's the way it's al-ways worked, and that's the way it's going to work. I'm responsible for this club winning or losing. That's the way it works."

So that was the way I had to pitch.

I went through four games. I pitched a game against Lefty Gomez and the Yankees in Bos-ton, and about the third inning Cronin had been on the mound about ten times, and he had me so screwed up I couldn't con-centrate on what the hell I was doing.

"Keep the ball down."

"Make him hit this pitch."

"Don't walk him."

Joe Cronin

He just kept after me. And finally, after about ten times he starts to the mound, and I hand-ed him the ball and said, "Here Joe. Why don't you pitch the Goddamn ballgame, and I'll play shortstop? How about that? I can't pitch with you in my ear all the time. If you want to pitch, you go ahead. I'll do something else."

I started to walk off the mound.

"You go back and pitch the ballgame," he said.

I didn't pitch for 27 days. That was it, right there.

Lefty Grove was the only guy who could pitch for him. Lefty Grove was a close friend of Tom Yawkey. They went deer hunting and quail shooting together in the fall to his place down South. Grove had been there for years and had Yawkey's ear, so Cronin stayed away from Grove. Grove didn't care for him. When Cronin walked to the mound, Grove would walk to the dugout. He never talked to Cronin in a ballgame. He pitched his own ballgame. But Grove was the only one. The rest of us had to pitch with him calling the signals and on the mound talking to you.

Jack Wilson had a lot of potential. He was a good pitcher, but Cronin drove him crazy. You never knew when you were going to start. Fritz Ostermueller about went crazy. He did this to the whole pitching staff. Of course, they had been used to it.

Ostermueller was a damn good left handed pitcher. Hank Greenberg almost killed him in Boston. I was with Detroit. Fritz was a left-hand pitcher. And Cronin was driving him crazy. He never knew when he was going to pitch a game. He called Fritz in from the bullpen one day to relieve. Greenberg was at bat. Fritz had a delivery where he finished very low, and he followed completely through. He pitched on the outside, and Hank hit it directly back at Ostermueller, and the ball hit him right in the face, shattered his jawbone, knocked out or loosened all of his teeth. We thought Hank had killed him. I didn't think he'd ever pitch again, but he did.

Hank was as white as a sheet. I didn't know if Hank was even going to finish the game, he was so upset by it. It hurt Hank, scared him, because he had hit the ball so hard. I think it was the first time he realized how dangerous he could be.

With Cronin, you never knew when you were going to pitch. You'd start a ballgame, maybe sit for another ten days, never start another one. Today you might be in the bullpen. You go out and think you might start. The only time you knew you were going to start was when you went to the ballpark, and he'd say, "You're pitching today." He might tell you the night before, "Get ready for tomorrow." That's the way it was all year. I was so messed up, I didn't want to pitch.

[Auker's record pitching for Boston in 1939 was 9–10 with a 5.36 ERA. He only pitched six complete games.]

Tom Yawkey and Mr. [Eddie] Collins called me in at the end of

Elden Auker

the season, and he said, "We want to sign you up for next year. We'd like you to sign your contract before you leave."

"Tom and Eddie," I said, "you just signed Joe Cronin to a five-year contract. I cannot do you any good. If Joe is going to be here, you are wasting your money with me. I can't pitch for Joe Cronin. I'll either quit baseball or else you can sell me or trade me, get rid of me. I'd love to pitch in Boston, but I just cannot do the job with him out there."

I liked Joe. I wasn't mad at him. But that was Joe. He was as nervous as he could be. He couldn't help it. He was sincere in what he was trying to do, but Jesus Christ, he just couldn't handle a pitching staff. He drove you nuts.

Fritz Ostermueller and Jack Wilson, Jesus, they were beside themselves. I thought Fritz was going to be an alcoholic. He'd go home and he was so frustrated, he didn't know what he was doing. And it was too bad, because we had a good ballclub. God Almighty, Bobby Doerr had just come up. We had Jimmie Foxx at first. Joe Cronin was a hell of a ballplayer at shortstop. Jim Tabor, Joe Vosmik, Ted Williams. We had a great team. And we had good pitchers. We had Grove, Wilson, Ostermueller, Dixon, a good pitcher, but Cronin drove him crazy. He couldn't pitch his ballgame. He couldn't concentrate.

Cronin would drive you nuts. We went on one trip. I was rooming with Jimmie Foxx, and Yawkey knew this. Yawkey said to Jim, "What would you do if you took charge of the pitching staff? I know that Joe is having problems. Would you take it over?"

"I don't see how I could do that and still play on the team with Joe being the manager and me managing the pitchers," Jim said.

"I understand the problem, but I don't know what to do about it," Yawkey said.

Cronin was a real politician with Yawkey. He named his first son Tommy after him. And Mildred, Joe's wife, was also a very good politician. She was a Griffith. [She was Washington owner Clark Griffith's daughter.] It was a political situation. Eddie Collins was kind of in between on the deal. He worked for Yawkey, and he knew what was going on, but there wasn't much he could do about it. They needed a manager, and though we had finished second, we should have won the damn pennant.

At the end of the 1939 season the Red Sox traded you—to the lowly St. Louis Browns.

Fred Haney, the manager of the Browns, called me.

"Elden," he said, "I've talked to Tom Yawkey, and he said it was all right for me to talk to you. Tom tells me you do not want to play in Boston next year, and there's a possibility of your quitting baseball."

"That's right," I said. "I will not play in Boston. I'm wasting my time. I can't put up with it here."

"Would you play for me if I traded for you?" he asked.

"Great," I said.

"I'll make the deal."

In 1939 the Browns lost 111 games. What was it like going from Boston to St. Louis?

Outside of Detroit, I had three of the most enjoyable years I ever had, and the reason they were enjoyable was because we had a nice bunch of ballplayers. They weren't great ballplayers, but we had a good ballclub, a good little team. We had a manager, Fred Haney, who was one of the nicest guys you ever saw. He was a great manager. He took me back to Mickey Cochrane. He was just like Mickey. He was one of us. He was with us all the time. He loved to win, and he was a player himself, so he knew what the game was all about. "When you walk on that mound," he said, "it's your game. Go get 'em."

Fred never bothered you. You knew when you were going to pitch. You were in a rotation whether you won or got beat. You were pitching, and you were on your own, and Don Barnes, who owned the ballclub, was one of the nicest guys in the world.

One night in Cleveland I pitched a ballgame against Mel Harder. I beat him 2 to 1, and in the 9th inning I loaded the bases. The stadium was packed. Cleveland was driving for the pennant, fighting the Tigers in 1940. The crowd in Cleveland was so loud, you couldn't hear yourself think. You never heard anything like it in your life. The crowd was crazy.

Haney came out to me, and he said, "You want to get out of here, or you want to stay?"

"Leave me here," I said. "I'm going to be all right."

"Okay, go get 'em," he said.

I struck out the next two batters, and got a pop up to the infield, and the ballgame was over. We stopped them. I beat them.

When the game was over, we were in the clubhouse, and Browns owner Don Barnes was in there. He had gotten so excited he had wet his pants. He reached into his pocket, and he gave me five one-hundred-dollar bills.

"That was the greatest ballgame I ever saw in my life," he said.

That's the way he was.

Don Barnes was very wealthy. He owned the Public Finance Corporation of America, the largest small-owned corporation in the United States, and he started with three hundred dollars as a youngster, and he built it into a fortune.

So why weren't the Browns better?

Well, I don't know. They had a good farm system with San Antonio and two other clubs. They weren't a wealthy club. Barnes owned it, but it was separate from his business. A separate entity, and he had only put in so much money.

But we finally got the people coming out in St. Louis. We drew pretty good crowds. And then we had the lights put in in 1940, and I pitched the first night game against Bob Feller, and he beat me 3 to 2. He hit his first home run in the major leagues off of me. Into the right field stands. I threw him a fastball. You could spit over that fence in right field. It was only about 230 feet.

Was playing under the lights exciting?

I had played under the lights in the Texas League. And we had lights in the American League in Chicago.

What was Sportsman's Park like when you came to play there?

It was in bad shape. They played 154 ballgames at that park. The Cardinals played in it, and the Browns played it. The groundskeepers worked their tails off trying to keep it in shape, but it was hot in the summertime. The field was baked. You walked out on that field with your steel cleats on, and your feet would almost burn off.

I pitched a ballgame there in 1936 on the 4th day of July, and the first game of a doubleheader, and I was in perfect physical condition. I pitched nine innings. I changed my uniform three times, and I lost 11 pounds pitching that ballgame. There was no air conditioning at the hotel or any place else, and it was 110 when I walked on the pitcher's mound.

What was the city of St. Louis like in 1940?
Beautiful. It was a great town. It was highly industrialized. They made textiles, had foundries, had steel mills on the river. They had all kinds of industries, a leather industry. Later on St. Louis had breweries. That was a river trade. In the old days St. Louis was a major industrial town in the West on the Mississippi River.

It was a good town. Fisher Body had a plant there. Ford had a plant there.

What did you and the other players do for recreation in St. Louis?
We went to picture shows like everyone else. We stayed at the Chase Hotel there. It was first class, great. They had theaters. We played cards, bridge, hearts.

In the winter of 1940 Don Barnes bought four pitchers, George Caster, Johnny Allen, Denny Galehouse, and Fritz Ostermueller.
That's right. Galehouse came over from Cleveland and Allen from the Yankees.

Allen was tough. He sure was. He was one of the most competitive pitchers you ever saw. Boy, he could throw that ball right through the wall. And he'd throw it right through your head if you got a good solid hit off him. He broke Gerald Walker's wrist one day. He was mean. He went out there to win that ballgame.

Again, the nicest family man you ever saw. His wife was a lovely person. He had a son who he adored.

Denny was a very quiet, soft-spoken guy. A first-class gentleman. A good pitcher. He had good years. He was a workhorse. He went out and did his job and never said much.

Fred Haney quit as manager after only 40 games in 1940. Luke Sewell took over. The team was not doing very well.

I remember. Haney left the ballclub and went to California as an announcer. He went into the radio business. He had managed the Hollywood team [in the Pacific Coast League] for several years. He had a lot of friends out there. And he became disgruntled. He and Barnes were good friends. No hard feelings between the two of them. He had this opportunity in California, and he became the announcer for the Hollywood Stars. He had been the manager. He was very popular.

Later, the Cowboy [Gene Autry] came to him and asked if he would go in with him to buy the Angels. And Fred didn't. Fred was the first general manager. He's the one who put the Angels together.

Tell me about Luke Sewell.

Luke was a good manager. He was a technician. His personality—he was not aggressive. A quiet guy. Luke was a good catcher. He was a playing manager.

You played .500 ball under Luke.

Yep. We had a pretty good ballclub. They had some confidence. We had a good first baseman in George McQuinn. We had Bob Heffner at second base. Johnny Berardino came up at shortstop. He was a good shortstop, and we had Harland Clift at third base. Walter Judnich and Rip Radcliffe were little Brownies. They weren't big guys. We didn't have any Greenbergs or Dickeys or Groves. We were all little guys, but they were good ballplayers. No big home run hitters. They had Chet Laabs, a little chunky guy. I was the biggest guy on the ballclub.

In 1941 Ted Williams hit .406.

I pitched against him. He beat me in Boston one day, broke my heart. I had Boston beat 2 to 1 going into the 9th inning. The first year Johnny Pesky came up was in 1941. We didn't know much about Johnny Pesky. We knew he could bunt and run like crazy. Run like a rabbit.

We went into the 9th inning, and I was working the ballgame against Lefty Grove. Pesky came to bat, and on the first pitch, he dumped it down the third base line and beat it out. The next hitter was Williams. Bobby Swift was my catcher, and Bobby came out to the pitcher's mound, and he said, "What do you think Williams will be doing? Hitting straight away or what?"

"Christ, I don't know," I said. "With Cronin managing, he might have him taking. We'll just have to wait and see. I'll keep the ball low and outside, keep it away from him and see whether he'll square around and bunt or hit."

I threw a pitch about two feet high off the ground—it was six inches outside—and Ted hit a line drive like a two-iron into the centerfield bleachers for a home run. The ballgame was over. He jogged around the bases, and he was waiting for me in the dugout when I came in.

"Get out of the way, you son of a bitch," I said. "I'll kill ya."

Ted started laughing. He put his arm around me, and he said, "You know what you said to Swift? I'll keep the ball low and outside, and we'll see if he's going to bunt or not. I was reading your mind. I knew exactly where you were going to throw that ball."

That was Ted Williams. "You couldn't throw a ball to an any better place," he said, "but I knew Goddamn well where you were going to throw it."

And he hit it in the centerfield bleachers for a home run.

That was Ted Williams.

He was thinking all the time.

In 1941 the Browns drew only 176,000 fans. Often you had 600 fans a game. Very few.

Why?

Because in the summertime it was hot in St. Louis. And that was not a stadium. It was a grandstands. They had to leave the grandstands open. You close it in, and people would smother. They left it open so the breeze would blow through.

The Cardinals had a winning team, and most of the St. Louis fans were Cardinals fans, because they had a winning ballclub. The 600 fans we had out there were Brownie fans, and that was the most fans we had until we started winning and doing a little better. But the Browns never had a good ballclub, and they never had too much of a following. They didn't put any money into the club. The guys who owned the club were operating from hand to mouth. They couldn't afford to have a good ball-club. It's a wonder they even survived.

Were you aware that Barnes and DeWitt were going to take the team to Los Angeles in 1942?

I had heard talk about that. I quit during the 1942 season.

They were going to have a meeting on December 8, 1941, to discuss moving to Los Angeles.

Once the war started, I wasn't going anywhere.

Where were you on December 7, 1941?

I was in Detroit. We were sitting in the apartment of the people right below us, a couple there lived there, Freddie and Edith von Bottom. He was a German baron. He was in the motion picture business. We had gone down there for a late breakfast on Sunday, and while we were sitting there, the report came over the radio. I'll never forget it. I couldn't believe it.

In February of 1942 a fellow by the name of Richard Muckerman bought the ballclub.

Muckerman was on the board of directors. I knew him. He was a great baseball fan. And very wealthy.

With Muckerman's money the Browns bought Vern Stephens and Don Gutteridge.

He put more money in when he came in. He was a great baseball fan. Barnes was the president. He had the president of Buster Brown's shoe company. Two fellows, one made women's shoes and this fellow was the president of the international shoe company, a conglomerate, formerly the Browns Shoe Company. This fellow was very wealthy. Rhythm Step Shoes, Emmitt Johnson, a very nice guy. Both of them came to spring training. We met them down there. They came in, and they had money.

Barnes was getting this group together that had some money. That's when he brought in Muckerman. I met him in spring training. I knew him.

We were pretty happy to get Stephens and Gutteridge.

The Browns never got much publicity. We had some good players. Harland Clift was a great third baseman for a long time. He never got much publicity. He never played on an All Star team. He didn't have the publicity. George McQuinn was a very good first baseman. We had good ballplayers. We got publicity in St. Louis, but not as much as the Cardinals.

We had good sportswriters in St. Louis.

In 1942 you finished the season 14 and 13. Remarkable, because most people who have records like that don't quit.

They didn't want me to quit, but the war had started. I was working for this aircraft company. The factory was in Michigan. I lived in Detroit. I started in 1938 and worked on these anti-aircraft guns. I was a specialist. And this was a hot issue. In the winter of 1941 I was hardly home.

What were you doing?

On the inside of the barrel of these guns, they had rifles in there—it's what made them shoot straight. We had a particular type of operation that cleaned them. They had to be less than three microwaves, had to be absolutely flawless, because they fired those things rapidly, and if they picked up one little grain of that shell, with the heat in there, it would melt, and it would fill up so fast with lead it would blow up the gun. It had to be perfect. And I was making thousands of these. They had a 20-millimeter and a 40-millimeter. That's what I did, and when the season was over in 1942, I left immediately and reported the next day to work.

That winter Mickey Cochrane had gone over to Great Lakes, and he wanted me to come over. He was in charge of their athletic program, and wanted to know if I would come over with him.

Captain Broadhead, the head of the Navy Reserve in Detroit, said, "If you come over, we'll make you a lieutenant junior grade, and I need help. I'd like you to come over here."

I went over to Great Lakes in north Chicago to see him. They had the best football team in the country and the best baseball team. Mickey was in charge. He had Bob Feller on his team.

I came back and called Mickey and I said, "If I'm going to fight a war, it isn't going to be in north Chicago. I can't contribute anything there. I'm on a job here, and I'm too old for the draft. I'm 31 years old. I'm married and have a child. I can do more for the war effort here."

So I announced I was going to quit.

I got a call from Don Barnes. I told him I was retiring. Clark Griffith called me, and he said, "I just talked with President Roosevelt, and he said all the older players who are not going into the service, we want to keep baseball going. I understand you said you were going to retire from the game."

"That's right."

"We'd like to have you stay in," he said.

"I can't do it," I said.

"We have to keep up the morale of the country," he said. "We'd like you to continue to play."

"Mr. Griffith," I said, "I wouldn't feel right playing baseball while guys were going overseas getting killed. I'm not going to north Chicago to coach baseball or football. I can contribute more where I am, and this is where I'm going to be."

The Browns offered me $7,500 to come back to St. Louis.

"No," I said. "I'm going into business. I get $500 a month from the company."

We were grinding 20-millimeter shells, big shells, cannons, and airplane parts. I was working on the aircraft parts. I had two guys working for me. We went all over the country.

After I quit, I never went to a ballpark for five years. I wouldn't go. I lived in Detroit for five years. I didn't want to be seen there. I was busy working, and if I went to the ballpark and sportswriters saw me, I'd get my name in the paper, and I didn't want my name in the paper. I was in business. I just didn't feel right. Guys were going to war. They were in the service. A lot of people didn't know what the hell I was doing. It was none of their business. But I knew what I was doing. I did what I thought was right.

And then when I really got into it, then things drifted away, and when baseball started up again, I lost my interest. A lot of the guys were gone. I didn't know the players. All I did was follow it in the papers. When television came along, I started watching television.

Are you a Tigers fan?

I just follow baseball. I like baseball. I was never a great fan of baseball. I played it for money. It was not a sport to me. It was a business. And when they quit paying me, I lost interest. I couldn't go out there and jump up and down and yell, get all excited. A guy hits a home run, he hits a home run. That's what he's paid for. A pitcher strikes someone out, that's what he's paid for. And I can't jump up and down and go crazy like some people can. It's a business to me. I was never a baseball fan before I started. And I was never a baseball fan when it was over.

I look at it now and admire good pitching, see the good hitters. I see the pitching staff that Atlanta has, which is amazing. To see what some of the young guys get paid today is also amazing. David Justice just signed a four-year contract for $28 million. Someone else signed one for $34 million. The owners have lost control. I don't blame the players. I hope they get ten million dollars apiece. I'd like to see them break some of the owners. It would be good for baseball. We have too many teams. The quality of the game is being lowered. You only have one or two hitters on each team.

After the war, Elden Auker worked for a company that made armaments. When he retired in 1975, he was the company president.

On August 4, 2006, Auker died of congestive heart failure at his home in Vero Beach at the age of ninety-five. He was the last surviving member of the 1935 World Championship Detroit Tigers.

CHAPTER FOUR

JOHNNY PESKY

Pesky Holds the Ball

*J*ohnny Pesky played shortstop with the Boston Red Sox from 1942 until
1954. He had a lifetime batting average of .307, and he was so beloved
that the right-field foul pole was named after him. It's now called the Pesky
Pole. For many Red Sox fans, the moment he is remembered best for may
well be the moment in the seventh game of the 1946 World Series against the
St. Louis Cardinals.

Enos Slaughter was on first base when Harry Walker lined a shot to centerfielder Leon Culberson, who was out there because star outfielder Dom
DiMaggio had been injured. Slaughter was running hard on the hit, and he
was heading toward third when Culberson threw the relay to Pesky at short.
When Pesky turned toward the outfield to catch the ball, he didn't notice
that Slaughter hadn't stopped. By the time Pesky threw home, it was too late.
Slaughter would score with the run that won the series for the Cardinals.

Some said that Slaughter had scored because Pesky had held the ball, but
that really wasn't true. Slaughter's hustle had won the day, but for the rest of
his life Johnny would have to put up with wise guy Red Sox fans who too often
remind him not to "hold the ball."

Johnny Pesky was attending one of the Red Sox fantasy camps when I interviewed him. He was gracious and happy to talk about his life in baseball.

~

*In 1942 you were a rookie, and Ted Williams was getting skewered in the
press at the time for asking for a draft deferment. In July Joe Cronin, the*

61

Johnny Pesky

manager, fined Ted $250 for loafing, and towards the end of the season Ted seemed so angry that he once told reporters that he did not want to be the MVP. He finished second. You as a rookie finished third for MVP. The question I still can't figure out is, Why did those reporters dislike Ted as much as they did?

Peter, I don't think all of them disliked Ted. A couple of them didn't think he was a true professional. They thought he was too cantankerous, and he resented the media trying to get close to him. But it seemed like a couple of them wanted to expose him as something he wasn't. That's just my impression.

Col. Dave Egan was always on Ted, but he was a guy with a flair for words who sold a lot of papers and had a nickname for everybody. It's hard for me to understand people who write controversy. I've seen them write some things about people I was very fond of, and I didn't think they were in their character.

Two of three didn't because he wouldn't answer their questions. He did a little yelling and carrying on, but to most writers he was very cordial. You talk about the fine, and he admitted it and accepted it, and that was the end of it.

Was Ted a controversial figure?

No, I wouldn't say that. One thing about Williams, Peter, he came to the ballpark early and he left late. He had great habits, great living habits and great work habits. I spent a lot of time with him my first two years. A lot of the time I was single and he was single. We got to know one another, and I think we understood one another. He was known as the game's greatest hitter, and I followed him around like a little dog.

Ted had fantastic seasons, including hitting .406. I have the clippings. Austin Lake, Huck Finnegan, a half dozen of them said the most horrible things about him. They talked about how he didn't take care of his mother, liked to dodge the draft. They made him seem to be a horrible person, which he wasn't.

You're right, Peter. He wasn't. I can recall some of those people you talked about. They were trying to make him out to be something he wasn't. I don't know why. They had an utter dislike for him as a person, but with us Ted was just great. Just great. You can ask Bobby Doerr and Dominic DiMaggio and Tex Hughson and Boo Ferris and all those people. We never had a problem with him, but one thing about Teddy, he always played. He went into the service. He did what the rest of us did. I went into the flight program with him. He went into the Marines and then in 1952 he had to go back. He lost almost five years, so he didn't shirk his duty.

Did he dislike people trying to find out things about him?

He was more of a loner, but he'd supper with us three or four nights a week in the old Kenmore Hotel. I can't image that anybody would dislike this man. To this day I have great affection for him. You said that no one got abuse like Ted did. Well, Joe DiMaggio got it in New York. Ted had great writer friends in New York like John Drebinger and Jim Leary.

The writers would go in the dugout. They rarely came into the clubhouse. But now the press and TV and the media have access to our clubhouse, and they will talk to a player, and then interpret what he says. I know Roger Clemens is going through it now. It's hard for me to believe, as good a kid as Clemens is, as nice a boy as he is, detrimental things were said about him. I didn't hear the TV reports on that, but I don't believe Clemens meant it the way it came out. Cause Clemens is a fine young man.

Did Ted and manager Joe Cronin get along?

Oh yeah. Ted liked you to fight him back. And they'd get going, but Ted had great admiration for Cronin. Cronin was a great player, a self-made big-league player and manager, a Hall of Fame player. I didn't see any animosity.

Ted would be in left field practicing his swing. Cronin would be at shortstop watching him do this.

He would probably say something to him. But Williams was always ready to catch the ball. To me Ted Williams was 25 years ahead of his time. He went through the Navy program like a ghost of salts. And I went along with him. I was on every sub squad. Navigation. Everything imaginable. One day he said to me, "How come you can't get this, Johnny?"

"I just don't have your kind of mind, Ted," I said. "I don't have your ability."

We were always in awe of him. And he never bothered anybody, Peter. He was fun to be around. He'd be here and there, signing autographs like a queen bee, and all the bees coming in, and he would sit patiently signing all the books and magazines, pictures, gloves, bats. He's that way.

Did you ever go with him to a hospital to see kids?

No. He liked to do that on his own. He's very involved in the Jimmy Fund in Boston. He's an honorary chairman. When he celebrated his 70th birthday, he raised a quarter of a million dollars. He did it for the Jimmy Fund. Because he doesn't like to expose himself.

For a long time he wouldn't tip his cap. He wouldn't hit to left field on an outside pitch. He wouldn't meet the writers halfway.

In those years we had the best owner in baseball, Tom Yawkey, and I'm sure Tom talked to Ted about it, because no ballplayer likes to be hassled, taken to task all the time, and he was the game's greatest hitter. You had to look at him like that. He had his own personality, his own make up. I think more people loved Ted Williams in this whole country than any ballplayer who ever played the game.

He had such great ability, and the reason nobody talked about the hat business, because when he popped out, they would boo him, and he said, "If I hit a home run, I'm not going to tip my cap." Now they hit a home run, and everyone gives you a high five, which is all right, I guess.

Ted Williams and Bobby Doerr

Williams was one of those guys, if he was the first or second guy lead-ing off the inning, he'd stand there watching to see how the guy threw, and the pitcher wouldn't like that.

I mind my own business. It's no concern of mine.

You were a rookie in 1942. What were some of the highlights for you coming up that year?

My rookie year we had Jimmie Foxx at first, Bobby Doerr was at second, I was at short, and Jim Tabor was at third. We had Williams, Dominic DiMaggio, and Lou Finney in right field. Jimmie Foxx only stayed until June, and then he went to the Cubs. Tony Lupien came in. That was a good ballclub. Our pitching was a little suspect at the time next to the Yankees, but you don't look at it like that. Then I went into the service, and we lost myself, along with Dominic, Ted, and Tex Hughson.

When the Korean War got over, we were still young enough. We were in our early 20s. The Navy did a lot for a lot of us.

You played alongside Bobby Doerr. Did he make it easy for you?

Yes, very. Bobby knew the hitters, and he moved me around a couple of feet. We used to take a lot of ground balls and feed one another, know where we wanted the ball, and this is where Bobby was a big help. Bobby was very, very helpful to me, and he was a quiet man. Bobby Doerr is just a beautiful man. We were fortunate to have people who were so fundamentally sound. Their thinking. Their living habits. Couldn't find a better guy than Bobby Doerr. Birdie Tebbetts, Tex Hughson, Dave Ferriss, Mickey Harris, Mace Brown all were just great. And the most important guy, obviously was Ted. He was great to all of us.

We came up a little bit after the Depression. A loaf of bread was a dime. A quart of milk was fifteen cents. I know when I got there, I signed a minimum contract, and I had a good year. I knew I was going into the service, and Tom Yawkey gave me a nice bonus. He gave me $5,000, and I'll never forget it.

I had chances to do other things, but I said, "No, the ballclub has been good to me. The man helped me, and he helped my family." Because my dad was an asthmatic. Money in those years, you had to scrape and save, and we knew the value of a dollar. I can't say enough about Mr. Yawkey. He was the best owner. As far as I'm concerned, there is only one Mr. TY.

I was supposed to go into the service in November, but I went in right after the season got over. We went up to Amherst then went up to Chapel Hill. Ted and I went to primary flight school in Indiana, and he went on to Pensacola. I became an operations officer.

Were you more mature when you returned?

Absolutely right. Eddie Collins was the general manager then, a great person and a great player. Mr. Collins was just a fine man. He wanted the players to play well, and he explained to us the meaning of a good attitude. For example, he'd say, "Do your work. Do your hitting. Run the bases. Take some extra ground balls. Stay out there for the whole time. Don't be a Swede. Don't shirk your duties. Do your work, and do it like it's game conditions."

Dominic [DiMaggio] was like that. Bobby [Doerr] was like that. The approach was pretty much the same in those years.

We had two Pullman cars, a dining car, and a car for the writers. We'd go in the dining car, and after dinner we'd sit around and play cards and talk baseball. We'd take the New England States out of Boston at two o'clock and get to Chicago the next morning at seven. You had all that time. Get up, have breakfast, sleep, go out to the ballpark. Those were the fun days because you're kind of young, but in those days you'd brush your teeth and shave in an eight-by-eight room. Ted would be there, and we'd go out into the dining car, and six or eight of us would sit around, and someone would say, "So and so is pitching tomorrow. This guy does this. This guy does that." And you pick little things up.

Of course, as players we watched the opposition a lot. The players today hit and go into the clubhouse. They don't sit out and watch. Ted, instead of going into the clubhouse, he'd sit out and watch the other team hit. He'd say, "Batting practice with the Yankees is entirely different."

Could Ted watch a pitcher and then tip you off as to what he will throw you?

I asked him that one day. We were playing the White Sox one day. One thing we always did once we got in the box, we didn't step out. If you did, they threw behind you. Anyway, the count was 2 and 2, and my mind just went blank. My hands were wet, and I picked up a handful of dirt and I walked towards Ted, and he said, "What's the matter?"

"What is this guy going to throw?" I said.

He started to laugh.

"For crying out loud, pick the ball up and hit it."

And that's exactly what I did.

In 1946 when everyone returned, when could you see that the Sox could really win the pennant?

We saw it from the first month of the season. First, Tex Hughson was pitching well. Ferriss was pitching well, and so were Mickey Harris and Joe Dobson. And we had good hitting. We were scoring runs, and at one point we were 55 and 10. We won a hundred and some that year, and we cinched the pennant one of the earliest times ever. But it took us two weeks to win the game that would take us over the hump.

We just got lackadaisical, things happened, and in the game that won it for us, Ted hit an inside the park home run at League Park in Cleveland.

The fielder tried to make a shoe-string catch, the ball rolled to the wall, and Ted just circled the bases.

I know it really bothers him that we didn't win the World Championship. He had great affection for Mr. Yawkey. It's unusual for an owner to get that close to a ballplayer. Mr. Yawkey had a nice way. He'd come in after we lost a game, and he'd say, "You have to give the other guy credit."

He was criticized for running a country club. It's *never* been a country club. He just wanted to be good to his players, because he had affection for them. People couldn't understand that. They liked the guy with the whip or the hammer over your head.

You couldn't do that today. I think everything's better. It's tougher to play than it was fifty years ago. You're going coast to coast, play a longer schedule.

Before the 1946 World Series, an article in the papers said that Yawkey was going to trade with the Yankees, Joe DiMaggio for Ted Williams.

There was some talk about that, but I don't think Mr. Yawkey would allow that. He never tried to interfere with running the ballclub.

If Joe Cronin had wanted to do that, or Eddie Collins at the time, no way Yawkey would let him do it.

I don't think so.

Your most vivid memories of the 1946 World Series.

I had a bad taste in my mouth because of that bad play. I don't even want to talk about that. It always comes up. I got blamed for something that I didn't think was my fault. Three weeks ago I was in the market, and an older guy climbed all over me. "You're a bum."

"You weren't even there," I said. "Where was it?"

He said, "In Baltimore."

"It was in St. Louis," I said.

I was kidding with the guy.

"If you want to blame me, go ahead," I said.

It's one of those things I had to live with.

As Joe Cronin used to say, "It's a game of inches." It really is.

Tell me what happened on that play.

I can remember it like it was yesterday. Enos Slaughter was stealing second base, and he got a real good jump. I'm covering second base. The ball was hit, and with two outs he just kept on running. I'm almost at second base when the ball was hit, and I'm in short left-center field, and by the time I got the ball I was way in the outfield, and I fielded the ball, and Arch McDonald, who was the announcer that day, said that I hesitated, that I took too long to get rid of the ball.

It's too bad we didn't have television in those years. We'd have had a better look at it. And the funny part about that, that was in the eighth inning. And then we had runners on first and third, and we didn't score. But those things happen, and that's what baseball is all about.

The two greatest players to ever play the game were in that series, and both of them [Ted Williams and Stan Musial] had bad series. They didn't hit a lick.

Too many people in our business think negatively. You take your plusses. If you get two or three plusses over one negative, you're that far ahead. Every once in a while the negative thing will pop up and hit you in the eye. That happens in baseball. It will happen until eternity. You're just going to have to accept it.

What was the reaction at the end of the 7th game?

It was a sad, sad experience. That was the all-time low for all of us. Boy, Ted was really down. He was almost in tears. I might have shed a tear. You think you should win, and you don't. I felt we had a better ballclub than the Cardinals. They had one guy who was outstanding in the series. And we didn't win.

I have too much affection for the game. I still think it's a great game, regardless of all that goes on today, agents, this and that. The thing I hate to see in the newspapers is the monetary thing. Some agents I think a lot of, and others I don't understand. I could name two or three. Also the reliance on stats. Sometimes you can have good stats and not be a good player. Look at people knocking Wade Boggs. How can you knock Wade Boggs? He scores 115 runs a year. To me Wade Boggs is the best hitter in the game. I've been a Wade Boggs fan since I watched him as a kid.

In 1947 the Red Sox did not repeat.

Tex Hughson had a bad arm, Boo Ferriss had a bad arm, and Mickey Harris had a bad arm. Hughson had circulatory problems. His middle finger would be ice cold. Harris hurt his shoulder. Mickey Harris hurt his elbow. And then in 1948, we got Ellis Kinder and Jack Kramer. I thought in '48, '49, '50, and '51 we had as good a ballclub.

In 1947 the Sox traded for Vern Stephens. How did that affect you?

I moved over to third base. I led the league in double plays in '48 and '49. Stephens was a hell of a player. He could hit home runs, he could run, he could throw. And he was someone who loved to play ball. Loved to play.

Joe McCarthy became the manager in 1948.

Best manager I ever played for. Ted Williams will tell you the same thing. He was a very quiet man. He always moved around the field, to center field, right field, the dugout, talking to the press. Best baseball man I ever saw. I loved him. I just loved Joe McCarthy. He was a guy who always talked baseball. I don't care. Whenever you saw him, it was always baseball.

What would you talk about?

About the old players. They would do this, they would do that. He just talked about baseball itself, talking situations, and he wore a uniform that didn't have a number, and he would stand out there, and if something happened, he'd call you over and talk like the teacher you fell in love with at school. He would say, "I suggest this to you." I never found him to be gruff. And he got along great with the writers. He always talked to them.

The '48 team.

We played very poorly the first two months. We had a good ballclub. We just played badly. We did the damnest things, hit into double plays, and we struggled to get over .500. The first few months we just played bad.

Forty-eight was the damnest thing I ever saw. McCarthy walking up in the tunnel. In the middle of the year he says, "We're going to be all right. We're going to win seven or eight in a row." And that's the way we did it.

Did Joe McCarthy contribute to the resurgence?

Oh yeah. He knew when a guy was getting tired, knew when he needed a new pitcher. To me, he knew more baseball than anyone I ever knew. He was a great person. And some players didn't respond to Joe like they should have or could have. I don't know why. I know how I felt. Ted Williams also loved him, said he was the best manager he ever played for. He played for Cronin and a lot of other guys.

Joe McCarthy

You were ahead by a game with five to go in '48.

I can remember Ted the last week of the season saying, "I never thought we'd be in this situation." As good as your players are, you hit the ball, and you have to find holes and not make errors and concentrate and be on your toes.

And then you won five of them including the last four games. But the Indians played one game better.

The Indians had a one-game lead with one game left, and we beat the Yankees in Boston, and Cleveland lost, so we had a playoff game in Boston. It was the first playoff game in the history of the American league.

Instead of starting Jack Kramer, the Red Sox ace, manager Joe McCarthy chose Denny Galehouse, who some Red Sox players thought as nothing more than a relief pitcher. Said catcher Matt Batts, "Of the twenty-five ballplayers, I don't think there was one of them that wasn't upset about it."

Galehouse didn't get through the fourth inning, and the Sox lost 8 to 3.

What do you recall about that ballgame?

That we got beat. They scored two runs in the very first inning. Then they got two more. A run here, and a run there, and we got beat 8 to 3. It was a ballgame where we got beat from the start. It was a terrible, terrible feeling. It was just a sad thing.

In '49 we had a game lead going into New York, and we lost both of those. Jerry Coleman hit a little blooper over the infield to score 2 runs. We got beat 5 to 2.

In June of 1950 Joe McCarthy quit.

When McCarthy left, we all felt bad about that. And Steve O'Neill took over, and he was another fine man.

Did Joe call a clubhouse meeting to tell the players?

No. We were coming off a trip, and we were at the ballpark, and we were told, "Mr. McCarthy has gone home." He was old, but he was still very sharp. He just decided to quit. Things happen. You feel bad about a lot of things, but you never can tell. The most important thing, Peter, is to win. I don't care what it is. If you win, they will remember you as a winner, not as a loser.

Some guys are affected by losses more so than others. Other guys scream and holler, but Joe took it inwardly, and you don't like it, but you have to live with it.

Tell me about Steve O'Neill.

He was a fine man and a good baseball guy. Very pleasant. Soft-spoken. Just a nice, nice man. We never questioned his authority. In those years when we played, we never questioned authority.

I got the sense with O'Neill that when Ted broke his elbow at the All Star game, somehow O'Neill got blamed for that. The Red Sox might have won the pennant if that had not happened. Ted missed a couple months and came back in late August.

How are they going to blame O'Neill? The guy goes and catches a ball against the wall, and it's not padded over there, and Ted broke his elbow.

And in the spring, he broke his collarbone. I didn't think he'd play the whole year, and he was back in two months. I was gone then.

Why did they fire O'Neill?
I don't know why they did. Lou Boudreau came in. He came in '52, and he had a plan, and he turned the whole thing upside down.

Lou decided to get rid of all the vets, and bring in all these young kids like Tommy Umphlett.
We were in first place when I got traded. They got rid of Stevie and myself, and Dom quit. They put Tommy Umphlett in center, White in right. Dominic DiMaggio and Al Zarilla had been there. It was just a mistake in identification. Boudreau came in from Cleveland, and he destroyed the whole thing. And Lou is a knowledgeable guy and a hell of a player. And a good manager.

Odd he got rid of all those guys who were loyal to the Red Sox.
You see, that's where things have really turned. The loyalty of the players to one team—even in those years, if you weren't happy, you kept it to yourself. A lot of times you wanted to stay on the ballclub, and if you got traded, you felt badly. Now these guys have an opportunity after so many years, they can become free agents. If you're a good ballplayer, you've got it made.

The reserve clause was in effect, and you had no bargaining power.
We couldn't afford to feed our families. If you're a pretty good ballplayer today, if you play eight years, you won't have to go to work. You read about guys who have lost everything. Their agents are going to do the best for them. Players should put some money away. I wish I was in the position to do that. I'm getting old.

Do you want to manage again?
No. I had that opportunity nine years ago. I said no. A one-year deal, and I was looking for three. A pretty good ballclub in the other league. If you win as a manager in the big leagues, you can manage two or three

other players. Take the managers today. Whitey Herzog might be the best manager. Sparky Anderson. Davey Johnson. You never see a manager say, "I won this game today." He depends on execution out on the field. Only Charlie Dressen said, "If you can win 50 games, I'll get you 30 more." That's idiotic. He had to eat those words when he went to Washington.

Being a manager on the Red Sox was difficult because Yawkey was taking away some of the manager's authority. If the players know he loves them, and if anything they do is okay with him, doesn't that make it harder for a manager?

I'm sure Yawkey liked a lot of players, but Yawkey would have done anything to win. Which he tried to do. He tried to buy a championship team. He built up the farm system. When an outsider came in, they were a little bit suspect about the way they handled things. I'll give you a guy who was a good manager: He should have never gotten fired here: Don Zimmer. Don Zimmer to me was as good a manager—if you look at his record, he won more games than any manager we've had in a number of years.

What about Dick Williams?

Mr. Yawkey didn't call him a great manager, and Dick said something. I like Dick Williams. I think he's a hell of a manager, but everywhere Dick has gone, he's had some pretty good ballclubs. When he walked into the Red Sox, he had Rico Petrocelli, Reggie Smith, Yaz, Dick Lonborg. A lot of managers didn't have these young kids.

At the end of the 1962 season Tom Yawkey made manager Pinky Higgins the general manager and named Johnny Pesky the Red Sox manager. The Red Sox were a second-division team. Higgins and Pesky were not close, and there was talk that Higgins was undermining Yawkey's manager's authority. In 1964 Higgins added first baseman Dick Stuart, a fine hitter who was such a terrible fielder he was nicknamed Dr. Strangeglove. Stuart made Pesky's life difficult, and at the end of the season, with the Red Sox mired in the second division, he was fired with two games left in the season and replaced by Billy Herman, a friend of Higgins.

It must have been hard for you.

One day I told Pinky Higgins, who was my general manager, "Christ Mike, I'd like to do this."

"Ah, it's all right," he said.

It just didn't work out. Maybe he didn't take to me. I had more problems with him than I did with the players. We had a couple of situations come up that I know I could have handled, but he stuck his nose in—a couple guys who didn't like me, and I didn't care for them—when they don't care for you, you have to get them off your ballclub. And he wouldn't. What are you going to do?

⌁

The Red Sox honored Pesky on September 27, 2006, his eighty-seventh birthday, by officially naming the right-field foul pole Pesky's Pole. It had been called that for years. Two years later the Red Sox announced they were retiring his number 6. Pesky died on August 13, 2012, at the Kaplan Family Hospice House in Danvers, Massachusetts, at the age of ninety-three.

CHAPTER FIVE

ALBERT "HAPPY" CHANDLER

"I Will Allow Jackie Robinson to Play for Brooklyn"

A*lbert "Happy" Chandler was one of the most influential figures in base-ball history. Elected governor of Kentucky and twice elected from Ken-tucky to the United States Senate, Chandler was the baseball commissioner from 1946 until 1951. During that time he shocked segregated America when he bucked the wishes of the baseball owners, who fervently wished to keep Major League Baseball segregated, when he gave Brooklyn Dodgers own-er Branch Rickey permission to bring up Jackie Robinson from his Montreal farm club to the Dodgers. Without the okay of this very southern politician, Robinson would not have integrated the major leagues.*

Chandler is also remembered for suspending Dodgers manager Leo Du-rocher for associating with gamblers.

I interviewed Chandler in 1981 for my book Bums. *As you will see, Chandler was bitter that he had not been elected into baseball's Hall of Fame. His election would come a year later.*

The owners held a meeting to vote on whether Robinson should enter base-ball, and the vote was 15 to 1 against him. The owners held their meeting at the Waldorf Astoria in New York. They took a vote over Rickey's intention to bring Jackie Robinson, who was African-American, from Montreal to Brooklyn.

The baseball owners took a vote, and they voted 15 to 1 to continue the current whites-only policy and keep Robinson out of baseball.

I asked Chandler about the 15 to 1 vote.

Well, that vote was supposed to be notice to me and to Rickey, you understand. They gave me all sorts of reasons why this black man couldn't play. They said they'd burn down the Polo Grounds, because it was located in Harlem, you understand. They cited all sorts of reasons why this boy shouldn't play, and none of them except Rickey said anything in favor of this boy.

Let me see if I remember who spoke at the meeting. Larry MacPhail spoke. He was against

Albert "Happy" Chandler

it, of course. He was violently against it. He graduated from the University of Michigan law school. He went to college at Maryland, and that's down south. Horace Stoneham had his place in the Polo Grounds. Stoneham was a good baseball man and one of my best supporters. I have nothing but good feelings for him. Mr. Griffith spoke against it. He was very much against it. Mr. Mack voted against it. It was fifteen to one, my dear boy. And I announced the results of the voting.

I was not surprised these people were so violently against it. I had foreknowledge of the facts that they were very much opposed to it. See, I had to go against fifteen fellows. [New York Yankees owners] Topping and Webb. Oh sure.

They didn't give good reasons, but rather excuses. I don't remember them except that one about burning down the Polo Grounds.

There was a lot of ignorance, as far as I was concerned. See, here was a fellow with talent, and there wasn't anything bad they could say about his character. He had a good record at UCLA.

Soon after the meeting was over, Rickey and I talked it over in my cabin on the backside of my home in Versailles, Kentucky, where I lived.

Branch Rickey

Rickey told me he wanted to come and see me.

I told him, "All right. Come on."

He came down here, and we talked about it for about an hour. I said to him, "Mr. Rickey, I'm going to have to meet my maker some day, and if he asks me why I didn't let this boy play and if I said, 'Because he's black,' that might not be a sufficient answer."

I said, "I will approve of the transfer of his contract from Montreal to Brooklyn, and we'll make a pact, so you bring him on in."

Rickey said to me, "I can't do this in the face of this adverse vote without the complete cooperation and support of the commissioner."

"Mr. Rickey," I said. "I know that."

See, I had known Josh Gibson and Buck Leonard and Satchel Paige, and of course Josh Gibson died without ever having a chance, and I thought that was an injustice. He was one of the greatest players I ever saw. He was a great catcher and a great hitter.

"Galbreath of Pittsburgh went to Landis, and he asked Landis to let Gibson play, and Landis would not let him," I said.

Wendell Smith, the man who writes for the *Pittsburgh Courier*, went to Landis too. As soon as I was elected, Smith came down to Washington to see me. So did Rick Roberts, a baseball historian and a longtime writer for the *Currier*.

"I am for the full freedom," I said. "If a black boy can make it to Iwo Jima and Guadalcanal, he can make it in baseball." And I said, "Once I tell you something, brother, I will never change."

"I always thought that was pretty special for a Southerner to say that," Roberts said.

I lived with black people all my life. I was born in Western Kentucky on a small farm, and I worked at the mill with a black man named Bill Blunder, who was the best friend I had. And we had to bring 100 44-pounds of shelled corn from the cellar to the railroad ties and got the corn to the mill. And I was the only white one.

But I had to work. We got about a quarter a day. I got along fine with the black people, and Bill Blunder was one of my best friends. I never had any trouble with black fellows in my life. We lived together and got along well together. And we played ball together. I thought the time was right for this fellow to play.

At the time I was talking with Rickey about bringing up Jackie, I was also talking with Pee Wee Reese. Yes, indeed. Pee Wee was the most helpful baseball player that we had. He wanted to get Jackie Robinson accepted in baseball, and he went out of his way to befriend him. I've known Pee Wee ever since he learned to play marbles. He won the marbles championship one year down here. I've known him practically all the days of his life.

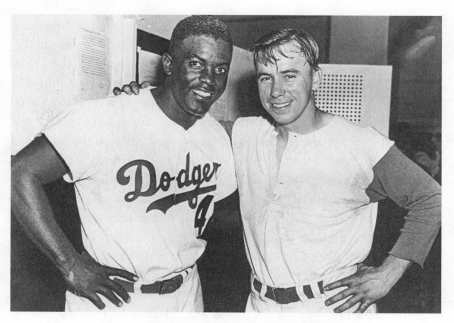

Jackie Robinson and Pee Wee Reese

Pee Wee and I talked, and he understood what I was trying to do, and I understood what he was trying to do. He was trying to help this boy gain acceptance into the major leagues, and he deserved a lot of credit for it. We didn't have a prolonged discussion, but each of us understood each other.

I went to training camp at Vero Beach when Robinson first broke in, and I thought all along without belaboring any point of discussion that Pee Wee was doing the best he could to get this fellow accepted and to counsel and advise him.

One of the things that happened, Dixie Walker, a Brooklyn player, threatened not to play. He said he was going to stay home and paint his house. He told me this to my face. I just happened to see him somewhere down south. I don't remember exactly where that was. But I remember he told me face to face.

I tried to persuade him. I didn't think he was serious, but he was. He said he was going to paint his house and he wasn't going to play. He's an Alabama fellow. He didn't like the idea at all of a black playing with whites. He and I were good friends. I had known him nearly all of his life and all of mine.

People don't know this, but I went to the University of Kentucky, Transylvania, and Harvard. I had been elected governor [of Kentucky] and twice elected United States senate. And I couldn't take [the job of baseball commissioner] right off, because the war wasn't over, and I told them they would have to give me some time, because I was on the Senate military finance committee. I had been on it all during the war. That was important in the progress of the war and the promotion of the war. I had quite a bit to do with that. I had a secure seat in the United States Senate in 1945, and I hadn't sought the job, so they unanimously elected me in Cleveland on the 25th of April of 1945. They called me and told me they had elected me. Each one of the owners was on the telephone. Yes sir.

I had been a good baseball player. I played in the Blue Grass League in Kentucky, and I played in the North Dakota State League, and in 1920 I played in the West Canadian League sixty-one years ago this summer with Saskatoon. I pitched 13 games for Jackson, North Dakota, and won 12 of them. I pitched a no-hitter against the Benoba Indians. I knew most of the baseball players in the country.

And so I approved the contract from Montreal to Brooklyn, and after Jackie Robinson came into baseball, Rickey never did credit me. He always talked like he had done it all by himself. Which he could not have done.

My goodness. I'll tell you. I don't want anything. See [Commissioners] Landis and Frick are in the Hall of Fame. They have ignored me so far.

Landis has a reputation he didn't deserve.

I know that, but I don't want to say a thing about him. Landis is gone. But his bark was worse than his bite, and I had his records when I was commissioner. I read them, and for 25 years Landis consistently dropped any chance to put blacks and whites on a big-league field. He didn't let them play exhibition games.

Leo Durocher had been a controversial figure since he was a kid shortstop with the New York Yankees. A rogue shit-shirrer from the poor side of Springfield, Massachusetts, as a rookie in 1922 he drew the wrath of veterans by spending more than he made on fine clothes. Babe Ruth in 1928 famously accused Durocher of stealing money and his expensive watch. After he was traded to the St. Louis Cardinals in 1933, he needed Branch Rickey, the Cardinals general manager, to pay off his outstanding debts. After Durocher was traded to Brooklyn in 1928, his spending and his penchant for gambling were troubling, but despite that, Dodgers president Larry MacPhail appointed him manager for the 1939 season.

By the end of 1946, Rickey feared that Durocher would get in trouble for his gambling and his friendship with such mobsters as Bugsy Siegel and Joe Adonis, and actor George Raft, who was mob-connected and had a serious gambling addiction. The friendship between Durocher and Raft was so out in the open that articles were written about them in the press. The Brooklyn DA even tapped Durocher's phone.

Rickey told Durocher to end his connection with these people. Meanwhile Commissioner Chandler saw that Rickey was not getting through to him, and in November met with Durocher. If he didn't clean up his act, Chandler said, there'd be trouble.

Complicating matters was Durocher's marriage to actress Laraine Day. In January of 1947 there were headlines that Durocher had stolen her from her husband. A California divorce court decreed they should wait a year to marry, but they went to Mexico, got a quicky divorce, and married anyway.

The condemnation was great. The Brooklyn Catholic Youth Organization threatened to boycott Dodger games.

Then in March Durocher in the New York Daily News *complained that MacPhail, who was running the Yankees, associated with the same gamblers that he did. MacPhail then sued Durocher and Rickey for slander. Chandler had no choice but to step in. Durocher apologized, and he and MacPhail hugged, but the damage had been done.*

As Rickey prepared to introduce Robinson to the world, he had no idea that Chandler would suspend Durocher, his manager, for a year.

"For what," Leo would ask. "To this day if you ask me why I was suspended I could not tell you."

I asked Chandler about it.

Strange as it may seem, I knew Durocher about as well as I know anybody. And I had to discipline him.

I met Leo while he was playing in Cincinnati. He played in St. Louis and he played in Brooklyn. He wasn't much of a gambler until later. See, George Raft was one of his closest associates. It was a bad thing, because Durocher and Raft gambled with everybody—even the baseball players—for more money than the players could afford to lose. Leo was just a bad boy, pardner. I think I almost made a good boy out of him. He had been in so much trouble. It's a long story.

I told Rickey, "You take charge of it, and if you don't take charge of it, I'm going to."

I had to have numerous meetings with Durocher. He broke a fellow's jaw with the brass knuckles that he got from the police in Brooklyn. He said the fellow slipped on the water trough, and that was not true. And they got together at the trial to pay this fellow off. And then he hit a little black boy after a game was over. But it turned out he didn't hit a little black boy. It was a Puerto Rican boy. And then another thing he did, he was dating Laraine Day. I met with him at a country club in Oakland. I had him out on hole 17, and we were standing on the green, and he told me the story of his being in the bedroom with Laraine Day and her husband arguing over who was going to take this man's wife.

"Durocher," I said, "if you do that, I won't have to deal with you, because they will kill you."

I was trying to convince him that this was something you just didn't do.

"You're in the man's bedroom with his wife," I said. "She's his wife, not yours."

I wanted a basis where he wouldn't be killed. I didn't know what kind of fellow he was dealing with. I told him, "If you come to Kentucky and do that, they will kill you."

I told him Bugsy Siegel would bring him nothing but harm. I did everything I was required to do to try to save this fellow before I suspended him.

I had a hearing, and it was Durocher's fault more than it was anybody else's fault. I said so. There was an accumulation of instants, and each one I had tried to put him on a straight path. And I couldn't do it. And Rickey couldn't do it. It was beyond his control. He was just a bad boy and undisciplined.

He didn't play by the rules, and he couldn't get out, and he never thought about how he was going to get out. He was not well educated. He was a fine baseball player, I thought, and a pretty good baseball manager with the exception of the fact he didn't know how to work with young players. The record will show that.

I never did have any reason to believe that he tried to throw a baseball game, although I will never forget when he stood with Jocko Conlan at home plate, kicking Jocko's shins, and Jocko started kicking him back.

Leo got into this bash with this fellow in Havana, who accused MacPhail of associating with gamblers. I took a good look at that, and that was not true. MacPhail did not associate with gamblers. Whatever you want to say about MacPhail, and I knew him about as well as I knew anybody, he drank whiskey, and when he drank too much whiskey, he'd hit little girls, but when he wasn't drinking, he was a graduate lawyer from Michigan and one of the best baseball men I ever saw. In the latter years of his life, after I left baseball, MacPhail would come down to my cabin, sometimes for a week at a time just to visit with me. He brought his wife with him. And I also appreciated his baseball knowledge. He was quite a baseball man.

Mr. Justice Frank Murphy was governor of Michigan before he was appointed [in 1940] by Roosevelt to be a member of the Supreme Court. While that business with Durocher was going on, he wrote me a letter.

"You're a man of honor, a man of integrity," he wrote. "I want to tell you if you let Durocher play baseball in Brooklyn this year, we will have the Youth Catholic Organization desert the field. They won't take part in baseball in Brooklyn because of this fellow's conduct."

What do you think of that?

He said, "You have to discipline him, and if you don't, the Catholic Youth Organization will not take part in baseball in Brooklyn this year. They will stay away for the baseball season."

And I'll tell you another thing. Leo had five or six wives. You can check that. [He was married four times, to Ruby Hartley, Grace Dozier, Laraine Day, and Lynne Walker Goldblatt.] One of them, Grace, who was from St. Louis, was one of the prettiest girls I have ever, ever seen.

The year I suspended him, I was sitting in Yankee Stadium, and she came to me, and my memory about this is about as clear as if it happened yesterday. She was no longer living with him. They were separated. A pretty girl. But she remonstrated with me, trying to take up for him, and I complimented her.

"Grace," I said, "I appreciate wives who take up for their husbands. I didn't do this to be offensive to you. It was something I had to do for the integrity of baseball. I'm sorry."

In the meantime, a year passed, and he divorced her and married Laraine Day. The same girl came to my box at the identical spot at Yankee Stadium, and she sat down and held out her hand, and she said, "Commissioner, you knew he was a son of a bitch all this time, didn't you?"

I never laughed so much in my life.

"Grace," I said to her, "I didn't say that. You said that. What a difference a year makes."

I remember it so well. I'll tell you, I'll be 83 in July, but my memory is crystal clear.

This was in 1947. That was the year they brought in the new manager, Bert Shotten. I sat Durocher aside for a year. That was necessary because that was a mild penalty. And he never appealed that decision, you understand. He just took it.

By the way President Nixon is a great friend of mine. We exchange notes. We have for a long time. He and I have been close for a long time, and I think they mistreated him. It's one of the great tragedies of our lifetime. He was a good president, and if it hadn't been for him, we wouldn't be associated with China now, you understand, and they are our greatest safety valve against the Russians. And if it hadn't been for him, we'd still be doing business with Taiwan.

Happy Chandler was baseball commissioner until 1951. The major league owners, still stung by his refusal to honor their 15 to 1 vote to keep African-Americans out of baseball, sent him packing at their first opportunity. When Kennesaw Mountain Landis was chosen as commissioner after the Black Sox scandal of 1919, Landis took the job under two conditions: 1. No one could overrule his decisions, and 2. He would have the job for life.

After Landis died, the owners gave Chandler a six-year term. No longer would the commissioner have unchecked powers for his lifetime.

I left the day before my birthday on the 13th day of July of 1951 in Detroit. That was after they refused to renew my contract. They changed the rules after I was elected. Old man Landis only had to get a majority of the vote. I always had a majority, but I had eleven at the time of the showdown, and they withheld five, and they did it deliberately, on purpose. Among them Topping and Webb. Fred Saigh from St. Louis, who later went to the penitentiary, and Bill DeWitt.

DeWitt and I didn't get along very well in baseball. I helped him get Muddy Ruel to manage his team for him. That didn't work out, and I thought he held it against me.

Saigh was just no count. He went to the penitentiary, and of course they all got mad.

You don't know this, but I was on the bench at Centre College when we beat Harvard in 1921. I carried the football out of the stadium on the subway after the game was over. I've been a football coach and a basketball coach and a baseball coach and a baseball manager and a baseball player and I'm still on the board of Kentucky University and still on the board of trustees.

I raised Adolph Rupp. The second year he won the national championship, they offered him a one-year contract. He called me and said, "Governor, I've got to see you."

"All right, son," I said.

"I've won the national championship," he said, "and they've offered me a one-year contract."

I said, "You go back and tell Dr. Funkhouser I will give you a better job," and he went back, and they gave him a three-year contract. I was with him the whole time he was here, and I was a pallbearer at his funeral. He said I was his best friend, and I suspect that's right. Whenever he got his tit in a ringer, I always got him out.

It was the only time anyone was elected twice in Kentucky.

Rickey was whipped 15 to 1 with his own fellows. All I had to do was say, "I'm not going to get in it. Why should I get in it?"

Transylvania, the oldest college west of the Allegheny Mountains, is celebrating its 300th year. They picked out their most important graduates, and I was the only living one. They had a special day and a special lecture for me. The chairman of the history department is writing my story. I told him, "I was sober, and I meant to do everything I did." I wouldn't take it back for anything, pardner.

Bill Werber and Pee Wee Reese and other fellows are trying to help me get into the Hall of Fame. They put [commissioner Ford] Frick in the Hall of Fame, and I have no objection to that, but if he's in, I ought to be chairman of it. I had the respect of the respectable people in baseball. I protected the integrity of baseball.

I'm responsible for the players' pension fund. MacPhail and I got it up, and the owners agreed to go for five years. It worked out good. In 1951 I met with Tom Gallery, you know him [he was director of sports for NBC Television], and I made the first contract for the televising of the World Series. It was so advantageous and lucrative, I put the money in the pension fund, so now everyone in baseball gets a pension, and I fixed it so it was actuarily sound. I'm more responsible for it than anyone else. That's just the truth, pardner.

I've been very lucky. Mom and I have been married for 56 years. I have four nice children and 13 grandchildren and six great grandchildren, and if I never make another dime, I don't need anything except the respect of the respectable. I covet that, pardner.

Let me know if I can be of any further help to you. God bless, son.

After the publication of Bums, *I received a package in the mail from Chandler. In it was a citation that I was named an official Kentucky Colonel. It was signed by Martha Layne Collins, the governor of the great state of Kentucky. With the honor came an open invitation to the Kentucky Derby.*

Albert "Happy" Chandler died on June 15, 1991, at the age of ninety-two. He was an important figure in baseball history. He should not be forgotten.

CHAPTER SIX

DEL WEBB

"Would You Be Interested in Buying the Yankees?"

W hen I called Del Webb to tell him I was writing a history of his Yankees, he invited me to his Los Angeles mansion. Webb had made millions in construction prior to buying the Yankees. In 1928 he developed the Del E. Webb Construction Company. In 1946 he built the Flamingo Hotel and Casino for Bugsy Siegel in Las Vegas, and in 1948 he built six hundred houses and a shopping center in Tucson. He also built the Poston War Relocation Center that housed seventeen thousand Japanese Americans who were ordered there after Pearl Harbor.

Later he would build communities across America, including one in Ocala. When I interviewed Moose Skowron, he was working for the Del Webb Corporation, and he offered me the chance to buy one of the Ocala lots for $25 a month for sixty months. When you're twenty-seven years old, you aren't thinking about your future. Making such a commitment seemed too much to contemplate. Had I accepted, I would have made a small fortune.

Webb greeted me and walked me to his office, which was festooned with Yankee memorabilia, including fourteen World Series rings. At his desk, I could see an array of telephones. Every once in a while during our conversation, one would ring, and he'd pick it up and talk business. Webb was a no-nonsense guy who could swear a blue streak when riled.

As lunchtime approached, he invited me to dine with him at one of his favorite haunts. He said the specialty was sand dabs, little delicious morsels of fish, and he ordered sand dabs for both of us.

I was in awe of the guy. We shook hands after we were done, and after I left him all I could think of was, No wonder the Yankees won all those pennants.

Del Webb

Weren't you a semi-pro pitcher here in California during the 1920s?

I pitched from the Canadian border to Mississippi to the Pacific Coast. Of course, I had quite an experience in baseball, which I don't think anyone else ever had as good an opportunity as I did to learn baseball like I did, because during World War I, I had signed with the Oakland baseball club. I signed on a little piece of paper. This was in 1918. That was the year they stopped baseball in July because of the war. They cancelled baseball. So I went to the Oakland ballclub and signed with a little fellow by the name of Herbert McFarland, who was then secretary of the club. I went in and signed this thing. He showed me a wire.

"We're sending the whole ballclub down to the Moore Shipyard," a shipbuilding company in Oakland. "We have jobs for all the ballplayers down there, and they are going to play in the Shipyard League."

I went down there. From the time I was 10 years old, my father gave me fifty cents a day to learn a trade, and I learned the carpentry trade. Incidentally, I always made a lot of money in the summer playing semipro and working in the carpenter trade, where I could make a lot more money than the average ballplayer.

So I went down there, and when they found out I had a carpenter's card, they gave me a shipfitter's job, which was the same thing as a carpenter on a ship. They gave me a helper. My helper was Clyde Wares, Buzzy Wares. I don't know how far back you go in baseball. He was a second baseman for Oakland and wound up his career as being one of the coaches of the Cardinals under Eddie Dyer, who used to be the manager there. Buzzy was my helper. I would get seven dollars a day, and he would get three and a half, and he was a veteran on the ballclub, and I was a kid.

I got thrown in in that shipyard league with these veteran ballplayers. I guess they thought I had some ability. I had a good fastball. They took a lot of interest in me. I remember Davenport, an old pitcher who we had, took a lot of interest in me as a pitcher. Harry Krause, an old pitcher was there too, so I got a lot of insider baseball as a kid.

I played in that league the next year when baseball opened up. I had a better job and could make almost twice as much money working in the shipyard. I still played in that league in 1919. A lot of old time ballplayers were still playing there, and those fellows helped me.

I got more knowledge of baseball in a short period of time that a lot of fellows ever would get any other way.

How long did you continue?

About a year and a half, two years I was in that league, see. And I was making more money than five guys in the Coast League was. This was where I got a pretty good knowledge of baseball, and I think I was one of the few owners of a ballclub who had the capability of managing a ballclub if I had to, knowing the plays and knowing baseball, and of course I was quite a student of the game too, and I will deviate a little bit here, we started—it was my idea—when we bought the Yankee ballclub, they had 24 farm clubs, and they had player/managers managing a lot of these ballclubs. It was an economical thing, paying them $400 a month to manage and play. When I saw that, I immediately told Weiss that I thought we ought to have more capable managers. Instead of paying someone $400, we should pay an old ballplayer like Billy Meyer or Casey Stengel or whoever you wanted to even if we had to pay them $5,000, so the kids could learn something down there. Cause I'd go down there and I saw they didn't learn from some guy who was a playing manager.

Who were some of the people you hired?

As manager to teach these kids? Billy Meyer was one of them. And Bill Skiff was another one. And Joe Devine. Joe managed one year, but he scouted mostly. Joe and I were raised together. That's another story.

We had a lot of capable managers. This gave me the idea. We had started to cut down on the farm system some. Then I come up with the idea.

"Why don't we bring all these kids to camp?"

We'd pick out the kids in our organization that we think have the potential of being a big-league ballplayer. Bring 35 or 40 of them to the big-league camp along with the pitchers, three weeks before spring training. And get them down there and help them.

I got the idea that they could learn a hell of a lot in that three weeks. Not only that, but it would give us a chance to look at them. And it would also get these kids acquainted with the big club. Just to take an example. Here's Joe Doakes playing down at let's say Kalamazoo, and he has a good year. We bring this kid up to Yankee Stadium. He's never even seen the Stadium before. He don't even know the ballplayers. Christ Almighty, this is a hell of an experience for him. But if he's been down to spring training, and he knows all the big league ballplayers, Joe DiMaggio might come up to him and say, "How are you?" He walks into the clubhouse, he don't know anybody, and Joe asks him how he's coming along or Tommy Henrich might ask him, and this gives the kid a lot better feeling.

I get this idea, and we did a lot. Of course Casey Stengel went with them.

Another reason I had this idea: I was on the Salt Lake Club one spring. We trained in a little town called Adesta here in California, and I landed in town, and I was there a couple days, and there were only two fellows on the ballclub, a fellow by the name of Mickey Shavers and myself, the only two on the ballclub who had never been in professional baseball before.

We went to spring training, and these guys like Bunny Brief and these old guys, shit, they wouldn't give us the time of day. The first thing that happened to me was, I was assigned a roommate, and the roommate happened to be a fellow by the name of Bill Rogers, Raw Meat Bill Rogers, and I think he's still alive, and he had been quite a ballplayer in the Coast League and had managed the Portland club the year before and been with Cleveland. He was kind of an idol of mine, and Jeez, I was elated that he would be my roommate.

He come in and talked to me, "Kid, how are you? Let's go down and have something to eat."

We go down to eat, and he asked the waiter, "Do you have a t bone steak?"

The fellow said yes.

"Let me see it."

He brought it out on a platter.

"Put it down and let's see it."

The guy put it down, and he got out and knife and fork, and he started eating the God damn steak. The blood started running all over the checkered table cloth, running this way and that off the block it was on. I was a kid. We ate beans. We hardly ever ate meat. It upset me so much, the waiter said, "What will you have?"

"I'll have a steak well done," I said.

He ate that steak raw, and he asked the guy if he had a couple eggs that he wanted to eat. He brought out raw eggs, and he ate them eggshells and all. He ate two of them. And that's what Rogers ate every night.

Incidentally, Ty Cobb and I were at the old Hollywood baseball park. It must have been fifteen years ago, and some fellow comes up behind me and hits me on the shoulder.

Ty Cobb said, "You know this fellow, don't you?"

I looked over and I said, "Raw Meat Bill Rogers."

His hair was all white, but his face was still rosy, and he was 80-something years old then, and everybody tells me he's ninety-something now and still alive down in Texas. [Rogers died in 1981 at the age of ninety-one.]

But what I'm getting at is, when I joined that ballclub, I was so lonesome, Bill Rogers was the only guy who took any interest in me at all. If it wouldn't have been for him, there wouldn't have been anybody.

I was throwing hitting practice one day, I had thrown for twenty minutes, and Jesus Christ, that's a lot of work, and I told the manager I was a little tired, and he said, "Holy shit, what did I bring you out here for? Come on, throw another five minutes."

When I complained, he said, "All right, run around the park three times."

He did that just to be ornery. Shit, I could hardly walk around, let alone run. I'd gone through all this, and I never did get into the ballgame. I never even got a bat in my hand. I didn't get to hit in hitting practice. They didn't even know you were there. Mickey Shavers and I got together, and we both felt pushed out of nowhere, see. The only salvation I had was when evening come, I get to talk to Bill Rogers a little bit.

This was 1917. I was only 17 years old. With this background, I put myself in the place of a kid coming up, so as I say now, the kid goes up to Yankee Stadium, maybe never seen the Stadium, maybe we had him up in the spring, so he comes up there and he has more of a feeling that he's wanted and that somebody knows who he is. That was the system, and we did a lot of good with that. We helped develop a lot of ballplayers. [See the experience of Rod Kanehl in chapter 13.]

Did any other clubs do that?

Some clubs tried to pattern after us a little bit. We were the first. In fact, we had that for several years before anybody even tried it.

I got the idea in 1951 in Phoenix, because I was around there all the time. Phoenix was my home. We traded spring training camps with [Giants owner Horace] Stoneham that year.

Why did you do that?

Because I wanted to get the club down in Phoenix.

You were a semi-pro pitcher until you got typhoid.

Yeah. I got typhoid in 1925. You know how I caught it? We used to play exhibition baseball games over at San Quentin prison. The prison allowed those exhibition games. They allowed two of them a year. I played in two places, the Folsom Prison and San Quentin. We had a first baseman by the name of Tom Lariat, who hit the ball over the centerfield fence, and a big colored boy said, "Whoa boy, I wish I was on that ball."

I went there to this game, an all star game, at San Quentin. Ray Kremer, the old Pittsburgh pitcher, was on the club, and we had had a party for him the night before. There was a wagon with three guard dogs that was 40 feet from the bus. The people in the bus needed guards. I was one person with three guards. I was late.

I ordered a glass of water, and a fellow brought me a water. They gave me a trustee to wait on me, and he brought me the water, and he sat down on the bench and held his head, and he said, "I feel bad as hell." Two or three weeks later I got sick. I thought I had the flu.

Well, I had typhoid fever, and I was laid up in bed for a solid year. This was the changing part in my life too, because I had developed a bad arm. I had an accident, sliding into home plate, and I tore my shoulder up all to hell. The next year I had a bad arm.

I didn't realize it at that time, so I was trying to pitch for three years with a bad arm, and then I got the typhoid, and I got to thinking I was through playing ball, and I was drinking too much, and I had to start over again, see. There were a lot of changes in my life.

For six to eight months I was laid up in bed.

What did you do for six to eight months?

I tell you, I weighed 204 pounds when I took sick, and then I weighed 99 pounds when I got through. It took me ten years to gain my weight back. I never weighed that much since.

Is that why you went to Phoenix?

Yes. I'm getting off on other things here. I could talk to you for two days about this.

You were an excellent carpenter when you got down to Phoenix. How in the world did you get started in government construction?

I knew this fellow, and he used to always write me a Christmas card. I would write him back. When I got sick, I got thinking about Arizona because I knew it was a good place for somebody to start. During the year I had a lot of time to think. So I wrote him where I thought in Arizona I could get well, and he told me to come down there, and we'd do something.

"I can get you a job in the industrial league," he said.

I went down there, I ran into an old catcher by the name of Roscoe.

"If you played in this league, you'd do pretty good," he said.

I told him I was a pitcher. He said I could be an outfielder.

I worked out with them. They had a rule that nobody could play in the league unless they were a resident of the city for 39 days. They didn't want a team bringing in people to win a pennant. Well, I went along, and we were in a ballgame, and in the late innings of that game, I hit a home run and won the ballgame.

Afterward they protested, because I had only lived there for 29 days instead of 39 days, and they threw the game out and they threw me out too. That was perfect for me because I had a good job. I was a carpenter on the Western Hotel. The superintendent used to work for my father. I fit in pretty good.

How did you develop that into what you eventually developed?

That job was finished, and I went to the union to get my clearing card to get out of town. I thought I'd go somewhere else, go to the Grand Canyon or maybe I'd leave the state. I didn't know what I was going to do.

"Here's another job you can go to Monday if you want to," they said.

It was a pretty good job. The fellow was looking for a foreman, and it paid two dollars more than scale. And I took it. That was a grocery store. Then I got into some trouble with that guy. The contractor got to chasing around, and one thing or another, and so I quit that job and went to get my check from the grocery store, and the check was no good. The check bounced. The bank wouldn't accept it.

Then I was stuck again, and I didn't know what the hell to do, and I waited over, and this Bayless stores wanted to know if I could finish this job up because this contractor was in trouble, and I said, "Sure."

So I went to work for them, and I built a lot of grocery stores.

For the second go-around, I was the contractor.

How did that person have the inkling that you were capable of contracting and finishing?

Because the job I did finishing up his store. I ordered the lumber and the material, and the list goes on and on, and I organized it all and finished it, and they were pleased with it, so they talked to me, and I came up with the idea to contract it.

And how did you get your first government contract to do some of that war construction?

That was several years later. We were well-established in the state. We were one of the leading contractors, so we were picked.

How did you build a fort on 149 acres in ninety days?

That was one of the things we did. Fort Huachuca [located in southeast Arizona, fifteen miles from the Mexican border], I came up with the idea. See, a lot of barracks were built for the army. All typical barracks.

I said to our people, "How long is it going to take to build nine of these barracks?"

"About 90 days," they said. If you multiply that by ten teams, goddamn it, we can build them in 120 days. The trick was getting more people to do the work. Of course, we had the ability to get the labor.

The greatest job we ever did was to build the concentration camp for the Japs in California at the bottom of that river. Jesus Christ, we built a house in every 14 and a half minutes down there.

Did it ever bother you that you were sticking all these people in the middle of the Arizona desert in 120 degree heat?

Well, I've been criticized for saying the greatest thing I ever accomplished in my life. This was after it was all over with.

Of course, when I made that statement, people took it different from what I meant. What I meant was, the *greatest construction accomplishment* I ever made. I wasn't even thinking about the Japs. That wasn't my problem.

And some of these fellows thought I meant taking the Japs and moving them down there. That wasn't what I meant. We had nothing to do with that at all. We had built the houses for them, and the government moved them down there.

It was a great accomplishment because we were down in the desert where there was absolutely nothing. You couldn't even drive a truck down there. We had to walk out there, and it was 120 degrees in that goddamn July, Jesus Christ. Rattlesnakes all over the place.

When did Larry MacPhail first approach you with the idea to buy this ballclub?

I'll go back. I first met Larry MacPhail with Leo Durocher, who I had known in Brooklyn. Leo come to Phoenix one time and called me, and MacPhail was with him, and I met MacPhail then. It was just a short meeting.

This was before the war, and as the war come on, Larry MacPhail was a lieutenant colonel under Robert Patterson, who was the Undersecretary of the War, and he was also in charge of the athletic development of the army. I run across Larry when we were finishing up these army base camps at the tail end. Larry would come along with his athletic program and check it, and the first time I met Larry was down in Tucson. We were finishing up a camp down there. This was 1941, '42, somewhere around there, in the middle of the war.

If you build a camp, the athletic director would come in, and he'd want some additional things for the camp, make a suggestion to the contractor, and that was us. The quartermaster might come in and do that too. They'd ask for things the architect wasn't thinking about. Larry was always full of ideas anyway. That's where I first met Larry, and I got to know him, and I'd go to Washington—I had to go to Washington a lot, and I'd see him once in a while there.

One time Larry called me. He wanted to know if I had time to have dinner. He came over and said, "Would you be interested in buying the Yankees? They can be bought."

Let me go back a little further on that. The Oakland ballclub was for sale too back then. And Carl Sandlock, the old first baseman/pitcher, had been a manager there, and he and I played ball together. Carl called me one day and said, "Del, this ballclub can be bought for $75,000, including the ballpark."

I thought a minute, and then I got a hold of my attorney and told him to take a look at it. He

Larry MacPhail

come back to me and said, "This might be a pretty good deal for you as a tax write off. You can write that off pretty well."

About that time we were called to Washington, and we were negotiating a very important military job. He called me in Washington, and I said, "We're too damn busy. Tell them we haven't got time to get involved."

But this give me an idea about owning a ballclub. A year or two later Larry come up with the same thing, and I got into it then. There were ten people involved in it. To make a long story short, the deal fell through.

One of the big things was that Ed Barrow didn't want anything to do with Larry MacPhail. So anyway, the thing fell through, and Dan Topping was one of the ten who was involved in it. He was down here at El Toro. We were having a golf tournament in Phoenix, and I was talking to Sammy Byrd, the old outfielder, and Sammy was telling me that we missed the boat.

I got a call from New York. Dan Topping, who then was in the Marine Corps, but was back on leave in New York, he had run across the girl who was the daughter of the president of the Manhattan Chase Bank, Manufacturer's Trust, and she talked to him about buying the Yankees, and he went to see her father, and she said he thought this thing could be put together.

Dan Topping

They had set a price for it, and Dan asked me to come back there.

"I have to go back," Dan said. "I'm about off leave."

I flew back in time to get him, and we talked for a couple hours, and we got MacPhail back in it, and so it was the three of us.

Topping and I put up half of what it was. We started talking two million two, and finally it ended up two million eight five. MacPhail put in half a million dollars of borrowed money that he got somewhere. And we put it together.

MacPhail would manage it, run it, and that's the way we finally put it together, and of course there are stories about that. I won't bore you with that.

No. Bore me.

Of course, Ed Barrow and MacPhail were like that, and Barrow was trying to keep MacPhail out of it. Topping's friend at the bank was trying to talk Barrow into doing this, because the bank had to get rid of it. By the way, Barrow was the administrator of the estate. The bank had to call him in, and so they put a lot of pressure on Barrow, and by God, he had to be reasonable, because the bank was gonna push in on him and do something.

I had never met Barrow. I never knew him.

When I was in Phoenix, I left the next morning and left the golf tournament. Nobody knew where I went. I told them I had gone to Washington, see. The same fellow happened to be in New York, and I knew he was there, and I called him, and I said, "Now Carl, you keep your room, and I will come and stay in your room, because I don't want anybody to know I'm there."

He left the day before. I never saw him. But his room was there, and I stayed in it. So we got together in this way. It was getting pretty hot. I had the newspaper men surrounding me in that hotel. They finally found out. I knew the people in the hotel and I knew where the elevator was. I knew the newspaper men were out in the halls. I got a hold of the bell captain, got him up there, and I said, "I want to get into this freight elevator that's right over here. The newspaper men are out here. Now you get those newspaper men around the corner of the hall."

"How am I going to do that?" he said.

"You go up and tell them if they go to the elevator over there, I may be coming out of that elevator," I said. "And I'll go down this elevator."

I went down that elevator, and I talked to MacPhail on the phone. He was over at the Ambassador. I knew the hotel and went down through the freight elevator to the basement and went over to the Ambassador and called MacPhail.

Ed Barrow was over at the Regency Hotel. He said, "I want to meet Webb before I make a deal."

I told MacPhail this, and MacPhail had to stay there, because Barrow wouldn't see MacPhail.

I went over to the Regency and went up to Barrow's floor, and I went into the living room, and he was in the other room, and he come out, and the first thing he said to me, "Webb, I never met you, but I hear you're a pretty good guy and a rough and tough old ballplayer."

"I don't know about that," I said.

"Well, I wanted to meet you and talk to you about this deal," he said. "That goddamn MacPhail, I've got no goddamn use for him. I'll tell you very frankly. It hurts me for him to have anything to do with baseball. I don't think he belongs into it."

Why was that?

They had a lot of problems when they were in baseball. I don't know what the problems were, but I think anyone in baseball can tell you that it didn't take much for MacPhail to irritate you.

He asked me, "How active are you going to be in it?"

"I'm going to have a lot of say in it, along with Topping," I said. "Topping is going to be here, and I'm going to work pretty close with Topping."

He said, "This is quite a decision for me to make, but I think I'm a pretty good judge of human nature. I've talked to you, and you look like you're a pretty good guy. Put it here, and we'll call it a deal."

We went to MacPhail and announced it.

Was Barrow finished with the Yankees?

Oh yeah. Absolutely. He was completely out.

It was the winter of 1944, and we took over in 1945. I kept thinking about what happened in 1918, when they stopped baseball. There was a lot of talk in Washington. This was in 1944, and the war was on, and this was the gamble we had to take. If they had closed baseball down, we'd have been in a hell of a shape. And that was one of the reasons we were able to buy the club for that price. Of course, me being in the construction business. The only time I had ever been in the Stadium, I could observe, being in the construction business, what a well-built stadium that was.

I visualized that when I bought this, this was the greatest deal I had ever made. Two million eight hundred thousand for Yankee Stadium, the parking area, for the Newark Stadium and the parking area, and 20 acres of land besides, and the Kansas City stadium and parking. We bought all that for two million, eight hundred thousand dollars. Plus 450 ballplayers. If you take George Allen here, he called me one time and he said, "Del, I want to talk to you about this football team. I think you can buy it for 18 million dollars."

"What do I get for that?" I said.

"You get the franchise and 85 ballplayers," he said.

"Let me tell you something," I said.

And I told him about the Yankee deal.

"You're talking about making a half a million a year," I said. "We make a million to two and a half million every year."

CHAPTER SEVEN

DEL WEBB

Stengel and Weiss and Victory

*T*he three-way marriage among Larry MacPhail, Dan Topping, and Del Webb was destined not to last. MacPhail, though a brilliant baseball man, was a volatile drunk who at some point was going to enrage the businessman Webb. It happened at the end of the 1947 season after the Yankees won the World Series.

Was Larry MacPhail instrumental in hyping the gate? Was he a good promo man?

Oh hell yes. He did a lot of things to commercialize the Yankees. He was a great guy but not too good a businessman. Of course, you know the story of how Larry got out of the business.

Please tell me.

Let me go back a little further. We won the World Series in '47, and Larry put on the Goddamnest party you ever saw. He bought all the goddamn champagne he could buy anywhere in the country, and Christ we had a bill for champagne for I don't know how many thousands of dollars. Nobody could have ever drank all the champagne he ordered. But he picks a fight at that party.

I don't know how well it was planned, but anyway, he punches this guy [a minor official from the Dodgers who he didn't want there]. He punched him in the nose and that started the whole riot. Then he went upstairs and fired George Weiss. I think he was just trying to stir up a lot of dissension so he could get the ballclub.

So after this happened, Happy Chandler called me about this. Chandler was the commissioner then.

"Goddamn it, we have to do something about this thing," he said.

"I don't know what you're going to do about it," I said, "but I'm going to tell you something right now what I'm going to do. I think this is a disgrace to baseball, and I'm going to offer MacPhail two million dollars for his share to get out. Whether he will accept it or not, I don't know, and I don't give a shit. I'm not a quitter, and I'm going to take this right to the end."

Chandler says to me, "I'll back you up on it. MacPhail shouldn't be in baseball."

"You made that decision, not me," I said. "I told you what I'm going to do."

MacPhail hired an attorney, this fellow Parke Carroll, who used to be the attorney for the National League, which I thought was a stupid thing to do. Carroll called me and told me MacPhail wanted to see me.

"What does he want to see me about?" I said. "Does he want to talk about the buy and sell agreement? There is no use in him seeing me, and if you want to make the deal you can make it. I'll give him two million dollars, and he has to get out of baseball."

"You can't do that," Carroll said.

"Let me tell you something, Carroll," I said. "You tell me I can't do it. I'm telling you I'm going to do it. I'm going to tell you another thing. You tell him that if he don't take the two million dollars, I don't give a goddamn. I'll tell you one thing: He's got to make up his mind by six o'clock tonight. I will be at the office at five o'clock. Today is Sunday, and he knows where his office is, and I know where my office is, and I'll be there at five o'clock. At six o'clock he can make up his mind whether he wants to or not. You just tell him so."

"I don't think that's fair," Carroll said.

"I don't give a shit whether you think I'm fair or not," I said. "That's what I'm telling you. I'll be there at five o'clock. And tell him I don't give a shit whether he does or not. We'll take other steps after that."

What would you have done if he had said no?

Well, we'd go to the courts, because it wasn't a fair thing to do.

What wasn't a fair thing to do?

What Larry did was this: We had a buy and sell agreement, see. And Larry got this fellow Zeckendorf to make a buy agreement. He made a phony offer of around three million dollars for his share. He used that as a basic to bargain on with Topping and me.

He had got a price for three million dollars, and we thought that was a phony thing he was using against us. He had a right to buy and sell at a price he could sell it for. These prices are sometimes set in the agreement and sometimes set by an appraisal and sometimes by an offer that's made.

He got this phony offer from Zeckendorf.

So he came down from three million to two million five, which he said he would settle for, see. Well, I said two million, even then I thought we were paying too much. But I said I would do that.

I was over at the office at five o'clock, and I was in my office, and MacPhail and Carroll were in their office when I got there. Carroll comes into my office and he said, "I don't think MacPhail will settle."

"I don't care if he'll settle or not," I said. "I told you that before. Don't bother me about it. I'll be here until six o'clock. Let me know."

"MacPhail wants to talk to you about it," he said.

"I don't want to talk to MacPhail," I said. "He has nothing to talk to me about. Just tell him to make up his mind."

"I don't think he'll do it," he said.

"I don't care," I said. "I'll be here til six. Let me know."

I was madder than a son of a bitch. I was really pissed off at this whole thing.

MacPhail had really upset George Weiss.

Oh man, it was terrible. George was crying like a baby. Just terrible. Mrs. Weiss was there too. I went up there and tried to help George. George was so upset, he didn't know what he was doing.

"George," I told him. "You still have your job. Don't worry about that for two minutes."

I was there, so pretty soon Carroll come in. He looked forlorn. He said to me, "MacPhail said he will accept your deal." And he said, "He'd like to talk to you."

"Well, all right," I said.

We went over to his office, and he was standing there all smiles. He put his hand out to me, he said, "Well Del, I want to say you've been a pretty good partner."

"You no good son of a bitch," I said. "You can stick that fucking hand up your ass. I'm not going to have a Goddamn thing to do with you."

I walked off and left them standing there.

And I never saw him for a year after that. I ran across him down in Miami one time. He was just as friendly as he could possibly be. That's the way the guy was anyway.

Judge Landis told me one time, "That is one guy who shouldn't even take a teaspoon full of liquor." MacPhail could be the most lovable guy and nicest guy when he wanted to do, and he was smart. But he'd get on these drunken sprees. You think he'd get to a point where he'd want to accomplish something. I watched the guy, and he'd be under pressure and work as hard as he could, and then he'd get drunk and raise hell about it.

He was an innovative guy.

No doubt about it. Goddamn, if he would just go along the way he planned things, but he'd always get on those Goddamn drunks, and it seemed to me it was in his planning. He'd go to a certain point, and he'd get drunk. He was a hell of a promotional man with a lot of good solid ideas.

He was responsible for night games at the stadium and for television.

He did a good job. I got along with him pretty good, except once in a while he'd get on a tangent about something.

Can you remember any of the major decisions you participated in during the MacPhail era?

I'll tell you one I participated in that started about the time we bought the Yankees. We were completing a profit-pension plan for our own

company. I got the idea that the profit-pension plan would be a good
idea for the Yankee organization. Of course, with MacPhail, if you told
MacPhail anything, if you give him an idea and he couldn't take credit
for it, he wouldn't do it. He wanted to take credit. So I got our man
Becker, who was our secretary at the time, to try to set up something
for the Yankee ballclub. We did, and Becker and MacPhail had a lot of
arguments back and forth, but we finally got it set up. And the next
step I made, was that I thought the baseball players ought to have a
profit-sharing pension plan. So I got Becker and a fellow by the name of
Nelson, who worked for Phil Wrigley, and got them together to get this
pension plan started.

I learned from my other experience that I better let MacPhail take
credit for this, or he'd fight the goddamn thing. So I got it started, and I
told Becker that and told Phil Wrigley that and told Nelson that. We had
to work with MacPhail to get the thing going, and so this was that way
that the profit-sharing pension plan started. It started from my idea. Our
own company brought in the Yankees as their own.

*You mentioned Chandler. I know for a fact he wasn't your cup of tea. What
is it that led to your kicking him in the behind and getting him out of there?
What did he do?*

He didn't do nothing, if you want to know the truth. He was a politician,
and that was not my idea. I get the credit for getting him in there, but I
didn't. I'll tell you what happened there. I wanted Bob Hannigan to be
the commissioner of baseball. He'd be a good man. Of course, baseball
was going along with no commissioner after a while. Goddamn it, [after
Kennesaw Mountain Landis died,] I found out I was acting as commissioner. Christ, everyone wanted me to do something down in Washington, like Christ. I remember I met one day outside the courthouse in
New York, and I told Horace Stoneham right there, "Goddamn, we've
got to get a commissioner."

MacPhail asked me who I wanted, and I said, "Bob Hannigan or
somebody. We have to get somebody."

They were going to have a meeting in Columbus, and they went down
there, and I met with MacPhail in Washington, and we were going to try
to get Hannigan in there. The first vote went around, and there wasn't

enough to carry it. And to this day I really don't know what the hell went on. I really don't know.

The next go-around, I'll be goddamned, MacPhail made a pitch for Chandler. Goddamn Chandler came up for a vote. A lot of people thought I was the one who put Chandler in there. Not so. That's the way it happened. And I wasn't at the meeting. I will always kick myself in the ass for not going to the meeting. I had some other things, and I didn't go.

One reason I didn't want to go: because I suggested Hannigan, I didn't want them thinking I was going to push him in there. But that's the way Chandler got in, and when he got in, I tried to do what I could to help him. I think I knew him better than anybody else. He'd go around to old Clark Griffith, Connie Mack, Walter Briggs and those older guys and pet them up, and they were in their second childhood, you know, and he made them think this and that.

I'll give you a couple of examples how stupid Chandler was. Right here in this town, big league ballplayers were playing an exhibition ballgame for a charity. There was a fellow named Lee who had the authority to put these teams together. He put them together every year. He'd been a ballplayer, and he'd been in the movies. Chandler heard about it and sent him a wire and told him the game would be cancelled, couldn't be played. He got the wire only a few days before the game was to be played. And they played the All Star game because they only had two days. Some of the ballplayers didn't play. Some of them did.

"Why did you send that wire?" I said to Chandler.

"These fellows are playing out there, and they have to get permission from the commissioner," he said.

"How do you know he didn't have permission from Landis," I asked. Because I knew he did. I knew something about this.

"Oh no no," said Chandler.

"Happy, I think you're wrong," I said.

This happened in the fall, and in the spring I went out to Wrigley Field with him to see one of the first workouts. Leo Durocher was there. Here he was sitting on the edge of the stands, and I'm sitting beside Chandler, and we saw Durocher in the middle of the field, and this shows how stupid he was.

"Durocher, come here," Chandler said. He motioned to Durocher.

"You know I'm going to fine you five hundred dollars for trying to play in that All Star game," he said.

Of course, all the newspaper men came around. And he holds the trial right on the curb of the dugout, for God sake.

Jesus Christ, we go back to the hotel, and he said to Durocher, "And I'm going to fine every other ballplayer a hundred dollars. You're five hundred because you're older."

I wrote back to him, "Jesus Christ, Happy. In the first place why in the hell did you put on an exhibition like that in the ballpark? Everybody saw you. You are wrong in this thing that the league doesn't have the authority to do this."

"No, I'm not," said Chandler.

"I'll prove it. When we get back to the hotel, I will call Lee, and he'll come down and show you the telegram he got from Landis."

"He don't have any telegram," he said.

"I know he does."

Lee had shown it to me.

The wire read, "You are hereby authorized to play this All Star game for charity, and this will give you the authority to play until rescinded."

All the newspapermen were out there waiting to see what the hell was going to happen. Well Lee comes down and shows Chandler the wire, and he has to rescind the whole goddamn thing.

I'll tell you another episode. Remember when Durocher hit that negro in Brooklyn? I was in Washington DC at that time. I was at the Mayflower hotel. Happy called me on the phone.

"Del, I have to suspend Durocher for life," he said.

"What the fuck are you talking about," I said.

"Leo just hit a negro down in Brooklyn."

"You don't know anything about it," I said. "Who told you about it?"

"The press," he said.

"Christ almighty," I said. "Let me come over and talk to you. In the first place, you don't know what the hell happened."

"Oh, yes I do. I know what happened."

"How do you know?"

He said, "You know Bill [Bojangles Robinson] the dancer. You know him, don't you?"

"Sure, I know him."

"He called me and told me about this," said Chandler. "Would you take his word for it?"

"No, I wouldn't until I found out just what the hell happened," I said. "Why don't you go to New York tomorrow and call Durocher up, and then make a decision. Don't haul off and decide."

He had the press all ready to tell it, see.

Chandler didn't like Durocher.

No, he didn't like Durocher, and Durocher didn't like him. But anyway—as for Durocher I can tell you a lot of things just as bad. So he went down to New York, and we finally got into the thing, but anyway, he didn't put him out for life.

He found out this guy had followed Durocher all the way from the dugout calling him, "You dirty no good cock-sucking son of a bitch, and you haven't got the guts to fight, and put your hands up."

Durocher finally hit him.

When Chandler found out—you know what I finally found out? I talked to Bill Robinson. I asked him, "Why did you call Chandler over this in Brooklyn?"

"I never talked to Chandler," he said. "Why the hell would I be talking to him? I don't even know what went on."

There's an example of it. He'd get himself in a pot like that and try to make an alibi for it, and he Goddamn lied.

He was just as incompetent as anybody could be. I said to George Weiss, "We have got to get rid of that guy. If he stays in baseball a long time, there will be no way to get rid of him."

They had a big meeting and they voted him out. I had a couple guys with me, and they backed out, but they finally voted with me, and we had a pretty good vote, and it was enough to get him out. He was giving a talk at the hotel, and we had to go up there and interrupt and tell him we wanted to see him and that he was through, and he came over and saw us. I let someone else tell him. I just listened. Phil Wrigley, after he got through, he said to him, "I feel real sorry about this."

Even so, Chandler wouldn't step down, and we had to go through a whole rigamarole to get rid of him again. He went around to all the owners and tried to sell himself. The trouble with Chandler was that I knew Chandler better than anybody in baseball, by far, and he went around giving them all this bullshit, and a lot of them would go for it.

I never will forget he said to me, "Goddamn, see what you've done to me and my poor family and daughters. My God, God will punish you."

He wrote a story in *Sports Illustrated* and he really took after me. There weren't too many true facts in it. The press called me, and I said, "The only way I can judge him, he's trying to run for governor again, and that's what he's using to try and become governor. Let's see how he comes out in the election."

Chandler got about ten percent of the vote.

I tried to work with him to try to help baseball, and I got to the point of selecting two commissioners, which I'm not proud of either one of them, Chandler and Ford Frick.

I got to tell you about Frick. Frick was one of the most loyal, devoted men I ever knew to baseball. A real honest loyal fellow. And a great guy and a good friend of mine, a dependable man. No idea that anyone could be better than him. He lacked the executive ability.

Frick did a real good job, but they needed a man who was more creative and more original than Frick was. I wouldn't want to ever say anything against Frick. Frick was a great man and a good friend of mine.

I might want to say one more thing than we're talking about Frick. I was the head of the committee for the commission, and we finally made the selection when we were in Chicago. It was two o'clock in the morning, and we couldn't get a decision. Frick made a motion to adjourn and continue the next day, and I said, "No sir. I won't accept that motion."

I took the goddamn key to the suite and threw it out the window into the trash.

"We're going to come up with a commissioner," I said.

It was between Warren Giles and Frick, and I think we picked the right man. Giles did a good job in baseball. He was a good friend, did a decent job, but of the two that's all we had, and unluckily, both times we had to pick commissioners we were in a position where we were in a war. We had the first World War and we had the Korean War. And you know who I thought should have been made the commissioner, an outstanding man, a man who stood out in my mind, well this was during Chandler's time, and I'm talking about J. Edgar Hoover. He would have liked to have taken it. He would have liked to have it, but Hoover was committed to the government.

Who were some of the people you interviewed for Chandler's job?
We interviewed 200 people. Dwight Eisenhower was one of them.

Would Eisenhower have taken it?
He couldn't take it because he was involved in the goddamn war, see. I would have liked to have him. We interviewed J Edgar Hoover and Earl Warren, the chief justice. Warren would have taken it. He was the greatest baseball fan in the country. But there was a war. He said, "I was the governor of California. I became the chief justice. How can I leave?"

Of all the people I ever interviewed, J. Edgar Hoover might have been a little old, but he was a man who was better than anybody. I interviewed Dick Nixon to take Frick's job.

What did Nixon say to you when you asked him?
I remember one thing he said.

"That's a pretty good salary," he said.

I recommended that we pay him a hundred thousand dollars a year. If I'd have stayed with it, I would have gotten that for him too. He said, "My god, that's a pretty good price, isn't it?"

I talked to him two or three times about it. He finally decided to stay in politics.

If we could get somebody in baseball, like Joe Cronin was considered. The only objection I had with Joe was Joe was getting a little old.

So Ford Frick was not your choice?
No. Because of the Korean War we couldn't get too many people.

At the end of the 1948 season the Yankees fired Bucky Harris and hired Casey Stengel. Why did you decide to fire Harris?

I'll go a little further about Bucky Harris. Bucky Harris was a real nice fellow, tough guy in a way and easy in another way. But Bucky Harris took the attitude he was a big-league manager. Bucky would leave the clubhouse as soon as the game was over, meet with the press if necessary, go home, and have an unlisted number. He didn't ever want to be bothered by anything. He'd be at the ballpark the next day at eleven o'clock.

He didn't take the time to work with the youngsters. I thought he might help them a little bit, but he didn't take any interest in them. We knew we had to do something with Harris, and this was a tough deal because in letting Harris go, he had lost the '48 pennant by only a game.

We hired Casey Stengel to manage the Kansas City club in 1944. I was president of the Kansas City club, and I got to know Casey pretty well. I worked awful close with Casey.

Casey Stengel

We had the worst fucking ballclub you ever saw. You have never seen a worst ballclub. We had a left-handed guy playing second base. The way he maneuvered around, I thought he did a good job.

Edna, his wife, said, "I'd like to see Casey get a job out on the Coast. We lived there, and he always goes East all the time. You could be in the Coast League, and we'd be home."

I got a hold of Brick Laws, the owner of the Oakland Club. I knew him quite well. I got him to hire Stengel, and Casey managed Oakland for three years. Of course, Stengel did the same thing he did there. He knew he had a lot of old ballplayers, and they couldn't play. One was Hershel Martin. He was forty-something years old and had a goddamn big gut and used a 42 ounce bat and could hit balls a mile but he'd strike out, and he couldn't run, and he had a lot of guys like that. He kept jerking them around like he did in Kansas City, see. Stengel got that idea of platooning from John McGraw, because the best year Stengel ever had, he hit .342 one time, and he played in and out all the time, about half the games.

I talked to Stengel, and we made a deal with Oakland, an off-the-cuff deal, and we took him and had an agreement to buy Jackie Jensen and Billy Martin.

Anyway, Stengel did a good job down there, and he won two pennants for them, and so when it came to Bucky Harris and the way he was, I didn't want to come out to George Weiss. There had been a lot of discussion. I was responsible for Casey coming because George Weiss and Stengel were good friends, but I didn't want to have me say we were hiring Casey as manager. I wanted George to say it.

George was jealous of a lot of publicity that I got Stengel. So I went out to the stadium one day. I just said to myself, *How can I do it? If I asked George if Casey Stengel would be the manager, and George would say no, then I would be in a hell of a shape. If I take a gamble and he said yes, then that would be fine.*

I thought about it, and we talked about managers.

I said to George, "If you had to pick a manager today, if we had to have one right today, who would you think would be the best manager to bring in?"

George thought about it, and he said, "I'd like to try Casey Stengel."

So then I got Stengel and brought him down to the Biltmore Hotel. I had quite a talk with him, told him he was going to the Yankees, and he couldn't jerk ballplayers around like he did in Oakland, and he agreed to all that.

The first year Casey had so many good ballplayers, he had to use them. Of course, when he got to where he was winning, then he got a little cocky about it.

When did you first become acquainted with Casey?
I first met Casey in 1923, the year the Yankees won the World Series.

You were a ballplayer, and he was a ballplayer. Were you friends with him in the 1930s and 1940s?

Oh yeah.

So Casey was it. You didn't think of Leo Durocher?

Of course we thought about that. We had a very good combination. Dan Topping was not a baseball man. Topping concerned himself with the stadium, the radio, the television business end of it, and of course, he was in on it, though the decisions generally were made by me and Stengel and Weiss.

What were some of the things you and Casey decided on?

Well, I'll never forget one time, we were fighting Boston, and we had a doubleheader. We had to win two games to win the '49 pennant. No use winning one game. We had to win both of them.

Well, Stengel and I went out that night. I left at two o'clock in the morning. We went to every Goddamn thing in the world. I can't remember all the details. Anyway, I picked him up, and he was still in his pajamas. This was about nine thirty. I looked down on the Goddamn floor, and here were a lot of papers all torn up. It looked like a mouse had been there.

"What in the hell is that?" I asked.

"I'm making up all these lineups during the night," Casey said. "Shit, I tore them up, this and that." And finally he said, "Here's the one I got."

And then we went out to the ballpark.

The strategy we finally worked on was to have Allie Reynolds pitch the first game. Reynolds won the first game 9 to 3.

Joe Page pitched the last six and two thirds in relief. In the second game Vic Raschi started and he was ahead 1 to nothing through most of the game.

That's right. Reynolds was going to pitch the first game, and Raschi was going to pitch the second game, and then we had all of the other pitchers to follow up after Raschi. And we talked about that, and if Reynolds got in trouble, we were going to follow with Eddie Lopat. If it got so far along we were going to follow with Page.

Casey brought in Page in the third inning. He pitched one-hit ball the rest of the game.

That's right. Page come in and pitched, and we picked up a couple runs and then another run. Finally, they got two runs and tied it, and Johnny Lindell hit a towering fly ball that went up into the stands. And then Raschi came along in the second game.

I used to call Stengel on the phone, and we used to talk a lot when we needed a ballplayer. This is when we traded for Johnny Mize and Enos Slaughter.

How did you ever get Mize out of the national league?

I can tell you about that too. We met up in Topping's apartment. Casey and I decided we wanted to get Mize. We went to Weiss on it.

How did you know he was available?

We didn't, but we thought he'd be the guy, a lefthanded hitter in that stadium. Stoneham was using him part-time, and so we thought may-be. We had Topping call Stoneham, cause Topping and Stoneham were pretty good friends.

Stoneham didn't want to make this deal. Because he said, "If we sold him to the Yankees, and he helped the Yankees, that would reflect on the Giants." Which was right.

Topping said, "Well, I don't think I can make the deal."

"How about fifty thousand dollars," I said.

Then we said to Stoneham, "We'll give you 75,000 if he helps us win the pennant."

Remember, it was up to George Weiss to make the decision.

Stoneham had left it up to Weiss to decide whether we would pay him 50 thousand or 75 thousand. Weiss decided we should give him 50.

Well, we got him. Stoneham reluctantly agreed to it.

As I remember, Mize helped us right away. He hit two home runs and won two ballgames in a very short period. He tailed off at the end of the season, and we were still leading.

He hurt himself. He hurt his arm.

Yeah, that's right. I remember he hit one ball and the guy caught in front of the fence, and he told me afterward, "Basically my shoulder isn't right."

Casey won his first pennant for the Yankees in his first year in 1949.

Well, he started in 1949, and he had something like seven injured. And Christ, he had to move fellows around. DiMaggio's heel and everything else. Weiss used to almost have a stroke. Casey would make some of

Casey Stengel

those moves, jerking players in and out, and Weiss would say, "Holy Jesus."

I used to tell him, "Goddamn it."

Finally, I told George, "I don't like it any better than you do, but there is no use getting all excited about it. Jesus Christ." So Weiss almost has a stroke over the moves Casey makes, jerking guys out and this and that.

"George," I said, "we've put up with this for a year or two now. We've drawn more crowds. The fans like it. As a baseball man, I don't like it either, but we shouldn't get ourselves all upset

about it. You know this as well as I do, that Casey ought to win these pennants by fourteen, fifteen games. Then we'd be playing in front of nobody."

I don't know whether that satisfied George or not, but he took it a little easier after that. I used to tell Stengel, "Jesus Christ, the way you manage guys, I can't complain. We gave you a ballclub, but you ought to win by fourteen, fifteen games."

What did Casey say to that?

He gave me a lot of double talk, like he always did. He'd say, "I don't know about that. When I was in Brooklyn in 1940, I hit a two base hit off Alexander. . . ."

And then I give him a watch. I don't remember what year. And I engraved on the back of that watch, "Everything considered, the greatest manager ever to put on a uniform." And when I gave it to him, I said, "You know what I mean by everything considered." He knew what I meant, all right. The way he handled the press, the way his appeal to the public was, the way he drew the crowds in there, and he won.

Was there a decision before the 1960 season where you felt Casey had run his course?

Oh yeah. We knew we had to do it in the middle of the season.

Did Casey know? What were the factors behind that?

Well, we knew he was getting older. The real story was this: We had Ralph Houk in Denver, and I was the president of the Denver club. I'd always been president of the minor league clubs. That was the set up that we had.

One of the reasons I did that and wanted to do it was that it gave me access to some of the younger ballplayers coming up, to see what they were. Stengel was getting old, so we had to be thinking about another manager. I suggested Houk. George Weiss didn't quite agree with that.

Who did George want?

I don't think George had anybody. George was thinking more about going out and trying to get somebody who was proven. We talked about everybody. Al Dark was number one on my list til I found out more about him, then Christ, I found out he wasn't a guy I knew at all.

[Dark, a devout Christian, was having an affair with an airline stewardess while he was married. There was also a feeling he was prejudiced against black and Hispanic players.]

He was not a discreet person.

No. A lot of things I found out about him. The thing was, what really made the decision, we knew Stengel was getting old. We knew we had to do something. The 1960 World Series didn't make the decision. That was made before. The World Series proved to us we were right in making the decision.

There were a couple of other things in that series too. The other thing that brought it home more than ever, Houk had managed in Denver for three years and done a good job. He won two pennants. Bobby Richardson had played for him, Ryne Duren really came to life there, and so did that catcher, John Blanchard. There were several ballclubs looking at Houk, see. If we didn't make a decision, we were going to lose him.

We got Stengel up to my suite in New York, told him we wanted to work out any kind of retirement thing that he wanted. Casey was pretty independent. He didn't want any retirement. He wasn't angry.

"You guys own the ballclub," Casey said. "I played for you, and I never had a contract a lot of times. Your word was good. I don't want to be around if I'm not wanted."

He wasn't happy about it, because he didn't really want to retire.

Casey proved that by going to the Mets.

Going to the Mets. I don't know if he proved that or not. Weiss talked him into that. He didn't want to, and he finally agreed to it. See, Weiss was going to retire when he was 65. Come 65 he didn't want to retire, and he was sympathetic to Stengel then, see.

We agreed there would be a press conference, and Stengel would go there and announce his retirement. Unfortunately, I wasn't there. What Stengel didn't like was to meet with the press and have a press release read to them. He'd never do that himself. He didn't like somebody else do it. I knew that. Nobody else knew that as much as I did.

"Any sonofabitch who has to read something to the press shouldn't even be talking to them," he said.

I wasn't there, and Friedman, our attorney, wrote up something. God only knows why Topping let him read it, but he up and read it before the microphone, and holy Christ, then Casey got mad.

He was supposed to say we had a memorable understanding that he was retiring and that everybody was all right. Instead, he got up and said, "Goddamn, they just fired me."

It was the only time I think I ever got mad at Stengel. I come back from California. I called him over to my office one day, and I really let him have it.

What did he say?

He didn't say very much, really.

"I told you what I thought, Case," I said. "We can be friends. You're mad at me alright, but I don't think you're right the way you treat us."

I didn't see much of Casey for years. Stengel and I are still great friends. I have a lot of respect for him, and he does for me too. We were in San Francisco one time, and he sat on the arm of my chair all the way on that damn flight.

Was Mr. Weiss annoyed about stepping down?

George couldn't come to grips with himself that he was going to quit. He wrestled with his own self about it. I remember he told me one time, "I know I ought to quit, but it doesn't seem like the thing to do."

If I remember right, I think we had to give him permission to go to the Mets. Because of our retirement plan.

George wasn't as bitter as Casey.

I was very close to George after he was over at the Mets. He used to come out and visit me, and I'd see him. And that reminds me, I have to go see Hazel when I go to New York.

I know Dan Topping remarried, and he had several children. Was there a point where Dan was losing a certain amount of interest in the Yankees, where he felt he should get out of baseball and sell out?

I told you that Dan ran the club, and he was the president.

I know in 1958 and 1959 he began taking an interest in some of the duties that Mr. Weiss had previously done. And Mr. Weiss didn't like it.

Yeah. Well, Dan was doing that because he thought Mr. Weiss was going to leave. To retire. As I told you, Weiss talked about retiring ten years before he retired. And he set a date of 65 years of age when he was going to retire.

Weiss was 67 when he left, and he worked two years after. I can tell you—and Dan doesn't like particular to have this said—but I think it's a fact, and it doesn't make too much difference now, but Dan's health was failing. That was his problem.

The doctors told him he had to get out of this. See, Dan had three quarters of his stomach removed, and he had a rectal operation, and then he developed emphysema. Might have been asthma. His mother died of emphysema at the age of 62. And then he had a heart condition develop.

He had two or three heart attacks, which people don't know, see. His doctor was telling me about the problems he was having, and he had to have a bowel operation too, see. He had all this done, and even then his health was bad. And he just couldn't take it anymore.

The doctor told him he'd have to do something. That was really what brought about the sale of the Yankees, and that also brought about me thinking about selling, because I couldn't run the Yankees. I was not a fulltime operator there, and Dan was the president. George Weiss had run it.

I told you what I did. I worked with Casey and the managers and followed the ballclub, and had a look at ballplayers. See, so that's what really brought about the sale of the Yankees.

I'll tell you one thing: Dan and I talked about selling several years before it was done.

I had three alternatives. I could buy Dan out. I could get another partner. Or we could operate the way we were, and I thought about it and thought about it, and finally one day I went to Dan, and I said, "You want to sell. We've had this ballclub for twenty years, and we've done pretty goddamn well with it."

All the time we had it, the worst we ever did was finish fourth once. Never out of the first division. And I said, "Let's see if somebody else can do any better. I'll sell with you."

I could see some of these other problems developing in baseball, expansion and the Goddamn restrictive draft. I had worked hard to keep that restrictive draft out. Clark Griffith and Bill Veeck were trying to get it in, and I kept it down. I went to every ballplayer when this fellow Lewis was the player representative, and I got him moved out of there. Who do you think was the one who gave us the most trouble? Our own representative, Allie Reynolds. I finally got him out. And I no more got out of there, then four things happened.

The unexpected draft and the representative of ballplayers, they got this Lewis out and got this other fellow in, and the reserve clause that I got the senators in Washington to agree on pretty well, and the fourth thing was the expansion of baseball.

I'll be goddamn. I wasn't out of there a year, and all four of those things got into effect within a year or two years' time. I could see this coming, and I just wore myself out fighting these damn things, and I could see maybe I was going to get licked if I didn't keep doing this, and I got tired. That was a lot of goddamn work, and I had other things to do.

You and Dan sold to CBS at the end of 1964.
Um hum.

Was there a point when Mr. Topping was feeling ill and he knew he was going to sell the club that it seemed expedient not to buy as many new ballplayers but instead to keep the money in the pot and make it a little more rosy?

I wouldn't say exactly that. I might put it another way. If we knew we were going to sell the ballclub, we didn't make any effort to buy additional ballplayers or buy additional farm deals for ballclubs, because if we knew we were going to sell. Thought maybe the new owner would have some other ideas. That wasn't going to benefit us any.

To be frank, not buying new players may have retarded things for maybe a year or something like that, but I don't think it caused a deterioration of the Yankees. CBS wouldn't spend any money.

Roy Hamey said the same thing.
Yeah.

⌒

Del Webb died on July 4, 1974, only a short time after I went to see him. I, like so many Yankee fans of a certain age, salute him.

CHAPTER EIGHT

RALPH BRANCA

The Ace of the Staff

*R*alph Branca, *the fifteenth of seventeen children, grew up in Mount Ver-non, New York. He pitched in the big leagues for twelve years, most notably with the Brooklyn Dodgers. Branca came up to Brooklyn in 1944 at age nineteen because a number of Dodger veteran pitchers were serving in the military during World War II.*

In 1947 he became the workhorse and ace of the Brooklyn Dodgers staff with a 21–12 record and a 2.67 ERA in 280 innings. Because Branca is primarily known for giving up Bobby Thomson's Shot Heard round the World in the final game of the 1951 playoffs, people forget just how dominant a pitcher he had been. A man with a great memory, Branca had interesting insights on his teammates, but most of all he vented about general manager Branch Rickey.

⌒

When were you first aware that the major league clubs were interested in you?

I was only 16 when my brother John and I went for tryouts, which they had in those days. We were New York Giants fans, so we went to the Giants first.

We were supposed to go on a certain day, and it rained, and we went the next day, and I don't know how many kids were there, and I never threw a ball, and I can see why. They looked at me, and they saw this blade. I was six-two and weighed about 135.

Ralph Branca

My brother threw, and they watched him. When they look for prospects, they look for guys who can throw the fastball. John just wasn't fast enough. But he knew how to pitch, and unfortunately in those days it wasn't enough.

We then went to Yankee Stadium, and they liked me. Years later [Yankees owner] Larry Mac-Phail used to give them hell because they had on my card, "Too young. Get in touch with him next year," which they didn't do. It was the war years, and they never got in touch with me.

For the third trip, a tryout with Brooklyn, my brother and I took the longest subway ride on the IRT. We went from 241st Street in the Bronx all the way out to Sheepshead Bay. We left at seven in the morning, and we took our sandwiches and our uniforms and went out.

I threw, and the Dodgers liked me. They had me come back and throw batting practice, and that was a big impression. I'm a 16-year old kid.

Who was the scout?

A scout named Joe Labate, another little scout named Jimmy Ferranti, and Art Dede ran the tryout. Even though I was pitching for the high school, the next year they had me come down and pitch batting practice. The Dodgers had just come home from spring training, which was at Bear Mountain, and they had the pre-season weekend series, and I went down and threw batting practice. I was 17.

The Dodgers were on the ball. They got me to sign that June right out of high school. I was 17. I got a new glove and a supporter with a cup in it. I didn't know what the hell that was. That's the truth, and I got ninety dollars a month to go to Olean, New York, in the Pony League, which played in Pennsylvania, Ontario, and New York.

What was Olean like?

Olean was a very small town. I liked it. It was the first time I was away from home. It had a big wide main street. Everybody except a couple older 4-F guys on the team stayed at the YMCA. Jake Pitler was the manager, and I loved Jake. He was a super guy. I played in June and July and came home in September, and when I got home, NYU asked me if I wanted to play ball. They gave me a basketball scholarship, and I told my buddy, "I can't go. You know I played pro ball."

"They don't know," he said. "Just go."

So I ended up going to NYU for a year. By the time I got to basketball season, I had started to mature. I filled out. I weighed about 178 my first weigh-in for basketball. I ended the season at 195, and by the time baseball was over, I was 205. I was still skinny. I wasn't fully matured. I was filled out, but I could throw a hell of a lot harder. I would say the next year at 19 I really matured and was able to throw the ball hard. I could muscle it.

In 1944 you pitched for Brooklyn.

Yeah.

Did you pitch for NYU?

Yeah. We didn't have a big schedule. We only played 13 games, and I started 12 of them. I pitched on Wednesday and Saturday. We lost to Navy our first game, and we lost to Columbia. We were 10 and 3. We lost to Army when the centerfielder made an error. It went through his legs, and we lost 2 to 1.

What was it like to be 18 and pitching for Brooklyn?

I had dreamed about playing in the big leagues. To be truthful, my best coach was my brother John. He was born to be a coach, and he had savvy. He knew enough about pitching and techniques in those days to help me, and coach Bill McCarthy at NYU was also good. He told me how to develop a change up, and so I worked on that. Here I was at the Polo Grounds on Memorial Day rooting for the Giants, and a week later I signed with Brooklyn.

It was a boyhood dream come true, to be 18 years old and be in the big leagues.

You're playing for Leo Durocher. Some players I talked to loved Leo, and some players hated Leo.

I was one of those who loved him. At that point in time, I loved Leo. I thought Leo was a good manager. He was very alert. He was ahead of the game, very sharp, and you could talk to him. I was only a young punk kid, but he liked me, and I liked Leo, and again, at 18 I could throw fairly hard. They didn't use me much. They used me in mop up relief.

Leo Durocher

You were 0 and 2 in 1944.

And then I went to Montreal for a month. I pitched there, and again I was on a twice-a-week schedule. I pitched Tuesdays and Fridays. Bruno Betzel was the manager.

I had really started to throw hard, and I had learned a lot. I had good stuff. Even though I was 18, I may not have had great control, but I got the ball over. I had a big overhand curve, which as a kid I called it a drop, and I used that.

I pitched very effectively, except they had an edict from Branch Rickey to pitch me every third day. Hell, I was pitching twice a week, and there were only two weeks left in the season. At that time I didn't care. Give me the ball. And I was always that way. I was that way in the big leagues. I would pitch.

The next year I really got strong. I matured. I was 19 and went from throwing the ball in the high 80s, maybe 85 or 88, to throwing the ball 95. I could throw it *hard*.

This time I went to St. Paul, Minnesota. Ray Blades was my manager. I started. I threw hard, but I was wild. It was a tough league. They had a mixture of kids and veterans, but I pitched well enough. I was 5 and 6. We really didn't have a good ballclub. I don't know what my ERA was. [It was 3.33.]

I came back to Brooklyn, and I really pitched very well. I mean, my record was 6 and 5, but without any prejudice for myself if you went over game by game, I could have been 11 and 2. That was really a bad ballclub. I pitched very effectively.

Did you live in Brooklyn?

No, I lived at home in Mount Vernon. I commuted. I couldn't afford a car, so I took the train into Grand Central, and then took the subway to Brooklyn. I could commute to the ballpark, because in 1945 and 1946 we played all day games.

I came back from St. Paul. Leo brought me in in relief against the Cubs, and I stood out. I struck out Phil Cavarretta to save the game. Then Leo started me, basically every four days. In the last half of the year, it was exciting to be a starting pitcher.

Did Leo ever give you advice?

No.

Did he ever put his arm around you and say, "I'll show you the ropes"?

No no, Leo just talked to me. He liked me, and he would discuss it. He was friendly. He was a very good manager then.

In the later years Leo got the Hollywood influence. After he went Hollywood, he wasn't quite as good a manager. To be utterly truthful, after he went to the Giants, he antagonized some of the Giants players by playing favorites with Willie Mays. Willie was his bobo, and he loved Willie, to the detriment of the other players, who resented it. Because I know players' reactions. *Hey, I'm playing right field, and he's playing center. I'm doing my job. I'm filling one position on this club.* And Leo was just too much for Willie. That's only an opinion.

Did Leo have any favorites on the Dodgers?

Yeah. He liked guys who were aggressive and who had the desire to win. I know he loved Pee Wee. Anybody would. Pee Wee Reese was a super guy and a good competitor and a hell of a shortstop. And Leo liked Cookie Lavagetto and he liked me as a pitcher, because if he wanted someone to knock them on his fanny, I'd knock 'em down. Which is a tool they have taken away from pitchers.

Leo was an excellent manager. Charlie Dressen was an excellent coach. That combination of Durocher and Dressen was great, because Leo was able to communicate with the players and had the wherewithal to communicate with the press. He was very bright, and if Leo would forget something, Charlie was there to help him. It was a good combination.

I was talking to Happy Chandler, and he said that one of the reasons he suspended Leo was that Leo was involving some of his players in some pretty high-stakes card games. Do you have any knowledge of that?

No. No. Had to be the older guys. I worked for Rickey. Nobody could afford high stakes. You crazy?

Tell me about Branch Rickey.

You don't have a week. If I analyze him and try to keep it short, I'd say Branch Rickey was very bright. He had theories about baseball, and he exercised them. He knew how to mesmerize players. He created a great image of being a very bright guy and a very holy guy. He had been in the game a long time, and yet my opinion is he took advantage of a lot of players and kept them down. He did not pay them near enough. I'd say he browbeat a lot of players with his image and with his vocabulary.

He had his pet likes. He loved guys who could run. And yet you couldn't steal first base. He brought up a couple guys to play with the Dodgers who were not good outfielders. They were fair outfielders with weak arms who could run, but they couldn't hit. He let Luis Olmo go to the Mexican League, cause he didn't want to give him $10,000. Luis was asking for ten, and he wouldn't give it to him, and he ended up going to the Mexican League, and Luis was a good hitter. Luis could have played for the Dodgers. He bailed out against right handers, but against left handers he was wicked. And he let go Frenchy Bordagaray, who was a very good hitter. He shipped him out of there.

In 1946 we could have used them. We tied for the pennant, and we lost in a playoff to the Cardinals.

Rickey signed a boy by the name of Joe Tepsic, a football player who came out of Penn State. He gave him a bonus and couldn't send him down, and the guy took up space and was of minus quality. He couldn't do anything. He just couldn't play the game, and yet they gave him a $21,000 bonus and he took up space on the bench, and we could have been better off with somebody who could have helped the ballclub.

He sold Billy Herman in '46.

Well. I guess he thought Billy was over the hump. Billy was still a good hitter. He had slowed up a little, but he was super. Billy is a super guy and a very knowledgeable baseball man.

Rickey made deals that didn't always pan out. Basically, Rickey had his pets, the guys he liked. He liked guys who could run. Heck, you got to be able to hit the ball and get on base to run and steal a base.

We had Dixie Walker, who was a super hitter, but he was old. He didn't have the greatest throwing arm, but he knew how to play the wall, and he played right, and Carl Furillo played center. We never did have one left fielder. Gene Hermanski played some left field. Not a bad looking hitter. Not a good outfielder. Good guy. We had Dick Whitman and Marv Rackley play out there.

Those days were exciting though. We had a good ballclub. In that ballpark Rickey wanted a team that could run. It was National League baseball, a team that could run and hit and run and squeeze and bunt. We played good old fashioned baseball. With the ball getting juiced up and with them moving in the wall, you had to have a blend of power and speed. And we had it. We had a young pitching staff along with a couple veterans.

It was a very young pitching staff. You and Rex Barney.

Hugh Casey was a veteran reliever. We had Hank Behrman in the pen in '47, and he was fantastic. He had a million-dollar arm. Hank could throw hard, and the situation would not bother him any. He had a good curveball.

And yet he had a rather short career.

Well, the next year on the first day of spring training, he just fired the ball, and he hurt his arm. Hank just wasn't the brightest guy in the world. He didn't take care of his arm, and boom.

Rex Barney could throw hard. He had one good half a season, and then he had a quirk where he couldn't get the ball over. Usually when a guy gets control, it's like riding a bike. Even if you don't ride it for ten years, when you get on a bike, you're right back. Well, Rex never got his control back. I look back at it, and I think he became what I call a hooker—instead of dropping his hands straight down, he would hook in his wrist, and it becomes very difficult to control a ball, especially a curveball. Most guys who hook their curveball, bounce it. Rex just got a quirk that he just couldn't get the ball over. They sent him out, and he just never was able to do it. And he had a pretty good curveball.

We had Hal Gregg, who was quick. His fastball was straight but had a very good curve and was fast. Unfortunately, they kind of shuffled him around. We had Harry Taylor, who had good stuff. He had chips in his elbow, but he was a tough pitcher. We had little Vic Lombardi. He was a cutie pie. He had a sneaky fastball and a good curve. He was a watch-charm-small, five seven, but he pitched effectively. And we had Joe Hatten, who had a good curveball.

Tell me about Hugh Casey. What do you remember about Hugh?

Hugh was a tough guy. He came out of Georgia, had a good sinker and a good curveball. He had the cool. He was cool under pressure, and he was a good reliever. He threw the sinker, which got guys hitting into double plays. He threw a good curve that they hit it on the ground and we got the double play. Later on relievers became fireballs a la Gossage, who would come in and strike you out.

Did you ever have the opportunity to hang out with Hugh after the game? Did you go with him and his cronies?

No, not really. There was a vast age difference. I was not a drinking man, so. With my background as an athlete, you didn't drink or smoke, and that stayed with me. I never did smoke, and I was never much of a drinker, and even today I don't think I have ten hard drinks a year. I drink white wine now, which is happening through the whole country.

The Dodgers in 1946 set a new National League attendance record of a million five, even though Ebbets Field sat about 33,000 people. What do you remember about playing in Ebbets Field back then?
Did you ever see Ebbets Field?

I never did.
You missed something. Really, Ebbets Field was a special place. It was a homey place. A Yiddish word is a *hamisha* place. The people, the fans, were special. They were right on top of the action, so they could feel like they were in the game.

The fans were so great. They really weren't fans. It was a love affair. They *loved* that ballclub. Through the 20s and 30s they hadn't a good ballclub, and now they had a good ballclub, and it was a dream come true for all these people who had rooted for them. The kids rooted for them, and they just loved all the ballplayers. The ballplayers loved going there because of the attitude. Everybody was so friendly. They didn't get on the players. They respected talent. Stan Musial got an ovation when he came to Ebbets Field, because they knew he was a talent.

Ebbets Field was a tough park to pitch in because it was small. The dimensions were small, but I loved the mound. It was a soft mound. The clay was soft, and I could dig my own hole and be comfortable with it. In other parks the mound would be scooped out, and you could put in three buckets full of dirt because it was all dirt piled into it, where at Ebbets Field they dug it out and put in fresh clay and pounded it down. The fresh clay was pliable and you'd have your own landing point. The elevation of the mound was good. The ground crew was excellent in Brooklyn.

When I pitched in Cincinnati, they had a concave mound where I overstrode the mound and landed on the flat, and Chicago was like pitching on concrete. It was so hard my feet ached. My feet hurt after pitching in Chicago. The Polo Grounds was a good mound, except again, they just filled in the landing area with dirt. You were pitching out of somebody else's hole.

Packed stands at Ebbets Field

You lost the pennant to the Cardinals in 1946.

I have to give Rickey part of the blame, and again, Durocher and Dressen. Those three blew the pennant for the Dodgers, because I had pitched very effectively in '45, and in '46 I had the temerity to hold out against Mr. Rickey. I had been on a USO tour, and he sent me a contract for the same money, and I didn't know protocol. I called home. My brother had gotten it, and I said, "Send it back. No letter, no nothing." So he put it in an envelope and sent it back.

Well, that rubbed Rickey wrong, and he never talked to me, never communicated with me from the end of January until I went on my own to Daytona Beach to talk to him about my contract. It was a year when they had all the veterans back, and I guess it was his way of punishing me and letting me sit home and come mealy mouth crawling back to him.

I asked him for $6,000, and again, another strike against Rickey, he lied to me. He said, "No young guy in your age bracket is making that kind of money."

I knew someone on the club—I won't divulge his name—was making more than that. He was making $6,500. And he was a friend of mine. Calling a spade a spade, he couldn't shine my shoes as a prospect or as a pitcher. But he was a friend of Rickey's, one of his favorites. He made more money than I did, and I had won a crucial game, started the playoff game, and I ended up signing for $5,000, not the $6,000 I wanted.

Tell me about your 1946 season.

I didn't report until March 17, and I pitched, and in one week I pitched three innings, then five innings against the University of Miami, and then seven innings. I was 20 years old, but I had worked out at home a little bit, but what do you do in the snow? By the time the season began, I was a starting pitcher.

Well, on the first of May I got hit in the arm by of all guys, Whitey Wietelmann. He hit a line drive knuckleball, and I went to catch the ball, and it dipped under my glove and hit me in the back of my elbow. I missed a couple starts. And then they forgot about me.

Two weeks went by, maybe three, and Charlie Dressen came up to me one day, and he said, "Why don't you pitch batting practice?"

"You can't make any money pitching batting practice, Charlie," I said. And Charlie got ticked off at me, and I got in the doghouse. And they didn't use me.

Well, finally towards the end of June, they put me in in mop-up relief. I got everybody out, and then again I got everybody out, and then I got everybody out. I had pitched five times and eighteen innings, and they got three hits off me and no runs.

So now I moved from mop-up relief to difficult relief, and they finally started me in a game in September. I pitched a shutout, and I came right back and pitched another shutout.

On September 14, 1946, I read you were to pitch to one batter.

It was a Saturday afternoon against the Cardinals. Dressen said, "We're going to start you, but we're going to have Lombardi warm up, and you pitch to one batter, and we will bring in Lombardi."

Did you question that?

No. I was 20 years old. Are you crazy? Today I would question it. I would probably refuse to pitch, but no. You just went out there. I was angry. I remember talking to myself, and I was saying, *You're a sacrificial lamb, MA.* My ass.

I was angry and the adrenaline pumped me up, the adrenaline got to flowing, and I got him out on five pitches.

"Keep pitching like that, Kid," Durocher said. "We're going to keep you in."

I ended up pitching a three-hit shutout.

I think that was the game that made me as a pitcher, because after that I believed in myself, believed that I could pitch in a crucial game. We went into first place by a couple percentage points, and then we lost on Sunday and went back into second. But I saw that I could pitch in such a crucial game against the Cardinals with Musial, Terry Moore, Slaughter, and Schoendienst. They had a tough ballclub.

I beat them 5 to nothing. And that really made me. That was the tempering of Ralph Branca. I became a believer in myself.

I lost the next game, but I pitched the first game of the playoffs. I'm a 20 year old kid, and I started the first playoff game. I got beat, but they didn't hit the ball hard. It was a lot of nub hits off me. I don't say that because I'm prejudiced. It's the truth. They hit a lot of nubbers off me, and I got beat the first playoff game.

The point I'm making: The Dodgers should have won the pennant in '46, because they really should have pitched me more. I made the starting rotation, but I never got a start until the middle of September. They should have won the pennant, but Rickey was pissed off at me because

Jimmy Powers was a writer for the *Daily News*, and I did an interview at NYU while I was working out with one of Jimmy's cohorts, and I told him, "I haven't made no money, and I'm looking to make a few dollars out of baseball."

I had made $90 a month at Olean, and now I come up to the Dodgers and I'm making $400 a month, and the next year I made $600 a month [$3,300], and now I'm holding out in 1946 and sign for $5,000.

You were pitching in the major leagues and making 90 dollars a month?

Yes. Listen, I wasn't the lowest price guy. Rickey had guys playing during the Depression for $200 a month at St. Louis. Do you see why they have a union? Because of Rickey. Because of George Weiss. Because of Sam Breadon. Because of Sid Weil in Cincinnati. They paid the ballplayers no money, and subsequently the players formed an association, and that's why the owners have all those problems now. Because the union is too strong. The pendulum has gone the other way.

I got a big raise to $6,500 in '47, but I didn't argue that year. I just wanted to sign and get down there and have a good year so I could make some money.

The 1946 season was the last full year for a number of the Dodgers. Pete Reiser, Ducky Medwick, Dixie Walker, and Billy Herman. Did these people add stability to the ballclub? Were these good people to have on the ballclub?

Yeah, they were good people. Billy Herman and Dixie were stabilizing influences. They had experience. It was a blend, a lot of young guys with potential and no experience, and a lot of guys with experience and who still could play.

In '47 we won the pennant, but we had a rookie manager. Durocher had gotten suspended, and Rickey brought in Burt Shotton, his friend from Ohio, which I think was another Rickey mistake.

Durocher was three or four steps ahead of everybody. To have this man Shotton a step behind or two steps behind as far as strategies go, was a big comedown for me. The man just wasn't competent enough to be a big-league manager, except he was a friend of Rickey's. I think it was a crime perpetrated on the people of Brooklyn.

Burt Shotton

And yet the guy won the pennant in '47.

Yeah. If you had a Cadillac, and you were racing against a Model A Ford, you're going to win the race. It's like Secretariat winning the Belmont. He had the horse. Again, it's what the jockey's got under him. Shotton just had such a super club. We did have a super club.

Was there any talk among the players that Hey, this guy isn't very good?

A lot of players thought that. They laughed at some of the moves Shotton made. You listen on the bench. If the count is 2 and 0, you have to anticipate that the count will be 3 and 0, and what are you going to make the man do? Hit or take? Shotton didn't give the signs. Clyde Sukeforth did.

Clyde would say to him, "It's 2 and 0, Burt. What do you want him to do?" And it was already 2 and 0. When the manager dictates what that hitter does, at least in those days. And he said, "Let him take."

"Now it's 3 and 0, Burt. What do you want him to do?"

To me he was behind. He should have said, "It's 1 and 0. If it goes to 2 and 0, make him take." "3 and 0, make him take." He had to have all that planned.

So Sukeforth was on the ball?

Sukeforth had to relay the signs to third base. We had Ray Blades at third base.

On September 27, 1946, Pete Reiser broke his leg sliding. Why was he so injury prone?

He played so hard. Even in batting practice, pitchers would be shagging flies and Pete would come out there. There'd be a fly ball, and Pete would take off, and you'd have to yell, "No no no no," because he would run into the wall in practice to catch the ball. The guy had no fear.

It's unfortunate Pete played in Brooklyn. If he had played in the Polo Grounds or Yankee Stadium, he never would have hit a wall. Brooklyn was a small ballpark. He hit the wall, and they put padding on the walls. Because of Pete, we started wearing batting helmets too, which were great innovations by Rickey. Pete got hit with pitches a couple times.

I didn't see him at his prime—'41 was his prime, and then he came back in '46, and you could see the guy had some talent. He could run, he could throw, he could hit, he could hit with power. He could do it all. Unfortunately, he was injury prone. It was because he played so fearlessly.

Pete stole home seven times in 1946. That must have been something.
And how, when you think about it.

What was Pete like as a person?
He was a good competitor and a good guy. I always marvel at his build. He's got sloping shoulders and his back muscles were like two tenderloins. His spine was five inches deep. His back muscles were so strong, and he could run. He could do everything. He was a shortstop, and they converted him into an outfielder. He had a good arm. He charged a ground ball, did everything right. He knew how to play the game.

Did Carl Furillo impress you as a rookie in 1946?
Yeah.

Were you close to him?
Pretty close to him. He was a line drive hitter, a very strong guy. He hit line drives, had a good arm, and got a great jump on the ball. He was an average runner, but got such a great jump on the ball. The ball off the bat, and he was off. Instinct and a great jump on the ball. And he was a good hitter.

If he had played with astroturf, he'd have hit 20 points higher or more, because he hit such hard ground balls. He hit the hardest ground balls you ever saw. On astroturf he'd handcuff the infielders today.

The season finished in a tie with the Cardinals. Was there disappointment to finish the season in a tie?

I don't know. Because you're thinking about winning the play-off. At least you're tied. Losing the play-off certainly made us disappointed. The Dodgers won the toss and elected to go to St. Louis to play the first game and then play the next two in Brooklyn.

They won the toss and chose to go to St. Louis? Who made that decision?

I really don't know who made the decision, but the Dodgers won the toss. We traveled by train to St. Louis, which was a 26-hour trip, and I lost the first game.

Tell me about that game.

They got base hits off me, but they didn't wear me out. They were nubby hits. Joe Garagiola hit one off the end of his bat. Cookie Lavagetto was playing in, and the ball spun in the dirt and didn't get to the outfield. He hit a broken bat blooper.

Harry Walker hit a chop over my head. They didn't wear me out. But I was just a 20- year-old kid, and I'm starting this game. I didn't pitch too long. I looked it up, and I pitched three and a third.

The next day you had to take the train all the way back to Brooklyn?

Right. We didn't fly in those days.

In that second 1946 playoff game Murray Dickson beat the Dodgers badly. Durocher used six pitchers in that game. What was everybody's reaction after that second ballgame?

The season was over, so it was disappointment and sad good-byes. We had a shot at them. We had a rally going, but Harry Brecheen struck out Howie Schultz. That's what I remember about the game. Brecheen struck out Howie Schultz on a screwball, and it ended the rally and the game.

That's a long time ago. We're talking 35 years ago. It was disappointment that we lost, and nobody knew who made the decision to play the first game in St. Louis. I'd have to say it was a Rickey decision, yeah.

You trained for spring training in '47 in Havana. Tell me about Havana in 1947.

In those days it was very nice. We stayed at the Nacional. We'd walk down, and Pee Wee and the guys would go bowling at night. Pee Wee's daughter came down, and she was a baby. They were there for a couple of weeks. We'd work out during the day and lounge around the pool in the afternoon. We'd go into town and walk around and buy souvenirs and trinkets. It wasn't decadent at that time. It was a good town, a tourist town. The weather was super.

Were you surprised when Leo was suspended for the 1947 season?

Yes. The way I remember that story, Leo was writing a column. It was ghost-written by Harold Parrott, and we were playing the Yankees, and Larry MacPhail had a known gambler in his box. Leo wrote a story criticizing MacPhail, saying that if it was him sitting in the box, he'd be suspended, and the next thing I know Leo got suspended. Don't ask me the reasons why.

On April 10, the Dodgers announced they had brought up Jackie Robinson from Montreal.

See now, we had played in Panama. We toured the Caribbean, played in Caracas, played the Yankees, and we came home and played Montreal in an exhibition game in Brooklyn. I pitched against Jackie, and he hit a ground ball and made out. We crossed paths and he said, "Thanks, Ralph." I didn't know what he was talking about. I guess because I threw the ball right down the middle and he hit the ball.

I was not aware of what he was thanking me for until several years later. We got to talking one time, and he told me why. He said that he knew that the Dodger players had signed a petition that they didn't want a black man on the team, and he knew that I didn't sign the petition. The petitioners never came to me. I was getting credit for something I didn't do. They figured I was from the North and I wouldn't sign it anyhow. And that's what Jackie was thanking me for. That I had not signed that petition.

I think back. I would not have signed it. Here I was going to play with Jackie. It didn't mean I was necessarily going to socialize with him, which

I did. I had breakfast or dinner with Jackie. Jackie was really a friend. He was one of my better friends on the club. I respected Jackie, respected him for his ability, respected him because he was a man.

Hell, I grew up in a neighborhood that was mixed. There were blacks who lived next door to me. It didn't matter to me. I was unaware of that petition that went around, but they did have it. Guys talked about not playing with a black guy. It's where you're brought up. The guys from the South had been ingrained not to do it.

Dixie Walker was giving Jackie trouble even after Jackie got to the club.

Dixie was a little cool to him. But eventually Dixie got around to where he respected him, and his position mellowed. He talked to Jackie. They weren't close friends, but they respected one another's ability.

And yet Rickey still traded Dixie away.

Right. Rickey traded him away. He traded a bunch of guys and got a lot of money for them. The Dodgers had such a wealth of talent that he could make those trades.

The Dodgers brought up Jackie. It seems he would need someone like Leo to protect him, and now Leo is suspended, and Rickey makes Burt Shotton the manager. Shotton wasn't the best guy to be Jackie's manager.

Rickey really controlled Jackie. They just bypassed Shotton. Rickey talked to Jackie all the time. He conveyed his feelings about what Jackie should do. And again, the minimum salary in the big leagues [in 1947] was $5,000, and Rickey knew what Jackie would do to attendance all over the league, not only at home but on the road, and yet he gave him the minimum salary.

Why? He knew what anguish this man was going to go through, just being there to be the first black to take all that abuse from his own players, not a lot of them but several of them, and from the opposition and from the fans. The heat he had to go through was worth more than $5,000.

We drew a million eight that year, setting a National League attendance record. We held 33,000 and we drew $1,860,000. Figure it out: in 70 home days how many are you drawing? A pretty good number.

Rickey had compassion for the blacks. Getting them into the big leagues was one thing, but when it came to parting with money, he didn't help Jackie that way. With all the abuse Jackie had to take, he could have given him $10,000. What's $5,000 to the Dodgers? It was a spit in the ocean.

Rickey let money dictate too many of his moves. He sold guys because he wanted the money. Rickey shared in the profits. His holier than thou attitude doesn't shine through when you analyze all the things he did. And yet there are people who worship Rickey and think he's God.

I happen to be the other way. I think he had a great knowledge of baseball and talent and how to appraise talent, but he didn't treat anybody like a human being. He let the dollar always stand in his way of treating them as human beings. I really think, in my own case, because Jimmy Powers wrote the article and branded him a cheapskate, El Cheapo, because I was the instrument by which Jimmy Powers used it, I took the brunt of salary negotiations with me.

You talk about Shotton, but under Shotton in '47 you won 21 games.

Because we had a good club. And I was a good pitcher. I went from not being pitched the year before, to this year. As I said, that game on September 14 in '46 was the making of me. That was the tempering of Ralph Branca. Now I could *believe*.

I went to spring training in '47, and I was able to pitch effectively. I was 21 years old now, fully matured, and I was a good pitcher. I pitched every four days. I never missed a start.

I didn't like to pitch batting practice. I thought batting practice would just teach me bad habits, because I would have to throw three quarters and I'd stop my motion. I said, "I don't like it," and so I'd go down the bullpen and I'd say, "If you need me for a man or two, I'm available."

I'd go down in the seventh inning, and I'd loosen up. Hugh Casey might have pitched in relief three days in a row, and they might need me. So that was my workout in between starts. I'd come in a pitch an inning or two, and I did it seven times.

You started the first game of the 1947 World Series, and you pitched four perfect innings. What happened in the fifth inning?

Joe Di got an infield hit to deep short, and looking back, my inexperience hurt me. Because I started pitching in a hurry. I'd grab the ball and throw it, not taking my time. I ended up getting a little wild, pressing.

I walked a guy, and a guy went to bunt. I threw the ball up and in, and the ball sailed, and it hit him. And then I made a bad pitch with a curve ball. I hung a curve inside to Johnny Lindell, and he hit a double down the left field line.

I had struck out five in the first four innings. My brother Johnny was sitting in the upper deck, and if he had wings, I think he would have flown down and talked to me on the mound. He said, "You started grabbing the ball and throwing. Nobody came out. No infielder came out to talk to you on the mound. No one came out from the bench."

I gave up five runs in the inning, I didn't complete the inning. They took me out. And I didn't start again, and then I relieved a couple more times. I ended up winning a game [Game 6]. Gionfriddo made the catch on Joe Di. Joe Hatten was the pitcher. But I had been in the game and held the lead, and I ended up winning the game. I won a game.

I would like to have had another start in the series. I carried the club all year. I just didn't get it. They thought they had to pitch lefthanders in Yankee Stadium.

Do you remember anything about Cookie Lavagetto's pinch hit to break up the Yankees' Bill Bevens no-hitter in the Series?

I was in the dugout. Al Gionfriddo stole second, which was a daring move. If he was out, the game was over. I would think they gave him a sign. Then they walked Pete Reiser.

"That's the winning run they are walking on," I said when it happened.

I knew Pete was hurting so bad he couldn't run. If he hit a shot into the outfield, they could throw him out at first. Well, they walked Reiser, and Leo put in Eddie Miksis to run.

Cookie was up, and he hit a ball high to right field, and I really couldn't see what happened. The ball must have come off the wall and hit Tommy Henrich in the chest, and he fumbled it. Gionfriddo was crossing the plate, and Miksis was twenty feet behind him. Miksis was off and running and he could fly. Two guys on the Dodgers who could go from first to home faster than anybody were Duke Snider and Eddie Miksis. They could fly, and Miksis was twenty feet behind him. He was a very good base runner. He was the winning run. We won, 3 to 2.

Bevins didn't pitch a very good game. He had a no-hitter going, but he walked nine guys.

Game 7 ended up Joe Page against Hugh Casey. The Yankees won.

The World Series went seven games, but it was tough. The Yankees had a lot of players with World Series experience. The Dodgers had two, Pee Wee and Hugh Casey.

How'd your negotiation go with Rickey after you had such a great year?

After winning 21 games, I was making $6,500. Not being a negotiator, I asked for $15,000. I just wish I had a tape recording of the conversation.

Rickey said I walked too many men. He said I didn't complete enough games. He belittled my record, and yet I had 36 starts, and I relieved seven times. I had the third best ERA in the league. I was second in strike outs. I gave up 230 hits in 280 innings, which is not bad.

I could have struck out more men if I wanted to, but I wanted to be a pitcher, so I let guys hit it. I had a 5 to nothing lead in Boston. I don't think I struck out two guys. Because I laid the ball in. I got ahead of everybody. I threw 85 pitches, and I pitched a shutout. They hit the ball. They hit some hard shots, but I got them out. I was trying to be a pitcher.

In those days I roomed with Eddie Stanky. Eddie'd say, "Go seven hard innings," and I would bust it for seven hard innings, and Leo'd bring in Behrman or Casey. I completed fifteen out of 36. I had a bad spell where I pitched lousy, got knocked out. I had fifteen wins early in the year, and it took me four games to win one and another four games to win another.

I remember losing a game 2 to 1. I remember losing 1 to nothing. But it took me four games to win numbers 17 and 18. The last game of the season I pitched five innings and left with the lead, and they brought in a young guy off the farm team who have up a run to tie it, and I lost the win. The Dodgers subsequently won. But it's a win I should have had. In fact, there was another game I pitched, where by today's rules I had to be the winning pitcher. Rex Barney pitched three and a third, and we had runs, and he got taken out. Casey came in. We had a lead. He pitched three innings, and they took him out and brought me in, and I pitched the last 2 and two thirds. I got eight out in a row. Yet they had leads and couldn't hold them, and I came in and stopped it, and they gave the win to Casey, and yet he wasn't effective. We had a big lead. I got eight out in a row.

When you asked for $15,000, what did Rickey do?

He said it was too much money for a young guy to be making. His same old line. And I didn't do this, and I didn't do that, and I didn't do this. I was under the gun because I knew how he negotiated. I said to myself, *I'll sign and have another good year, and then I'll really stick it to him.* I had confidence.

Rickey belittled my record, unfortunately. I went back with arguments, but I was not a good negotiator. I just wasn't. After going 21 and 12, I signed for $12,500.

CHAPTER NINE

RALPH BRANCA

The Shot Heard round the World

The third game of the National League playoffs between the Brooklyn Dodgers and the New York Giants took place on October 3, 1951. Ralph Branca was on the mound for the Dodgers in the bottom of the ninth inning in relief of starter Don Newcombe. The New York Giants batter was Bobby Thomson. The game was heard on the radio by millions. Russ Hodges did the play by play.

"It's a 4 to 2 ballgame. The Giants have the tying run on second base. It's going to be. I believe. The Giants win the pennant. The Giants win the pennant. The Giants win the pennant. They are going crazy. I still don't believe it."

For Brooklyn fans of a certain age, those words still sting. For Ralph Branca, who threw the pitch, that home run left a legacy that haunted him for the rest of his life, as you will see. Ralph, a prideful man who felt his legacy deserved better, died on November 26, 2016, at the age of ninety.

❧

Jackie in 1947 played first base in the final four exhibition games for the Dodgers. He was sitting out there all by himself. Did any of the players try to make him feel at home and to talk to him? He was older than you, I know that, but he was in a rather vulnerable position.

I was sitting in the old dugout in St. Louis. It was a two-tiered dugout, and I happened to be in the first row, and Jackie was playing first. As

Jackie came running for a short pop fly, I came out of the dugout and tackled him, because he had tripped over the mound, and by instinct, I moved and caught him on my shoulder and tackled him and stopped his progress where he would have gone into the dugout. He could have hit his head on top of the ceiling.

Jackie always said that was a big incident in his life because it was St. Louis, and I came out and caught him. I didn't care if he was black. He was my teammate, and he was going to get hurt. I sometimes wonder what I would have done if it was the opposition coming over that mound. Would I have reacted the same way, a guy wearing the other uniform? I probably would have let him go. Because he's the opposition, but Jackie was my teammate.

At the beginning of the 1947 season Kirby Higbe predicted he would win 42 games.
I guess he thought he was going to start every third day.

I heard some funny Kirby Higbe stories. Do you have any Kirby Higbe stories?
I didn't hang around Kirby. The only thing we had in common, I liked number 13, and he did too. In fact, in '46 he took 13, and I wore number 20. And then when he got traded, I took back number 13. But the story was that he got a letter from some broad on the road and told his wife, "It must be some other Kirby Higbe."

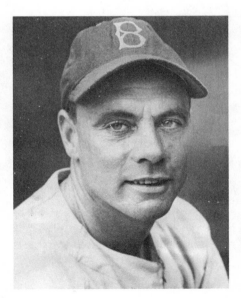
Kirby Higbe

Did you enjoy being with him?
Oh yeah. He wasn't going to hurt you. He was just wacky, that's all. He did some crazy things. He was a drinker, and he'd get drunk, and he'd get a little braggadocio. He had good equipment. He could throw hard, and he had a good curveball.

Unfortunately, they had an expression, and I won't say it about him, but there are a lot of guys who have million-dollar arms and ten-cent heads. They had the equipment, but they put the cart before the horse. Their idea was to go out and have fun first and playing baseball was secondary.

Kirby was the best pitcher in the league in the early 1940s.

Shoot. He had good stuff. He had a good fastball, a good curve, and he threw a knuckleball and threw it hard. He was the first guy I ever saw throw a knuckler hard. He could pitch. He was a good pitcher. He got heavy though. I can't fault his equipment or his attitude. He thought he could beat you, and he'd go out to pitch.

Were you able to hear some of the things Ben Chapman and the Phillies were yelling at Jackie?

In Ebbets Field the dugouts were close. I know the Phillies were on him. I knew Chapman was on him. Chapman was the most vociferous of all of them. "Hey, get your watermelon, boy."

On May 13, 1947, Reese put his arm around Jackie, and according to what I read, the crowd became silent when that happened.

The players might have been hesitant to warm up to Jackie very fast. They were afraid of peer pressure. I just remember the one incident. Jackie was playing first base, and Pee Wee walked over and put his arm on his shoulder. I think it was in St. Louis. He was saying, "He's on my team. He's my teammate. I don't care what color he is." Pee Wee walked over and put his arm over his shoulder and yakked with him in a time out.

Would the fans in St. Louis be on him too?

Yeah. The blacks sat in the right field pavilion of Sportsman's Park. They had open bleachers in left field and in right field, because it was so short, they had a screen, and to hit a home run you had to hit it on the roof of that pavilion, where left field was open. They had a big scoreboard in left field. And they had a screen. Well, that was the black section in St. Louis. Blacks had to sit in right field.

Jackie in those days did not stay with us in St. Louis. He stayed in the black section. When he was there in '47 alone, he stayed with black folks. I don't think he stayed in a hotel. When Campanella and Newcombe joined us in '48, then they stayed in a hotel down in the black section.

We stayed at the Chase Hotel. I don't know what year the Chase de-segregated. I'm going to say 1949.

There was a game on June 24 when Jackie Robinson stole home against Fritz Ostermueller of Pittsburgh.

Jackie was daring. Jack had such quick acceleration. In two steps he was full speed. I could see why he was a sprinter and why he was a great broken-field runner in football. He could change directions and go the other way. He'd round the bag and you'd think, *He's going to take the base.* And he'd jam on the brakes, and he'd be going the other way. He had quick speed. Two steps and he'd accelerate, boom.

You were elected to the All Star game in 1947. The game was played at Wrigley Field.

I didn't pitch. I had pitched on Sunday. I wasn't available.

It must be something to be 21 years old and be on the All Star team. You must have thought you were going to be in the Hall of Fame.

As a kid I dreamt about playing in the big leagues. I was in the big leagues, and I was a good pitcher. At 21 I wasn't thinking about the Hall of Fame, but I had potential, the equipment. I had Hall of Fame equipment. I could throw the ball 85 miles an hour. I had control. I had a good curveball. I was coachable.

Because I threw the big overhand curve, the strike zone was tough on me. The umpires would not give me the strike. It broke about 12 inches, and if they caught it below the knees six inches, it was too low. If they caught it over the knee six inches, it was too high. That's not a strike. Umpires don't give high pitches.

When I couldn't throw my curveball for strikes all the time, I switched and threw a slider, because I could throw it for strikes. I taught myself.

It got to the point I could throw the slider over the plate with control equally as good as my fastball. I'd get nine out of ten for strikes.

On July 18, 1947, you pitched a one-hitter against St. Louis.

That was a big game. I was going to tell you about that incident. I had 21 out in a row, but about the fourth inning Slaughter grounded out, and Jackie was playing first, and stretched out, and Enos stepped on his leg. Jackie went back to the bag, and Stanky got the ball and threw him out, and Slaughter stepped on Jackie's leg, just below the calf. He hit Jackie in the middle of his spikes, right on his instep.

"I'll get that son of a bitch for you, Jackie," I said.

"No, no," Jackie said. "Just pitch Ralph. Just get 'em out."

I pitched a one-hitter. I got 21 outs in a row. Slaughter got a ground ball base hit to lead off the inning. I got the next guy out, and then I walked a guy, and I got the last 21 in a row.

Was it the only time Slaughter did that?

The only time I can remember. Slaughter was a tough competitor. He slid into second base hard a couple of times. I wonder what he would have done had he played second or third where guys would have had a shot at him. He played the outfield, so no one had a shot at him.

Is that why Slaughter isn't in the Hall of Fame? [My interview with Ralph Branca took place in 1982. Slaughter was elected into the Hall of Fame in 1986.]

He hit .318 for 20 years, and he hustled. He was a hustler. He was coarse. He was a country boy. That's why they called him Country Slaughter. When you see some of the guys in the Hall of Fame, he deserves to be there. A Hall of Famer is a guy who is head and shoulders above everybody else. That's the way it should be.

Pee Wee Reese and Phil Rizzuto deserve to be in the Hall of Fame. They were local guys. They were two of the top shortstops. Too much is put on the hitting end for the Hall of Fame, though they could hit. Pee Wee had a .275 lifetime average. Did all the right things. He could field. He had a good arm. He was a good runner. Good competitors. He could steal a base. He stole 27 out of 30 one year. He was a team leader. You talk to any Dodger. Pee Wee was the captain. He really was the captain. The guys really had great respect for Pee Wee. [Reese was elected into the Hall of Fame in 1984. Rizzuto was elected in 1994.]

Roy Campanella

After the '47 season over the winter Rickey sold Dixie Walker to Pittsburgh, and he got Billy Cox and Preacher Roe. During spring training he traded Eddie Stanky to the Giants.

Dixie was the People's Cherse. The fans were up in arms, but that was part of the game. The Dodgers always had phenoms. There was a backlog of talent in the Dodger organization. Rickey traded Stanky to open up second base for Jackie.

Our catcher, Bruce Edwards, hurt his arm and couldn't throw. The first year he had a super year, but after that they had him play a little bit at third and in left field, but he couldn't catch anymore. Rickey wanted to bring Roy Campanella up, so he moved Gil Hodges from catcher to first base, and Jackie went to second.

You trained in Santo Domingo in '48.

We trained in Santo Domingo, because they were enticed by Trujillo to go there. The weather was super. We stayed in a hotel, the Jaragua, not a bad hotel. The Dodgers didn't want to train in the states because of the black situation, and that prompted Rickey to invest in Vero Beach, where he would have his own complex, and he could bring the blacks and whites to live together.

Stanky and I roomed together in Santo Domingo, and Stanky had pneumonia. He got traded to the Giants in spring training of '48.

I know Rickey loved Stanky. He was a guy, he said, who couldn't do this, couldn't do that, but the only thing he could do was beat you. Stanky was a very heady guy, did all the little things to beat you, slid into the base and kicked the ball out of Rizzuto's glove, got hit by pitches, worked a walk, just fouled off pitches. He was very competitive and aggressive.

Leo Durocher became the manager again in '48. He got on Jackie, because Jackie had gained weight, and Leo said he was too heavy. So they had a hassle going. That started their feud. They kept it. They didn't get along. Jackie resented him getting on him because he was heavy, and they were two guys who were very fierce competitors. To me they never really got along.

Did you see a change in Leo when he came back? Dick Young wrote that Leo was afraid of losing his job, that he wasn't the manager he used to be.

The only thing I remember about 1948 was that we got off to a bad start. We were in the cellar, and finally we got to jell and go. I would say that at the end of May, the beginning of June, we started to win.

The team was moving, and then Durocher left. It was July 4, and he left and went to the Giants. If he had stayed, we would have continued winning, and we would have been very, very tough.

It must have been shocking for Leo to go from the Dodgers to the Giants.

It was. As I said, I thought Leo was a very good manager. And Rickey brought Burt Shotton back. We had won with him managing the year before, so I could see why they brought him back. I would have preferred that Leo stayed.

Rickey didn't want him anymore, and when the Giants asked, he let him go.

Campy began catching in early July of 1948.

And Don Newcombe came up.

In July Carl Erskine came up, and in early August Duke Snider came up. Did you have any idea how good this team was going to be?

Yup. I knew we had a good ballclub. The only weakness was that we never had a solid left fielder. We had Furillo and Snider, and Hodges and

Robinson, Pee Wee, Cox, and Campy, and we had some pitchers on that club: Newcombe, Erskine, Branca, Barney, Jack Banta, Erv Palica. All young arms, all these guys had great equipment. If they didn't have Hall of Fame equipment, they had damn close to Hall of Fame equipment.

Jack Banta too?

He was a skinny string bean who could throw hard, but he came up with arm trouble. Palica had very good equipment, but I think that he was lazy. If you throw hard, you have to work hard and practice, and Erv tried to be Tom Edison. He threw a screwball and a sinker, a slider, and soft pitches, trying to be a pitcher and not exert energy, instead of exerting all the energy of being a hard-throwing guy like Goose Gossage. I say guys who throw hard, who throw a lot of fastballs, last longer. Bob Gibson lasted a long time. Warren Spahn came over the top, and he pitched a long time. But Palica was a little lazy.

Let me ask you about Hugh Casey.

He opened the bar on Flatbush Avenue. But he was having marital problems, and that really was eating at him. He never said anything. He was a hard-drinking, tough guy, and it ate at him. He ended up committing suicide because of the situation. I have to say it gnawed at him.

The Dodgers were leading the National League in 1948 at the All Star game. You were their ace. You then were injured, and the Dodgers ended up losing the pennant to the Boston Braves. It wasn't a coincidence.

I got off to a bad start. I was 2 and 3, and then I won seven in a row. I was 12 and 5 at the All Star break.

I got hit in the leg, and I got an arm infection, and in 1948 I ended up 14 and 9 with a 3.50 ERA, which is not bad pitching in Brooklyn. But if you look at my record, I had two seasons. At the All Star break I was 12 and 5, and then I hurt my arm, and I only won two more games.

How did you get hurt?

It happened in St. Louis. Tommy Brown was warming up playing pepper. Tommy was playing burn-out with somebody, and he threw the ball low, and the guy let it go, and it took one skip and hit me in the leg. The ball hit me right above the ankle.

The night before I won a game 1 to nothing. It was a hot day the day I got hit, and I went out and ran on it. If I had known what I was doing, I should have gone and seen the trainer, and he might have put ice on it right away, and it might have stopped the injury. But the lining of the bone became infected, and the infection settled in my arm, and I won two games the rest of the year.

In '48 the Dodgers were doing well. You were in first place for a while, and then the team collapsed. Warren Spahn beat the Dodgers a couple times, and the Braves ended up winning the '48 pennant.

Spahn and Sain and pray for rain, but they also had a pitcher by the name of Vern Bickford. I had arm problems. A leg infection affected my arm. I won a game, and I remember being hurt and being out. We took the train to Philadelphia, and my left ankle had blown up very big. I had an infection. The lining of the bone got infected, and subsequently I was in the hospital for ten days. They opened it up, and they put in a drain, and I only won one more game.

The Boston Braves won the pennant with a 91 and 62 record. St. Louis was second, and the Dodgers third, seven and a half games back. Had you not been injured, the outcome might have been different.

In 1949 with Jackie, Campanella, and Newcombe on the team, the Dodgers decided to test the racial barriers of the South. You went to Atlanta and Birmingham to play exhibition games.

I remember Atlanta. Jackie had gotten a death threat. The stadium was jammed. [Because of segregation] the blacks were all over right field.

We knew Jackie had a death threat. Somebody was going to shoot him. Gene Hermanski, who had a pretty good sense of humor, said, "We have nothing to worry about. We'll all put on number 42, and they won't know which one he is."

Of course, guys kidded Jackie.

"I'm going to stay away from you today. If I avoid you today, don't be mad at me."

We drew tremendous crowds coming through the South. They had trains coming through the South going north, and we would play in Cincinnati, and the stands had a tremendous amount of blacks who came from the South, and Sunday especially. The stands were filled with black fans.

Jackie is as important as anyone in the civil rights movement.
He was the first one who started it. Jackie did a lot for black people.

In June of 1949 you had a 10 and 1 record. Then you got hurt.
Actually it was a carry-over injury from '48. The back of the arm. A muscle. That's where I hurt it in the back of the shoulder. It was a carry-over from the previous year. I really learned how to pitch. I wasted my fastball and got by throwing a curveball and a change. I was 23 years old, and I really had to learn how to pitch, because I didn't have a fastball. I was 10 and 1 on July 1, and then I went on the disabled list. I finished 13 and 5.

The Dodgers won the 1949 National League pennant, but lost to the Yankees in the World Series in five games. The next year the Dodgers lost the 1950 National League pennant to the Philadelphia Phillies by but two games. For Dodger fans, the cry became, "Wait til next year."
In August of 1950 the Dodgers trailed the Phillies by six and a half games.
Shotten was the manager, and I ended up being the relief pitcher.

Did you balk at this?
No, because I wanted to pitch.
Dressen said, "Do you think you can do it?"
"I don't know," I said, "but I can try."
I ended up throwing the last few innings as the relief pitcher the last seven weeks. When I went to the bullpen in August, I began to throw hard again. I was throwing every day, and I became a relief pitcher, and I pitched very effectively the last seven weeks of 1950 in relief.

Do you recall the day Don New-combe started both games of a doubleheader against the Phillies?

I talked him into it. He want-ed to pitch the next day. I said, "You're crazy. Your arm will stiff-en up. Just make believe it's an extra inning game. Change your shirt and freshen up. Your arm will still be loose. If you wait, it will stiffen up and you won't be able to throw."

And Newk pitched very ef-fectively. He did a good job.

Don Newcombe

In 1950 Duke Snider hit 31 home runs. How good was Duke Snider?

Duke was a super player. Duke was a great outfielder. He got a great jump on the ball. He had an accurate arm. He had power. His weakness was left-handed pitching, because we didn't see it too much. We had such a dominant right-handed hitting club, Duke didn't see much of it.

Guys told me Duke would moan and groan when they pitched left-handers.

Yeah. But that was immaturity. That's all.

Did you ever get on him?

No, but the guys had this thing in the locker room. He would moan and groan, and they would say, "Somebody stole his lollypop. Somebody stole his candy."

Who got on him?

Pee Wee. Duke and Pee Wee used to live out in Bay Ridge together, and Pee Wee would get on him all the time.

"For crying out loud, who stole your candy? Stop moaning."

He'd be blunt with him.

But Duke was something. He could fly, he could run, he could hit with power, and he was a good outfielder. I'm prejudiced, so when they ask, "Who was the best, Duke, Mays, or Mantle?" there is no contest.

It's Duke Snider. He was a better outfielder than the other two guys by far. He got a far better jump on the ball. He had a much more accurate arm than either one of them, and he played in the toughest ballpark. He played in Ebbets Field. You have to worry about running into the wall. The other guys could run all day. Duke charged ground balls super. He's a Hall of Famer. He belongs in the Hall of Fame.

The Dodgers moved to California, where rightfield was three hundred miles away. Had they stayed in Ebbets Field for the rest of Duke's career, who knows how many home runs he would have hit.

One play against the Phillies in '50 cost the Dodgers the pennant. On a ball hit to the outfield, Cal Abrams was thrown out at home plate. Had he scored, the Dodgers would have won the pennant.

As I look back, Cal Abrams was not a good base runner, and Shotton had Eddie Miksis sitting on the bench. Eddie Miksis could fly and was such a good runner. Ashburn threw out Cal, because they faked him back. It was a bunt play. They took a step back to second, and then he made such a bad turn at third that Ashburn's throw was 20 feet up the line, and they still got him. Miksis would have been across the plate.

I was down in the bullpen at that point in time. But after it's over and you analyze it, shoot. it was Cal's first year up, and the guy is not going to be that aggressive. The game is on the line. He got on base for us, so he was a little cautious, and they faked him back to second—the shortstop ducked in behind him, and he took a step back—and then Duke hit a one-hop liner, and Ashburn was coming in to back up the play, and it happened to be right at him. If the ball was ten feet over, it would have gone on by him, and the game was over. But it was hit right there, one hop right to him. It was lucky for them.

Russ Meyer told me it was a pick off play, and that's why Ashburn was coming in.

The pitcher missed the sign. It just shows you.

[The year 1951 was another memorable year for Branca and the Dodgers. The season would end in a tie between the Dodgers and the Giants. There was a two-out-of-three game playoff. In the final game, Ralph Branca would earn a lifetime of infamy by giving up what is perhaps the most talked-about home run in baseball history. It's been thirty years since it happened, and as you will see, it isn't Ralph Branca's favorite topic.]

In August of 1951 the Dodgers were leading the Giants by 12 and a half games. The Giants then won 16 games in a row. A Giants rookie named Al Corwin won five games in a row, and the lead dropped very quickly. Were the Dodgers looking over their shoulders?

No. We just played lousy. We kept saying, "If we can just play .500 ball, we're in." If you look back in the last seven weeks, we really didn't hit much. If you want to fault anything, we had a short pitching staff. Dressen used five pitchers extensively, and the pitchers ran out of a little bit of gas.

I started ballgames, and we scored one run in each game. My record was 12 and 5, and I ended up 13 and 12. I started a game in September, and we scored a run. We just didn't hit enough. I can remember Erv Palica said he had a sore arm, and Charlie pitched him in the Polo Grounds. They got three runs in the first inning, and Bud Podbielan came in and shut them down, and we lost the game by 3 to 2. Don Newcombe pitched the next day, and he lost 2 to 1, and I pitched the next day. That's the day Willie Mays made a catch running into right center, and he made a perfect throw to the plate and got Billy Cox at the plate, and we lost that one 3 to 1. So we lost three in a row to the Giants, and that's a big swing. The Giants kept winning, and then the lead dropped to five games.

I pitched a shutout Friday night, and they had no one to start on Monday, and I pitched another shutout with two days rest. The thing was, I had a no hitter. It was a twilight game, and I was really busting it, and I hurt my arm, and I lost to Sal Maglie by 3 to 2. All we had to do was win one more game.

On the last day of the season the Giants were ahead of us, and we had to win on the last day to come back and tie. It's five years since 1946 when we won the toss and elected to play the first game in St. Louis. It's five years later. We're in Philadelphia, and the Giants are in Boston, and we have a playoff, and they tossed the coin, and the Dodgers win again.

This time no one is around because they are all in Philadelphia, and a guy named Jack Collins, the ticket manager, made the call. He remembered that the decision in '46 was wrong, that we went all the way to St. Louis and all the way back, and the Cardinals just stayed in St. Louis, so he made the decision that we will play the first game in Ebbets Field and the next two in the Polo Grounds.

Which was not apropos. It should have been reversed. We should have played the first one in the Polo Grounds, and the *next two* in Ebbets Field.

You never hear that story. In the first game Bobby Thomson hit a home run in Brooklyn off me, a ball that would have been an out in the Polo Grounds. And the ball he hit off me in Game 3 would have been an out in Ebbets Field.

Again, that was the wrong decision. The Dodgers twice won the toss, and they lost both playoffs because they made the wrong decision as to where to play the games. They won the toss and lost the war.

Do you remember the first game of the playoff against the Giants in '51?

I remember. Thomson hit a home run on a high fastball. It was a high fly with no authority, and it just drifted and drifted into the first row of Ebbets Field, and Monte Irvin hit a home run in the eighth inning. I only gave up four hits. I give my old line, "I scattered four hits, two inside the ballpark and two out."

We had the bases loaded on Jim Hearn with one out, and Carl Furillo popped out. Hodges swung at a bad curveball to end the inning. We only got one run, and we lost 3 to 1. I pitched effectively. [He only allowed six hits.]

The Dodgers won the second playoff game by the score of 10 to 0. Clem Labine pitched the shutout for the Dodgers.
    Tell me about Game 3.

I relieved Friday, relieved Sunday, and I started Monday. For Game 3 on Wednesday I was back in the bullpen, and I can't throw the ball sixty feet.

I started to lob toss in the fifth inning. I was doing all right, but I knew how stiff I was. I used a counterirritant called Capsulin, hot stuff, on my arm, and I started to throw, and I kept throwing, and finally my arm loosened up. I basically got to where I could throw hard again. I was really throwing the ball well.

Dressen called me into the game in the ninth. There were runners on second and third. We were leading 4 to 1. I don't remember walking in, but I met Jackie and Pee Wee at shortstop, and they both said, "Go get 'em," and I remember Charlie saying, "Get 'em out."

He went in the dugout, and Rube Walker and I went over the signs.

Thomson was up, and I wanted to get ahead of him, and so for the first pitch I threw a fastball. And it had mustard on it.

For the next pitch I wanted to waste a fastball. I tried to throw it up and in, and I tend to believe I probably aimed it, because again, I was a pitcher, and I was making a pitch, and he hit it down the line with an uppercut, and as it was heading towards the stands it was sinking.

I was saying, "Sink, sink," and it just went into the stands at the Polo Grounds. It went in over the wall by six inches. He probably hit the ball 300 feet.

From there to the locker room, I don't remember. I remember sitting on the steps and Barney Stein taking pictures. [Reporter] Will Grimsley was giving me a hard time. He wanted to talk to me, and I didn't want to talk to him.

"Leave me alone. Just leave me alone," I kept saying.

The season was over. I look back and think it was crazy, because a normal guy who couldn't lob the ball from 50 feet would have said, "I can't throw." But I didn't have an excuse because when I came in, I could throw hard. I had pitched two shutouts in four days.

When I look back at it, it's funny. I went to a dinner with Sal Maglie three years ago, and I told that story. I sat down, and Sal said to me, "If you wanted Thomson to hit a curveball, why didn't you just throw the curveball? Why waste a fastball?"

Sal was so right. If I wanted him to hit the curve, why didn't I throw it? He was the winning run. One out, man on second and third. If I wanted him to hit the curveball, why didn't I throw it?

I was 25, and I should have known better. If I had thrown it inside, a brushback, I would have been better off. After all those years, it really doesn't bother me. It does bother me lately. In 1976 I went to an Old Timers Game in Texas, and they got me out on the field, made the introduction, and they played the Russ Hodges record.

After two weeks in a row, I asked myself, *Ralph, What are you doing? This is crap.* It just kinda got to me. The Mets annoyed me last year. They showed a picture of me in their ad, without asking my permission. I probably would have given it had they asked. But lately it bothers me more than it has the previous 25 years.

It's good because people know who I am. I've achieved notoriety. It hasn't hurt me business-wise. I look back at my record. In '47 I won 21 games, and I won 12 in the middle of the next year, and 10 the next year. Put them all together, and I have a lot of wins. Unfortunately, they didn't have the training methods. They had one trainer instead of two in those days.

In 1952 I hurt my back, which is my only regret in baseball. During spring training I sat on a chair, one of those folding chairs, and the chair slid out—they had waxed the floor in the lobby in Vero Beach in the Dodger barracks, and I landed on a coke bottle. It hit me right next to the anus, and it cut me. I landed right on it, and it tilted my pelvis backwards. My left side was up an inch and a half.

I went to the trainer. He should have popped me back in and gotten a realignment, but he didn't, and that whole year of '52, I pitched a couple games, and then I couldn't throw effectively, and the next year I came home from spring training, and Dr. Kenneth Rowley made an adjustment. He said my pelvis was up an inch and a half. He asked if I had any pain, and I really didn't. From that point on I could throw hard again, but not consistently.

I got traded to Detroit, and they worked on me, but I had a pelvis that was twisted a little bit. I look back and I can see that I lowered my arm position, and unfortunately they didn't have videotape so I could make a correction. Coaching techniques and medical techniques have so much improved. Today they have it so much better. I go into the Dodger locker room, and they have Nautilus machines and bikes. My legs would be like tungsten steel if I had had those machines. If I could do it over again, I would be ten pounds lighter, get into jogging and be ten pounds lighter, to play at 215 instead of 225.

I was with Bobby Thomson last night. I like Bobby. He's a humble guy. He knows it was his moment of glory. He knows he's not a Hall of Famer, and I know I'm not a Hall of Famer. We both achieved notoriety.

And yet a couple times you know you've been invited because he's been invited.

Like last night. But I've gotten over it. I may not go to the next one that has that theme. It's been thirty years now, and it's time to bury that. Bench hit a home run to win a playoff game, and Mazeroski hit a home run off Ralph Terry to win the World Series, and Chambliss hit a home run off Mark Littell, but you never hear about those. Bucky Dent hit a home run to win the pennant. You don't hear about them.

This was the shot heard around the world.

Because it was in New York, and it was the great rivalry between Brooklyn and the Giants. That game wasn't even televised. You'd be surprised how many people told me they saw it on television. Or said they were there.

I've met 135,000 people who were at the game, even though the box score says there were 34,000. And that floored me. Only 34,000 for the final game of the playoffs. A Wednesday afternoon. A shock.

Someone said if Campanella hadn't been hurt and been catching it would have ended differently.

Not true. Rube Walker was a super receiver. He was a very heady catcher. Newcombe pitched a hell of a game, and really the first hit of the inning could have taken them right out of it. The ball went off Hodges' glove. If Gil catches the ball, there is one out. The next batter is two outs, and that's it. You have to make three runs to tie. Forget it. The inning is over. And that's the difference. If Hodges catches the ball, he's out, and the next guy is out, and that changes the Dodgers' attitude and changes the Giants' attitude.

When you were in the bullpen, you were there with Carl Erskine. Were you and Erskine talking to each other?

You talk about the game. I was staying loose by throwing the ball nice and easy. Dressen was talking to Clyde Sukeforth on the phone, and

Sukey said, "Erskine just bounced a curveball." And Sukey said, "Branca." He could also have said Erskine.

Is that what happened?

Erskine said that's what happened. He said that when he bounced that curve, it was the best pitch he ever threw. I think it's a true story.

And I wanted to pitch, even though when I started to warm up, I couldn't throw the ball fifty feet. But I was a competitor. As a competitor, I always felt, give me the ball. Even when I pitched in relief, I enjoyed it. I relished coming in in a jam. I got revved up.

You are sitting in the clubhouse, the game is over, the season is over, how does Ralph Branca feel?

That day I sat for a long time as the guys drifted out. I showered and dressed and finally got out to the car. Anne and I were going out for dinner.

What did Anne say?

She started to cry. And she had a cousin, a priest, Father Pat Rowley. His brother Jim was the head of the Secret Service. I said to Father Rowley, "Why me? Why me? Why couldn't it have been somebody else?"

"God chose you because he knew your faith would be strong enough for you to bear this cross," he said.

I accepted that this was something I would have to bear for the rest of my life. And I went about my business. I was going to get married in two and a half weeks. People would call the house and say to my mother-in-law. "Why doesn't your son in law learn how to pitch?" It was tough on the family. I just resigned myself that this was part of the game. At that point who knew how big it was going to be? Really, it was over for me in an hour.

The surprise is that 30 years later people are still talking about it.

My regret, as I said, is that the following spring I hurt my back. The writers were saying how much I had let the home run affect me. You know, they didn't pick the worst pitcher they had on the staff to pitch to Thomson. They picked the best pitcher.

I went about my life. It would unsettle me every once in a while. I was warming up in St. Paul, and some guy was giving me a hard time.

I said to him, "What team did you play for? Did you play for the Bloomer Girls? What league did you play in?"

And when I would be introduced to people, "This is Ralph Branca."

And he'd say, "Oh, Bobby Thomson."

I'd say, "My name is *not* Bobby Thomson."

I have nothing to be ashamed of. My name is Ralph Branca, and I was one of the best young pitchers in the history of the game.

CHAPTER TEN

BOBBY THOMSON

The Shot Heard round the World

*D*uring the spring and summer of 1981, I was the host of my very own *talk show on WOR radio, the biggest, most popular AM radio station in New York City. My show, modestly titled* Peter Golenbock's World of Sports, *aired on Saturday nights between the hours of six and eight. I loved doing the show, but in order to do it right, I would arrive at the station on Wednesday and spend the next three days lining up guests and doing an occasional interview to get ready for Saturday's show.*

For my efforts, the station manager of WOR paid me $100 a week. I did the show for about six months. One of the joys was working with Charlie Steiner, who did the news. Charlie was incredibly smart and amazingly glib, and he would come on the show, and we'd talk sports, and always he would be interesting. I was not surprised when he became the voice of the Los Angeles Dodgers. Charlie was a natural.

I thought that after six months I deserved a raise to $300 a week. I was writing my books from Sunday to Tuesday, and I was spending too much time for not enough money preparing for my Saturday radio show. When management said no to my pay raise demand, my run as a big-time radio talk show host came to an end.

Among the many sports personalities I interviewed for my show was the personable Bobby Thomson, whose home run off Ralph Branca in the 1951 National League playoffs ensured him an important place in baseball history. The following was my interview on the radio with Thomson, who died at age eighty-six on August 16, 2010, in Savannah, Georgia.

⌒

The gentleman who hit the Shot Heard around the World. On October 3, 1951, which was 30 years ago today, Mr. Bobby Thomson got up against Ralph Branca. The score was 4 to 2 Dodgers with two men on in the bottom of the ninth, and Branca threw a pitch to Bobby Thomson, and Mr. Thomson deposited it in the left field seats. The Giants won 5 to 4. They won the pennant. And they went into the World Series against the New York Yankees.

Bobby, in August of 1951, the Giants were losing by 13 and a half games. Was there any feeling that the Giants had lost, that this was just another losing year?

Certainly at that point in the season, and that far behind, we didn't think we were going to win the pennant. We weren't thinking very seriously about winning the pennant.

Something started to happen with this team. What exactly was it? What happened to the Giants in August that caused it to catch up?

Bobby Thomson

First of all, we had ballplayers on the team who had the ability to go out there and win ballgames. We had good pitching. We had some good offensive players, and we had a guy by the name of Leo Durocher, who could take people like Eddie Stanky and Al Dark and really cut them loose out there. He knew how to play ball. As far as I was concerned, Leo always put pressure on the other team.

Take the team around the infield and the outfield.

We'll start behind home plate. We had Wes Westrum, and at first base we had Whitey Lockman, Eddie Stanky at second, Al Dark at short, and I was playing third. I started off in the outfield that year, but they brought

Leo Durocher

in Willie Mays, and then they moved me to third base. And right field was Don Mueller, a fine hitter, and Willie was in center, and Monte Irvin in left. Monte was our big strong guy, our key guy playing left field.

Where did Hank Thompson fit into all this?

Hank was sitting on the bench for a good part, but he was quite a utility player. He could play regular for most clubs. He was in and out of the lineup, filling in here and there when we needed him, but for the most part, we played those same eight fellows.

And the people starting on the mound for you?

Of course, we had the Barber, Sal Maglie. He might have won 20 games that year. [Maglie had a 23 and 6 record with a 2.93 ERA.] Larry Jansen I know won 20 games. [Jansen had a 23 and 11 record with a 3.04 ERA.] Then we had Jim Hearn [17 and 9 with a 3.62 ERA] and Dave Koslo [10 and 9 with a 3.31 ERA], a fine lefthander, and we had Sheldon Jones and Alex Konikowski.

I did a little bit of research, and I discovered the Giants won 18 games in a row coming down the stretch, and there was a fellow by the name of Al Corwin. Corwin won six or seven of those games. Who was Al Corwin and what was he doing winning all these games?

I can see his motion now, and he could throw the ball, and he kept the ball low, and his ball moved, and he got the ball over the plate. You got to be lucky too in baseball. If someone hits the ball pretty well, if you have someone in the general vicinity to track it down, and we had fine defense.

At what point did you believe the Giants could possibly win this pennant after being down by 13 and a half games?

We didn't really believe we had a real crack at it until the last week. But within the last two to three weeks, we started getting up there pretty close, and we thought, *Wow, this is interesting.* We were giving it all we had, but you don't dare to think we have a real crack at this pennant, not till we get real close, and when I say real close, that means within a couple of games, because when you're even six games out, that's an awful lot of games to make up in two to three weeks.

The Giants and Dodgers in 1951 had to play a three-game play off. Could you describe for our listeners the first two games, please.

I'll never forget. We thought we won the pennant on the last day of the season, because we had won our game up in Boston against the Braves, and the Dodgers were losing to Philadelphia by six runs, so when we got on the train to head to New York—we were still taking trains then—we thought we were winners, and it wasn't until halfway down that we got word the Dodgers had won.

So all of a sudden from a great feeling of jubilation, we felt pretty badly that we have to go play those darn Dodgers, a team we knew was tough. We didn't relish the thought of having to play them in a three-game playoff in order to win the pennant.

Anyway, we showed up at Ebbets Field for the first game, and we were losing by a run. Ralph Branca was pitching, and I hit a home run off Ralph with a man on to put us ahead 2 to 1. And then Monte Irvin hit a home run, and that made it 3 to 1, which was the final score.

So we got off to a pretty good start, and we felt good about it. Jim Hearn pitched a great game, a fine game, so now we're really up and at 'em at the Polo Grounds the next day. We were out to win the pennant with an advantage like that, and goodness Clem Labine pitched against us, and he beat us 10 to nothing.

I remember I got up when we had a chance to score some runs. I got up with the bases loaded and two outs and I struck out, and that kind of typified the day we had. So now we're back down in the doldrums again. We didn't feel too good about losing 10 to nothing. We weren't even competitive.

And with Don Newcombe pitching the next day. Of course we had Maglie. It was quite a ballgame. The Dodgers got off to a one-run lead, and later in the game, I hit a fly ball into center field to get Monte Irvin in from third, and so there it was a 1–1 ballgame going into the eighth inning, when all of a sudden the dike broke, and the Dodgers scored three runs.

The score was 4 to 1 in the last of the eighth inning. Don Newcombe was still pitching great ball, and he just mowed us down in the eighth inning.

What is the attitude of everybody sitting on the bench? What is Leo doing?

There wasn't much Leo could do. He can only manage. He can't hit or field. When his ballplayers aren't hitting, there isn't much he can do for us. Anyway, Newcombe mowed us down in the eighth inning.

He struck out the side, didn't he?

Yes. Leo did get his fingers into the act by sending up Bill Rigney. Bill was a fine hitter and a great pinch hitter, and gee whiz, Newcombe struck Bill out without too much trouble, and we thought, *Wow, that isn't very good for our side.*

We felt pretty badly. So now we go out there for the top of the ninth, and we brought Larry Jansen in to pitch, and Larry got the Dodgers out. So with the score 4 to 1 we go in for our last at bats.

I'll never forget, I felt totally dejected. I thought we weren't good enough to go beyond this point, that we were only good enough to get this far, which just wasn't quite enough to win the pennant. That thought ran through my mind, and I also realized too that I was the fifth hitter, and heck, *I'm not even going to get a chance to hit against that guy New-combe, the way he's throwing.*

Well, of course, you know what happened. Al Dark led off with a single, a ground ball right up the middle into centerfield. Don Mueller hit a ground ball past Gil Hodges at first base. Hodges was holding the runner on for some reason, and the ball just got by him. So now we had a runner on first, and Dark went to third.

Monte Irvin was the next hitter, our big strong guy the whole year, and he just happened to pop up to the first baseman. So it was now one

out with men on first and third. My roommate, Whitey Lockman was
the next hitter, and he hit a double to left field which scored Dark. Mueller was heading into third base, he slid into third, and he hurt his ankle
severely, which stopped the game.

So now we had Mueller who was hurt on third and Whitey Lockman
on second. And I was the next hitter.

It's now 4 to 2 Brooklyn.

Mueller's injury stopped the game. He wasn't in good shape. He was
in pain, and we were all down there. I felt badly for him. They carried
him off the field, and that's when Ralph Branca came in to pitch.

Newcombe had been replaced by Branca, and I didn't even know this,
because our thoughts were all on Don Mueller, a guy who had been a
great ballplayer for us that year and a guy everybody liked. So really, looking back on it and rationalizing a little bit, that incident got my mind off
the game. It kind of broke the tension.

*Bobby, you are up there with men on second and third and you have the bat
in your hand, and the pennant is riding on what you do. Is there any thought
in your mind, where you say to yourself,* Gee, I'm going to hit a home run?
What are you trying to do when you're hitting in this situation?

Well, that's a good question. Actually I certainly was *not* thinking about
hitting a home run, but Leo Durocher was, because after they carried
Don off the field, I still had the bat in my hand. I was heading toward
home plate, and Leo comes up behind me and puts his arm around me,
and he said, "Bobby, if you ever hit one, hit one now."

I thought, *You're out of your mind, Leo. What a crazy thought.*

It was the furthest thing from my mind. I didn't even answer him.

I headed on back to home plate. What was on my mind was to go up
to bat and give myself a chance to hit. In other words, when an athlete
gets in a spot where he has to produce, he does a couple of things: he
becomes tremendously determined and he's got to relax himself, and he's
got to stay composed but very determined and patient.

I was psyching myself out, calling myself a few names too to get mad
and get up there and give yourself a chance to hit, but basically, to wait
for the ball and watch it. Wait and watch. And sit back and not get overanxious, because when hitters get overanxious, they get out on their front

foot and they have nothing left, no power, and so I told myself, *Sit back, wait and watch. Wait and watch.*

The first pitch was right over the plate, and all I can think of, I was *really* waiting and watching. But the second pitch I can still see—I got a glimpse of it coming in a little high and inside, and I jumped at it, and I was lucky enough to hit it.

Where did it go?

It took off. I thought it was going over the roof, because I hit the ball well, but it must have had tremendous overspin. I never hit a ball like that in my life before or since, and it had tremendous overspin and started to sink.

Then I thought, *Geez, I don't have a home run. It's just going to be a base hit.*

And the next thing I saw was the ball disappearing in the stands, and that was it.

What was your reaction in a momentous moment like that?

Well, it's hard to explain, but I was overcome with emotion. I never had a feeling like that before. Athletes go out on the ballfield every day, and they are heroes and are not heroes. They have chances to win ballgames, and everybody has their day where they do something great, whether it's making a fine catch or getting a hit at the right time. And there are days when we don't do the right thing and maybe are responsible for losing the game, but we do have our exciting moments. Very exciting moments.

This was the bottom of the ninth of the last game of the season.

Well, this was an experience I just never had before, where so much was riding on it, and of course the fact that the rivalry we had with the Dodgers was just an unbelievable thing, and it meant so much to us all, and I was caught up in this thing, and I got a little excited and started jumping around the bases.

Do you recall the reception?

Oh sure. I remember Leo tried to reach out and grab me coming around third. In fact, he stepped on my shoe and practically cut it off me. His spike ripped the back of my shoe, and then I remember the gang waiting for me at home plate, and I took one last big, long leap.

I had never run bases like that before, but there was nothing I could do about the way I was reacting. I just was so excited. I was out of breath and it's just hard to describe.

Have you ever heard Russ Hodges describe that home run?

Yes, I have. He did a tremendous job. I think he described it as well as any home run could be described.

[I played Russ Hodges' call on the air that evening.

Russ Hodges: "He's hitting .292. He has a single and a double, and he drove in the first run with a single. There's a long drive, I do believe. The Giants win the pennant. The Giants win the pennant, the Giants win the pennant. Bobby Thomson hits it into the lower deck of the left field stands. The Giants win the pennant, and they are going crazy. They are going crazy. Hey, ho.

"I don't believe it. I don't believe it. Bobby Thomson hit a line drive into the lower deck of the left field stands and the place is going crazy. The Giants won it by the score of 5 to 4 and they are picking Bobby Thomson up and carrying him off the field."]

Bobby, it's thirty years later. Do you still think about that day? Is it on your mind?

Well, I don't wake up thinking about hitting a home run thirty years ago.

Certainly not, but there must be times. You must have pictures.

I have a few pictures around my office. Nothing too prominent. When I think about it—I do think about that home run more days than not, because people seem to talk to me about it. If not every day, almost every day.

I was talking with Ralph Branca last month, and he said that the one thing that amazed him about the home run was that unlike so many other home runs, that people still talk about it. Is that amazing to you also?

Yes. I wonder why it is. At the time when I hit it, I never in the world thought they'd be talking about it five years later, much less thirty. All it meant to me was that the Giants beat the Dodgers. That's all it meant to us all, and of course, as the days went on, I began to realize, *Gee whiz, everybody listened to that ballgame.* That's when I began to see it in a different light when I heard so many different experiences people had. Around the country, and some of them were very comical.

Bobby Thomson, thank you very much for being with us this evening. It's been my pleasure. Good night.

CHAPTER ELEVEN

DONALD HALL

My Love of the Brooklyn Dodgers

D*onald Hall, the great American poet, grew up in Hamden, Connecticut, within earshot of Dodger announcer Red Barber. Hall loved the Redhead. His love affair with the Dodgers began in the late 1930s and was an important part of his life and that of his father as well. The memories Hall cherishes most are those of the Dodgers of the early 1940s, the Leo Durocher–led team featuring Pee Wee Reese and Pete Reiser, Dixie Walker and Dolph Camilli. Hall especially reveled in the coming of Jackie Robinson and in the Dodgers finally beating the Yankees in the 1955 World Series. The love affair ended for him, as it did for so many others, with sadness.*

In February of 1981 I went to Donald's farm in New Hampshire to interview him about his love for the Dodgers for my book Bums. *I felt bad when my editor, Phyllis Grann, who was the head honcho at Putnam, cut Donald's chapter out of the book. She said it interrupted the flow of the narrative. This is my opportunity to make it up to Mr. Hall.*

Donald Hall died on June 23, 2018, at the age of eighty-nine. His way with words was magical.

I remember the beginning of it all. I was ten years old, driving in a Studebaker automobile on a Sunday afternoon. Everyone in America who had a car in 1938 went on rides on Sunday afternoons.

My father knew every road because he had delivered milk when he was a boy. I thought he had Magellan's instinct for geography. He could get anywhere. And we'd arrive at a place where we'd have an ice cream

Red Barber

sundae, and we'd always come at it from a different angle, and I'd never know how we were going to get there, but we got there.

And when April came, he would turn on the radio, and we would listen to Red Barber broadcasting. Red came in the 1930s. It was dad's hand who turned WOR and later WHN rather than turning to the Giants or the Yankees. That's what started me on the Dodgers.

We lived in Hamden, Connecticut, seventy miles from Brooklyn. We could get the New York stations perfectly well. I don't know how my father got to be a Dodger fan, but it may have been Red Barber. We all loved him, and I still love him in memory, that wonderful soft voice coming down, the wonderful gentleness and calm, yet managing to rise to the pitch.

We loved his cliches, his individual expressions, "the bases are COD," chock full of Dodgers, and when we were playing the Pittsburgh Pirates, the enemy was "FOB," full of Buccaneers. The Catbird Seat was something he popularized. Later James Thurber would use it as the title of a story. I can't believe it didn't come from Red Barber. Ever since then no baseball announcer ever seems quite the authority if he did not have the gentleman Southern tongue. Vince Scully, who prepped with Red Barber, is the best one going. I liked Ernie Harwell in Detroit, who spent time with Red Barber.

So baseball for me began with the radio. Radio was a lot better than television because there was not the selective vision, and Red Barber was such a colorful talker. He would talk about the crowds and the fans at Ebbets Field, so this was something we went there expecting, and when I arrived at the park, I found this totally loose, expressive, gathering of people.

I was at Oxford just a few years later going out to a cricket match and seeing the visiting Australian team play the Oxford team, which is like the Yankees, and when the Australians were bowling, suddenly an Oxford player lifted a ball out to the outfield, and an Australian settled right under it, and it popped out of his hand. There were several thousand people there, and they all went, "Oh, too bad. Pity." Except for one person. I yelled up, "YYEEEEAAAAAAHHHHHHH." And that was pure Ebbets Field. I sat down again, blushing like crazy. They knew what nation I came from.

Every once in a while, we went on vacation to see the minor league team in West Haven. I remember one time the big attraction was that Ralph Branca's brother was pitching. We didn't go very often, but we did drive every Sunday, and we'd listen. My mother, who at first was totally disinterested in baseball, began to listen more and more. The three of us would sit in the front seat.

I remember that sleepy voice, the Southern tones coming off the radio. And the great pleasure would seem to be characters on the team, all exaggerated, names that carried captions with them, or slogans. Barber would say, "Luke 'Hot Potato' Hamlin is coming in from the bullpen." I'd think to myself, *Uh oh, watch out. The home runs are going to start popping out of the park.* I remember Hamlin threw a straight fastball that would rise if he was lucky. When it didn't, the ball left the field. You know why "Hot Potato"? He had a nervous habit: he couldn't hold the ball. He would throw it up in the air and catch it. I suppose I learned that from Red Barber.

One of the first things I remember—I didn't hear it on the radio, I heard it when I got home from school—this was when there were afternoon games—Tex Carlton pitched a no-hitter for the Dodgers. That was my first Dodger no hitter. A lot of the early Dodgers, like Carlton, were castoffs of other teams, acquired by trade, players who weren't supposed to be so good like Dixie Walker. Joe Medwick was not quite a cast-off, but somebody from elsewhere who had come to the Dodgers and put it together and played well.

Whitlow Wyatt, another discard, was a great pitcher, and there was Kirby Higbe, a fast-baller who everyone knew the Yankees would plaster out of the place [in the 1941 World Series], and they did. I never trusted him as a pitcher. My sense of him was that he threw one pitch, and he threw pretty hard. But if he got in trouble, if he lost something off his fastball, he didn't have anything else to go to. He was a strong back, but you couldn't trust him. Curt Davis, another old one, was a wily side-armer. Freddie Fitzsimmons, who pitched about once a week, was wonderful. You could count on him to win Sunday.

I remember when Ralph Branca came up the first time. I remember when we were playing St. Louis, and St. Louis was pitching one of their good fellows, like Howie Pollet, against us. Wyatt did well against St. Louis, but we couldn't pitch him every night. Joe Hatten, a left hander, was pretty good, and he was supposed to start, but very mysteriously we started Ralph Branca. Durocher—My Dodgers, when I began, were the Dodgers of Leo Durocher—had Hatten warming up under the stands. Ralph Branca—a kid who wasn't very well known—came in to start the game. Melton was then supposed to come in to pitch against the pla-tooned left-handed hitting lineup of the St. Louis Cardinals, and then, by God, Branca went out there and was throwing aspirin tablets, throw-ing heat, and they couldn't touch him. He went on to finish the game and pitched a hell of a game. But people only remember Ralph Branca for one pitch. I remember him as a hell of a pitcher. He was terrific, a mar-velous pitcher day in and day out. It's like Snodgrass' muff in the World Series. One thing gets recollected forever. One pitch to Bobby Thomson.

Pee Wee Reese was a rookie shortstop coming up right from the Lou-isville Colonels, a young kid who you'd think didn't have to shave yet. Billy Herman played second base before Eddie Stanky. He also came in a trade. I remember watching him, an incredibly big man, not lithe and skinny. He was playing second base, but he was light and quick and he could pick it, as they say, with wonderful delicacy, that delicacy you always find so strange in someone who looks stationary, cumbersome.

The young Reese looked like he could gallop over and get the ball deep in the hole and fire him out, which indeed he could. But Herman didn't look as if he could. But I remember being at Ebbets Field with my father—man on first base and a ground ball hit to Billy Herman's left—he twirls around with a beautiful balletic move and flips it underhand to Reese coming over the bag, double play. It was absolutely gorgeous. I was also hungry. Right after I finished seeing the end of the move, I turned my head and ordered a hot dog, which my father said was all right to order. He turned and said, "You didn't see it. You were ordering your hot dog." I said, "No, I saw it. I saw it."

I was putting things in their proper place. I saw the play, and the moment it was over, I turned to the hot dog man, but my father was disappointed in me. He thought in my greed and gourmandism, I had missed the play. The way he was with me was just the way I have been with my son, finding fault. It's true. I can remember that move, I can see it, it was wonderful, that elephantine delicacy, of the stubby ballet dancer on second base.

They were still my Dodgers when Jackie Robinson came in, but I'm thinking about my first time, which is perhaps your most intense one, the one you take to your grave, the first team you knew and loved—I can go around the infield—Dolph Camilli at first, Billy Herman at second, Pee Wee Reese took over at short, and Cookie Lavagetto and Lew Riggs at third, and later there was Billy Cox, who Roger Kahn wrote about in *The Boys of Summer* tending bar in Pennsylvania with the big gut—he was terrific.

Dixie Walker, Joe Medwick, and Pete Reiser were in the outfield, and Mickey Owen behind the plate. I remember Mickey Owen terribly well. He was quick around the plate. He could move. That's why the dropped third strike in the fourth game of the 1941 World Series was so stunning. I presume he called for a fastball and got a curve. It just went right by him. And that was the Series.

Fitzsimmons pitched seven innings beautifully. Casey, the great fireman, came in and pitched very well. He was indestructible—until the dropped third strike. I believe I was listening to it when it happened. No television, of course. Radio time.

It was going to be the third out. It was all wrapped up. And then he couldn't get anyone out after that. It was a typical nightmare where everything comes apart, and you can't stop it.

After Owen, Bruce Edwards caught briefly—he looked good and then hurt his arm, and then the great Campanella came in later on.

Durocher was a wild man. He was a calculating kind of wild man, a shrewd manager who was fiery and difficult, combative, reminded me of Billy Martin. Leo seemed appropriate to the Dodgers and their improvised bunch of eccentrics like Joe Medwick and Dixie Walker. Of course, it was an incredible disappointment to root for Dixie Walker, The People's Choice, only to discover he left the team because he wouldn't play with a black man in 1948.

What I loved about Walker was the manner he seemed to have. There was a nonchalance and apparent modesty, a gentleness toward the fans, a deference, and at the same time the ability to hit line drives and hit them often when they count. He was a singles hitter mostly. Camilli was the home run kind, but he struck out usually. He hit the most on the team, but it was Walker who would go up there and hit .300. He was very reliable, very steady.

Pete Reiser and Pee Wee Reese, the rookies, were the most exciting players. If you remember, when they both came up, Reese and Reiser worked on the Baltimore chop. They were young and fast, and they did this all the time. They would get a ball they could pound right in front of them, that would bounce high in the air, and they'd cross first base before the other team could throw them out. Reiser was a lot faster than Reese. Reiser was incredibly fast. He could steal home. Reiser was one of the most exciting players ever to come up. He was a magnificent center fielder who could run anywhere and catch the ball and throw, a fantastic gun, and of course, he could hit like all hell. He could do it all. He was Willie Mays who injured himself out of the game. The story of Reiser is well known. Reiser would not hesitate to run into a wall. He had many concussions on the baseball field. He played when he was seeing double.

He'd get out there and try to hit the ball, and he was foolish, I suppose. My, he was foolish in a way, that, aw, he was Homeric. Ajax was stupid, and I don't want to call Pete Reiser stupid. He just had an incredible ferocity of intensity of desire to let nothing stand in his way.

He did that, and other things that injured him, even more than Mickey Mantle. He was hobbled by injuries and held down and had a short career. But heavens, what an incredibly powerful and exciting ballplayer he was.

Pee Wee Reese was something else again. He seemed very talented, but he was more of a personality, more of a character. Perhaps because he was around longer, and I saw him getting older.

I think I learned about aging from baseball. Because it seems such a brief time when Pee Wee Reese was the kid with fuzz on his face, when Pee Wee Reese is the seasoned veteran, then the grizzled old man. All this happens between the time you first follow baseball and when you're out of high school, an accelerated idea of aging that in a way has a whole curve to itself. The whole riddle of the Sphinx: what is four-footed at dawn and two-footed at noon and three-footed at twilight—in baseball that happens in the space of ten years, sometimes more with other players, of course, depending on how late they come into the game.

But another thing that I recall, which has to do with aging—fathers and sons. The male lineage and the aging of the male seems to me deeply wound into the story of baseball.

Carl Hubbell was the great Giant pitcher. He was the great old man with a screwball, the left arm that hung oddly at his side. One time the Dodgers and the Giants were playing, and we were listening to this on the radio, and late in the game, a tied game, Carl Hubbell came out of the bullpen to pitch, which was not done. It was late in the season, and the Giants were doing well. And Durocher sent up Reese the kid up from Louisville, to hit against him. My father was a Dodger fan, but my father was also very fond of Carl Hubbell, and Pee Wee Reese hit a double off the wall to win the game, and I cheered and shouted for the Dodgers, and I looked over at my father, and he wept that the old great King Carl should be beaten by a punk kid coming up.

My father was not much older than Carl Hubbell at that point, if at all.

Oh, the wartime years were wonderful! We had a sixteen-year-old shortstop, Tommy Brown. Eddie Miksis played second base. We had a 44-year-old playing, and I can't remember who else, but I remember Red Barber trying to whip up interest saying how Miksis had a unique way of tagging second base and making a double play.

"Come out and see it. It's really interesting."

A bunch of Triple A ballplayers, very old and the very young coming in. But we did good, and it was terribly exciting. And here we were in Connecticut, seventy miles away, a big trip, during a time when it was hard to get gasoline. You had to save up your coupons if you wanted to get to New York, and every now and then my father would be able to get tickets, and we'd drive down in the morning and see a doubleheader at the Polo Grounds between the Dodgers and the Giants, and come back at night.

I remember seeing Mel Ott win a game, picking his foot up and slamming the ball in the close foul line at the Polo Grounds to beat the Dodgers. For us, in Connecticut, there was nothing magic about the notion of Brooklyn. We had no emotional feeling about the borough of Brooklyn.

But what I remember about Ebbets Field was a tremendous warmth and friendliness and the eccentricities. We didn't have a San Diego Chicken on the field, but we had a million feathers flying in the stands: the people in their getups, with their cowbells and whatever else they had.

From the age of 12 or so, I came up to New Hampshire in July and August. My grandfather was a great Red Sox fan. My grandfather in the 1890s went down to Boston, and he saw a game between the Boston Red Stockings and somebody. And he went down again in 1949. My father took him down, and he saw Ted Williams play. For fifty years he was a total Red Sox fan, totally in love with the team.

People will find it hard to imagine now that you could love a team and follow it closely without having seen it play. Which he did. That's what most people did. They knew their baseball team from playing it and watching the town teams play, and then they read about their favorite pro team in the newspapers. And this was true all over the country. We were a rural country for a long time.

My grandfather agreed to be for the Brooklyn Dodgers in the National League, and I would be for the Red Sox in the American League. I used to read the *Boston Post* every morning to find out about the Dodgers. I'd work on poems every morning. I took care of the chickens, but mostly I worked trying to be a writer, and then in the afternoon we'd go haying. And in between loads we'd come in and have some well water, spent about five minutes cooling off, turn on the radio, and we would hear three or four pitches of the Red Sox game, possibly to get the score, and go back and hay again.

Of course, you worked Saturday all day as much as you did every day, so my grandfather never got to listen to a game, because on Sundays you did not turn on the radio to listen to baseball. No way! That was breaking the Sabbath. Once or twice, when things got serious in late August, my grandmother, who was running the Sabbatherian roost, would allow us to turn it on long enough to get the score.

My father and I would go up to the car, and we'd take rides and listen to the radio in the afternoon. My father and I put two gloves and the ball in the truck, go out, and park the car in the road and play catch on Sunday afternoons. I speak of fathers and sons, as Roger Kahn does and many others as well: we had a tremendous thing between us. And we had lots of bad things between us. We didn't agree about everything, but this was always something solid between us. I never did go through a latency period when I decided baseball was beneath me. Some people do that and come back. I wasn't one of those.

And when he was dying—he died of lung cancer at 52 in December of 1955—he got to see the Dodgers win. I knew he was dying, of course, and he knew he was dying.

And when they won the Seventh Game—Johnny Podres pitched incredibly—I was way up in New York State, going to join my relatives of my first wife's, who were up on the St. Lawrence River. I stopped at a bar somewhere where there was a television set about four inches square, and lots of snow, and I waited until they won the game until I went on to join them. I called up my father. He had been following them all those years. When he was dying, I had wanted to arrange the world so everything would turn out the way he wanted it. I couldn't really arrange that World Series. I would have if I could. I wanted the Dodgers to win because I wanted him to have some pleasure. And he did take pleasure in that. And then for them to win didn't quite compensate for such things as dying, I won't say that, but it was something between us.

I had borrowed a neighbor's set, which was as big as a chest of drawers, with a tiny little picture in the middle, and moved it into the room where he was. And he could see the games and see them win. It was something we had together for sixteen wonderful years.

CHAPTER TWELVE

ELSTON HOWARD

For the Yankees, the First

*J*ackie Robinson came to the Brooklyn Dodgers in 1947. It would not be for another eight years—1955—before the New York Yankees brought up their first black player, Elston Howard, a star in the Negro Leagues with the Kansas City Monarchs and the Most Valuable Player of the International League with Toronto in 1954.

George Weiss, the general manager of the Yankees, was wary of signing black players, for fear of losing part of his robust white audience. By 1955 the Dodgers had signed Robinson, Roy Campanella, Don Newcombe, Junior Gilliam, Joe Black, and Sandy Amoros. In that the Yankees had won pennants in 1949, 1950, 1951, 1952, 1953, Weiss didn't feel the need to sign black players was particularly acute.

When the Yankees brought Howard up, they sought to change him from an outfielder to a catcher. Since Yogi Berra was the mainstay behind the plate, some wondered whether the Yankees were doing this to lessen Howard's playing time. It wasn't so. Manager Casey Stengel called him "my four-way man." Casey played him at catcher, first base, left field, and right field.

Ellie Howard, a sweet, thoughtful, modest man, played for the Yankees for fourteen years, and he was chosen for the American League All Star team twelve times. Ellie played in ten World Series. In 1963 Howard became the first African American to be named the Most Valuable Player of the American League. That year he hit .287 with 28 home runs and 85 RBIs.

Howard remained with the Yankees as a coach from 1969 through 1979. That he was never hired to be a manager in the major leagues broke his heart.

He died of a rare heart ailment on December 14, 1980, at the too young age of fifty-one.

As you will see, it wasn't easy to be the first black player on a team, even a team like the Yankees, during the waning days of segregation.

Elston Howard

While in high school you were a member of the St. Louis Braves.

That was a semi-pro team. I played when I was going to high school with that team. On Saturdays and Sundays. In high school we only played two games a week, and on the weekend I played with the St. Louis Braves, which was a semi-pro team in St. Louis. It was an all black team. I give Teeny Edwards, the man who used to run this, a great deal of credit for my baseball, because he used to stay after me a lot. I used to like to play basketball and football, and I used to like baseball a lot—I could hit the ball good. I played a lot of softball, and I give Teeny Edwards a lot of credit, because he worked a lot with me as far as the techniques of baseball.

What did he teach you?

He was a catcher, and he played a little bit in the old Negro Leagues, and when I went with the Kansas City Monarchs, he was responsible for it. They had been scouting me a lot, and I heard from the Dodgers, the Braves, and then the Yankees came along, and that's when I signed.

As a kid I played baseball. I used to like to play stickball, we used to play the bottle caps and all the different games. We played cork ball. For cork ball you used similar to a fungo bat. And you get one strike. You either hit the ball or strike out. It's a little bit bigger than a golf ball. This was a big game in St. Louis. I haven't seen it played anywhere else. They have cork ball nets built in St. Louis where you can play this game. We also used to play that with a tennis ball.

In the evening we'd come home and play all kinds of games. During the winter we'd skate and play hockey. I played everything. In high school I was a four-letter man. I participated in every sport.

Do you remember the shotput championships?

I won shotput the first time I went out for track. I won that.

For the entire state, wasn't it?

Yes. It was the public-school state championship, which was a big event. All the high schools in the county entered, and I won the county. It was the first time I went out for track. It must have gone fifty feet. I couldn't run fast, but I was also second in the javelin.

In high school you received scholarship offers in both basketball and football. Were you offered a scholarship in baseball?

One, from Western Michigan. My baseball coach in high school had been a football coach at Western Michigan, and I could have gone there on a baseball scholarship.

Why did you choose to play professional baseball over going to college?

My parents were educators. My father was a principal down in New Madrid, Missouri, at the O'Bannon High School. My mother was a dietician for many years, and they wanted me to go to college. I went to Stowe, a teacher's college, a little school in St. Louis, but I dropped out and started playing professional baseball.

I went into the black leagues. I played with the Kansas City Monarchs. Ernie Banks was my roommate. We won the Negro American League, which was big in black baseball. Today we have many black stars in the major leagues. It wasn't that way then.

When I came in, there were still racial barriers. We couldn't live in the same hotel with the white ballplayers. We'd go down to spring training in St. Petersburg, and we would stay with a private family. We stayed with Del Williams, who had a shoe repair shop. The food was great. His wife used to fix us real good food. Bob Gibson, Bill White, and Sam Jones used to stay at their home. They were playing with the Cardinals.

At the time I was the only black member with the Yankees.

We had a rough time during spring training. Camp would break for the day, and you had to cross the tracks into the black section to dress, while the white boys would go to the hotel and dress. They'd jump on the bus, while I had to jump in a cab with my uniform and come to the ballpark and go back and then jump back on the train, see.

Didn't this make you angry?

Oh yeah. Being a young man, I was really upset at it. The only time I would get *really* upset was when you'd hear racial remarks. In those days you heard a lot of racial remarks, and I still get mad today when I hear it. I get offended by it, and if a guy gets on me about it, I go right after him.

Were there any opponents in particular in the American League who used to razz you?

No. I never was razzed. I can recall only one incident, and that was Jimmy Piersall. He called me "black," which is a common word today. He said, "You lucky black son of a bitch."

After that Piersall was one of my best friends. And today, right now, Jim Piersall is a hell of a guy. I know he had a lot of mental problems, but he's a great friend and I overcame the whole thing. But as you'd go through the south you would hear things like that from the stands. They would say different things to you.

As far as ballplayers, when I came up to the ballclub I was with some good men, like Phil Rizzuto. I give Phil the most credit of anyone. Being I was the lone black ballplayer with the club, he would call me up during the day, and he'd take me up to various places, take me to the movies, introduce me to nice people around the league. Right

Phil Rizzuto

now I call him the Great White Father, because he was the type of man I respect, and I give him a lot of credit.

Hank Bauer was a great friend of mine and so was Andy Carey. The whole ballclub was great.

In June of 1955 Detroit led in a game 2 to 0. Berra hit a two-run home run, and then Noren singled, Eddie Robinson was hit by a pitch, Collins walked, and you lined a hit up the middle to win that ballgame. You were just a rookie that year. You came into the dugout, and they had a surprise for you.

Yeah, they had towels lined up from the door to my locker. Joe Collins and Billy Martin lined the towels up as I hit the door and went to my locker.

It was a funny gag. Yeah, I was surprised. Being the first black ballplayer, when they did that, that's when I figured I was accepted just like anyone on the ballclub. They had some great ballplayers on the club, and me being a rookie just coming with the club, naturally you want to fit in and do a job, but there had to be a little pressure on you, but when you get a base hit, the tension is eased, and this made me feel very good.

I shouldn't say accepted. I was accepted when I first came to the team. The ballplayers on the club, from Allie Reynolds right on down, did everything to make me feel accepted. I caught Allie the first game we played against the Philadelphia Athletics. I never will forget.

"Look," he said, "just sit back there and call what you want. You're the catcher."

Things like that would make it easy for you.

When you hear things like this from older ballplayers, that means a lot. Allie Reynolds was one of the greatest pitchers in baseball. He told me that, and that made me feel *really* good.

Hank Bauer was a hell of a man who would help you out a lot. Of course, Mickey Mantle, Whitey Ford, and all the ballplayers were regular. If anything went wrong with me, they would come back to my side.

Problems were there. I would get sick of it at times, but then you had men like that who would make things easier.

I couldn't stay in the Muehlebach Hotel in Kansas City. We'd go to the hotel in Chicago called the del Prado. You couldn't stay in that hotel, which surprised the hell out of me.

All things like that have been eliminated. Maybe there are still some places like that in the South. To show you how things run, my wife is a light-skinned black person. We all are different colors. My mother was practically as light as you are. My wife is very light, and when I received Most Valuable Player, I received a letter from a nut in Delaware saying, "I never did know you were married to a white woman. You ought to go back to Africa."

He saw the picture of my wife and I when I was named Most Valuable Player. So you get a lot of incidents. You get all kinds of mail.

A kid named Billy Rohr was pitching a no-hitter. It was the ninth inning. I hit a line drive to right field. I must have gotten about 300 letters, a lot of good letters and a lot of bad letters. Some would write, "Why would you break up a no-hitter?" and they would call me nigger and everything else.

Because I got a base hit? That's my job to come to the plate and get a base hit. They were getting on me because I broke up this kid's no-hitter.

They wrote some letters to Ralph Houk. I couldn't believe some of the letters. But you overcome that. But if a fellow says something like that to my face, I really get offended about it.

There was one teammate by the name of Bill Miller. He used to pitch for this ballclub, and he used some racial remarks. I didn't like that. I didn't say anything about it. Now you never hear anything like that.

I never could have gone through what Jackie Robinson went through. I don't think I could have taken that. I probably would have been in fights every day. I give Jackie a great deal of courage in opening the way for me.

I remember when Jackie came into the majors in 1947. I was just coming out of school. I went with the Kansas City Monarchs that year. I give Jackie a great deal of credit because he went through a lot. I don't think the modern-day players would even think about going through that, but he opened the way up for me, and I think every ballclub should appreciate a man like Jackie Robinson, who opened up the way for all of us, to be in a position to play this game.

Did you hear racial comments from others?

[Yankee teammate] Enos Slaughter would mention different stories, and I didn't like it. You hear all kinds of stories. That's something I don't go for.

Racial stories?

Yeah. I don't go for, as I call it, shit. I never did go for it. Anything like that. Enos was from the South, and it was one of those things that I guess they are used to saying that kind of crap. I was from St. Louis, which you could say is part South too. They call it the Midwest, but it's still a southern city. I went to an all-black school—I played football and basketball with all-black ballplayers. It wasn't integrated, but later on it integrated, and everything in St. Louis went along extremely well. Everything has opened up a great deal.

When you played against white teams in semi-pro ball, you would hear different things like that. But you try to overcome it. I recall when I heard them say the word "black," blood would rush across my head, I would get so mad. But today I've overcome it, and "a black guy" is a common word.

If they say nigger, that's something else; it's different. The meaning of the word nigger is an ignorant person. I think anyone could be that, but naturally always the black guy is a nigger. You know what I mean?

You played with the Kansas City Monarchs in 1948 when you were 19. What kind of club did you have with the Monarchs?

We had the best team. We had a fellow by the name of Bob Thurman, who later was with Cincinnati. Hank Thompson later played with the Browns and the New York Giants. Earl Tabor later went into organized baseball, Triple A. Willard Brown was with the St. Louis Browns. We had Ernie Banks, myself, and other older black ballplayers who were outstanding like Jim Lamar. Frank Barnes, a pitcher, went with me to the Yankees. The Monarchs was a good ballclub that would be up there every year. I only played that year and a half. We battled for the Negro American League pennant.

Did you play against Satchel Paige?

He was barnstorming then, so I only played against Paige one time. I was playing with a white club, the Kansas City Blues, from the American Association. He pitched against us, and my first time up, I hit a double off of him.

What kind of year did you have on the Monarchs?
I hit about .375. I had a very good year.

Did they pay well?
The Kansas City Monarchs gave me $3,000. When I left there, I got $2,800. During those days there wasn't too much money given out, like the big bonuses. The Yankees paid the Monarchs a package price for two ballplayers, Frank Barnes and myself. I didn't get a penny from the Yankees, no. I only got a penny from the Yankees when I started hitting the baseball.

Why didn't the Yankees sign Ernie Banks?
The Yankees had a chance to sign him. They could have signed anybody on the ballclub.

Why didn't they?
That's a good question. Willie Mays was still playing with the Birmingham Barons too. The Yankees knew about him too. The New York Giants came along and got him. At this time the Yankees weren't signing too many, see.

You certainly knew who the best players in that league were.
There were a lot of other ballplayers in that league who could have made it. Sam Harrison, George Crowe played in that league, Al Smith, who went up. A lot of the top black ballplayers who played, like Maury Wills. Henry Aaron played with the Indianapolis Clowns.

You could tell Henry Aaron was a great ballplayer, couldn't you?
You could tell. But in the beginning teams weren't signing a great deal of black ballplayers. They had the opportunity to. But they never did sign many of them.

Why did the Yankees sign you but not Henry Aaron?
Well, that's a good question. I was up before Aaron. I never did play against Aaron in the black leagues. I played against Willie Mays. I don't

know why the Yankees didn't sign him. The Birmingham Black Barons used to own Mays. The Kansas City Monarchs owned me. The Kansas City Monarchs used the Kansas City Blues ballpark, which was the Yankees Triple-A club. This probably had something to do with their signing me. They said, "If we had any ballplayers eligible to go up that we would take them right up."

Did you have a lot of scouts on your trail?

Oh yeah. We had a lot of scouts. The Boston Braves were after me. The Dodgers. The St. Louis Cardinals.

Another incident: I went to a try-out with the Cardinals in my hometown. I popped a double, a triple, and a single the first three times up, and they said, "We will send you a letter." I'm still waiting for the letter. I never did hear from them.

Why did you sign with the Yankees?

The reason why is, as a young kid, you always hear about the Yankees being a great club. I had an opportunity.

They want me, I thought. *I have a chance to make this ballclub.*

I'll never forget, scouts Johnny Neun and Billy Grimes approached me, and the next thing I knew, I was told, "You've been bought by the Yankees."

I was tickled to death. I was in Chicago when they told me this. Pitcher Frank Barnes and I went to Muskegon, which was a Class A club in the Central League. I played there for a year, and after that I went into the service for the next two years.

Was it difficult being a black man in the Central League?

Oh Jesus. When you would play in Dayton, Ohio, you couldn't go in restaurants. If you played in Charleston, West Virginia, you couldn't live in the hotel. In Dayton and Charleston, they *couldn't* accept a black man. The team would go into a restaurant, and I had to eat in the owner's house. They had a table for us. When we played in Michigan: Grand Rapids, Saginaw, Muskegon, Flint, those cities were great.

Couldn't the team exert any pressure to do something?

They could have. The same as the Yankees did in St. Pete. Mr. Topping exerted a lot of pressure when we weren't allowed to stay in the Soreno Hotel.

I admired Dan Topping and Del Webb. When we couldn't stay in the hotels in St. Petersburg, they said, "Next year we're going to Fort Lauderdale."

When we went to Ft. Lauderdale, they didn't want you to go into the dining room. Which I say was a lot of shit. What's the use of staying at the hotel if you can't go into the coffee shop? It didn't make sense to me. I went into the coffee shop anyway.

What happened?

Nothing. My wife went too. It's still tough in Florida. You ask for an apartment, and it's still pretty tough. For a lot of [black] players, you can't get an apartment.

Still? [The interview took place in 1974.]

Oh sure.

I respect Mr. Topping for doing that. I say he was the best owner I ever played for. He was a man who I had great respect for. He did a lot of things for me. He owned a hotel down in Nassau, and we won the pennant, and he said, "You and your wife go down to Nassau, stay at the British Colonial Hotel as long as you want. It won't cost you anything."

We did this for about three years. I went down and presented a Sportsman of the Year award for him. The man was great to me all the time he was the owner of the Yankees. He was a true first-class man. Mr. Webb was the same way.

You were in the service in 1951 and 1952.

I was drafted into the army. I wish to hell I wasn't drafted. I think I'd be in the major leagues. I'd have had twenty years in by now. But I was drafted, yes and had to go in.

I was based in Camp McCoy, Wisconsin, and I went over to Korea and then back into Tokyo. I didn't like Tokyo. I was there long enough.

I was in the special service, and I played baseball. Del Crandall was over there doing the same thing. We played against each other. Overall, my duties were running the gym and playing baseball and basketball. But staying over there so long was really rough. I had to go. It was for the country. I'm not a draft dodger. I went in, and I stayed in for two years, and I got out just in time to go to spring training in '54 with the New York Yankees.

The Yankees had Gus Triandos, Lou Berberet, and myself for catchers. They sent Triandos to Triple A Kansas City Blues and sent me to Toronto. I caught every day up there.

The next year Gus was traded to Baltimore, and I came up and made the Yankee ballclub. I had a better year than he did. In '54 I was the most valuable player in the International League. [He hit .330 with 22 home runs and 109 RBIs.]

A lot of clubs followed me around when I was in the International League. I was playing on a strictly older ballclub which consisted of Sam Jethroe, who was a former major leaguer, Ed Stevens, Mike Goliat, Hector Rodriguez, and a lot of old ballplayers. I was the youngest ballplayer on the club. A lot of scouts followed me around. We won the pennant.

Was Toronto a good place to play ball?

Toronto is one of the better cities I've ever been in. The people were outstanding. As far as I'm concerned, the Canadian people treated me as well as the people in New York City.

Branch Rickey sent Jackie Robinson to play in Montreal his first year because of the racial tolerance of the Canadians. Could that have been one of the reasons the Yankees sent you to Toronto?

It might have been. Jack Kent Cooke, who was the owner of the L.A. Lakers, was the owner of the Toronto ballclub. I enjoyed playing for Mr. Cooke because he did a lot for me. He let me know that I was important to the Toronto ballclub. I admire him.

What sort of things did he do?

Mr. Cooke would take you out. His general manager, Frank Pollock, would do a lot of things for you and gave things to my wife. I still communicate with Jack Cooke. I wrote him a letter, and he got me four tickets to the Muhammed Ali/Joe Frazier fight at the Garden. They weren't free. They cost over a hundred and a half.

When did you actually switch to catcher? Did Bill Skiff switch you?

Bill Skiff bought me the first catcher's glove that I ever had. And Bill Dickey gave me my first true course in learning the fine points of being a catcher. That was in 1954. I went through the mill my first spring training, and I was sent out to Toronto. Bill taught me everything about catching, if you want to say it like that.

Did Dickey work you hard?

Yeah. He worked you hard. In fact he worked you hard in your room at night. If he'd see you in the lobby, he would talk to you about different things. I admire him for that, because he was a conscientious man. He wanted to help you.

He didn't throw you grounders in the room at night, did he?

No, nothing like that. He would talk to you about different things. He'd say, "Get rid of that ball quick." Showing you different things like that. If he saw you in your room, he'd tell you about hitting. You'd stand in front of the mirror.

"Every man has rhythm as a hitter," he'd say.

He'd tell me, "Look. Don't worry about your hitting. You don't need any help. Just go up there and swing the bat."

And that's what I did. I never did like to talk to too many people about hitting because you get all mixed up.

What else did he teach you?

Blocking balls is one of the fine points. Maneuvering, shifting, getting rid of the ball quick. We call it the groundhog. Falling down in front of the ball and blocking it all the time. You have to block the ball if you're going to be a catcher. Being a good catcher is eliminating passed balls and blocking the ball and keeping the ball in front of you.

These were some of the finer points of catching I didn't know. Catching is also learning how to work with pitchers. Whitey Ford was a good

Whitey Ford

man. He helped me. I learned a lot through Whitey about how to master calling the game.

One thing: Jim Turner was the pitching coach, and I talked to Jim a lot. Because I wanted to learn. I wanted to be a good catcher, and the only way to get to the top is talking to someone who went through this. Jim Turner right now is one of the best pitching coaches in the game. He has been in the game over 50 years. And I talked to him constantly, because I wanted to improve myself and learn how to communicate with pitchers.

I never did get mad at them. I wanted to help them, and I wanted them to help themselves. So we worked together as a unit. I worked the same way with Whitey Ford. I call him the Chairman of the Board, because he was the best pitcher on our staff.

You were the first one to call him that.

Yes, I named him that, because he was a master at pitching. He could do more things than any pitcher I ever caught. He could throw a curveball at any time. Some pitchers cannot master a curveball. He could throw a curveball, a change up, any pitch he had at any time he wanted. At three and two. Some pitchers when it's three and two can't throw a curveball. They have to throw a fastball. But Whitey could throw a changeup three and two and get it over the plate. He's an outstanding pitcher.

I began to learn the pattern of Whitey Ford—fellows like that are smart pitchers—and I learned a great deal more about catching from Whitey Ford than I did from anybody, because he was a master at pitching.

I learned a great deal from pitching coach Jim Turner. I would talk to him a lot about pitchers before the game. "What is this pitcher's best pitch?" And it would help me. You learn a great deal.

Ralph Houk helped me when I first went down there. He had number 32, and because he left the ballclub to manage in Denver, that's when I got 32.

Ralph Terry said you were a big figure in his career.

Ralph Terry was one of the best control pitchers I ever caught. Ralph and I would work together a lot. He was outstanding. Ralph could do almost the same as Whitey. He could pinpoint the ball, had a good curveball, and a lot of guys said Ralph Terry would throw a lot of shit, as we called it, slow stuff, but they didn't realize when he would throw that slow stuff, Ralph Terry could also throw the ball right by you. He pitched one of the finer games in the World Series. We beat the Giants in 1962. We got McCovey out. He was the last out. McCovey hit a line drive to Bobby Richardson. Ralph pitched one hell of a game. He did a job on Willie Mays. He did a job on the Alou brothers, McCovey, Cepeda. He pitched one hell of a ballgame.

Did Yogi work with you?

Yogi as a player didn't have a great deal of time, but he still talked to me a lot. I talked to Yogi more the year we won the pennant in 1964. Yogi was the manager. Yogi was instrumental. I had one of my best years for him. How many games did I catch? 150 games. And I hit .313 for him.

How did you do in the 1955 spring training?

I hit over .400. I was hitting the shit out of the ball. I had a chance. I wanted to make this ballclub. I didn't care. I was down there to make the ballclub. I'm down there, and I played with a lot of guys I knew at Kansas City, and I wanted to make this ballclub. That was my main asset, to hit that ball.

What do you remember about spring training of 1955, the time you made it?

I had played with a lot of guys in the minors: Norm Siebern, Jerry Lumpe, Lou Berberet, Bill Virdon. We had a lot of good ballplayers down there.

Bill Skowron came with his wife and picked me up at the train station. He took me over to the ballpark. He's one of my real good friends. I run into Moose all the time. Moose is a hell of a guy.

Did anybody give you trouble during spring training?

Nobody on this club. Everyone tried to make everything pleasant for this black guy, the first one. Phil Rizzuto was there, and God damn he was great. I never will forget that man. He was one hell of a guy. At times I had problems going to a place. A wise guy would say something, but other than that, I never had any problems.

In 1955 in Birmingham, Alabama, there was a law that forbid interracial competition.

I remember that. My wife came down from St. Louis with my brother-in-law. In Birmingham, you couldn't do anything. A white club with a black guy playing on it, you couldn't do anything down there.

I skipped Birmingham, went on into Memphis, and I met my wife down there. I had a cousin living in Memphis, so that was a little vacation for me. I enjoyed it, because I hadn't seen my wife. It was my first year in spring training. She came down a little bit, but she was pregnant, and so I enjoyed seeing her. But the law was in.

Did this make some of your teammates angry?

A lot of them couldn't understand it. They couldn't believe it. They were told it was a law in the whole town of Birmingham and in the whole state of Alabama. No black man could play with a white team. And if you were black, you couldn't go anywhere. None of the places were integrated.

"Where the hell have you been at?" the fellows asked me.

"I went over to Memphis," I said. "I couldn't play in Birmingham."

"What do you mean?"

"They have a law that no blacks can play with whites," I said.

They knew I was missing. A lot of them kidded me.

"Hey, you got a vacation, huh?" they said.

Any other vivid remembrances of that 1955 season, things that happened to you?

I was happy to have made the ballclub. I wasn't playing every day, but I was platooned in the outfield with Irv Noren. Later Irv was traded, and I was two-platooned with Norm Siebern. I would catch in certain situations and played right field and played first base. But overall, I always enjoyed hitting the ball. When I got a base hit, yeah.

My first time up against the Brooklyn Dodgers, I hit a home run in the World Series. That was the first time a rookie ever hit a home run his first time at bat in the Series.

How was it you played the entire World Series after you were a platooned ballplayer throughout that 1955 season?

We were having problems in the outfield. Enos Slaughter was in left, and Billy Martin told Stengel to put me in the outfield. I played in every game.

Jim Turner and Frank Crosetti were on my side, so Casey put me out there, and I did a pretty good job out there for them. I got a few hits in the '55 World Series, and I never will forget—I made the last out. I hit the ball to Pee Wee Reese for the last out against Johnny Podres, and they beat us in '55. We came back the next year and beat them.

Did you get an opportunity to know Jackie Robinson?

Yeah. I knew Jackie. I first met him with the ballclub. We used to stay at the Sir John Hotel in the black section of Miami, when you couldn't stay at the white hotels. I stayed there with Joe Black, Junior Gilliam, Roy Campanella, as well as Jackie. It was in the black community, but it was one of the best hotels in Florida.

I talked to Jackie a lot, and I talked a lot to Campanella about catching. Jackie was a smart man. He was an inspiration for every black ballplayer. I don't think the young ballplayers today could go through what Jackie Robinson went through when he first came in. Times have changed a great deal.

I played against him in the World Series. There was a base hit to me in left field. Jackie rounded second base, and I charged the ball real good, and me being a rookie I asked myself, *Who is this guy to take this much lead?*

You know the saying, "Never throw behind the runner"? I threw behind him, and he took off and went into third base.

The next day I said to him, "I'll get you for that."

Jackie was laughing about it.

Jackie was a smart baseball man, a good hitter, a great base runner, and one of the most exciting baseball players I've ever seen. He'd break down that line, and the average pitcher would balk because he didn't know whether or not he was stealing home.

I give Jackie a lot of credit for opening the way for me, and all the other black ballplayers in baseball should feel the same way. I was one of Jackie's pallbearers along with Bill Russell, Don Newcombe, Monte Irvin, and Henry Aaron. I admire him and always will. I've always looked up to him as a real fine ballplayer.

Was it frustrating to have to play behind Yogi all those years?

I played a lot. Yogi to me was one of the best catchers. Yogi and Roy Campanella were the two best catchers I've ever seen. A lot of times I'd get a little upset because I wasn't playing. I wanted to play. Every ballplayer likes to play. One thing I had going for me. I didn't have to sit around and wait only, because I also played outfield, played first base and played right field.

You ever ask to be traded?

No, I never asked to be traded. I know I was mentioned in a lot of them. It never did materialize. One time I was talking to Buzzy Bavasi, the general manager of the Los Angeles Dodgers. The Dodgers didn't have a real good catcher at the time, and they wanted me to come out there with them, but.

I read where Paul Richards wanted me to come with his ballclub in Baltimore. Washington wanted me.

In 1956 you only played in one World Series game. The last game.

I just got out of the hospital. I had a strep throat. Dr. Gaynor put me in the hospital because he didn't want me being around the other ballplayers. It was contagious.

When I got out, I was so damn weak I could hardly stand up. I came out and had to build up, because I was laying down a lot, and that throat made me weak as hell. The last game they put me in against Don Newcombe, and I had a pretty good day. I had a two-run home run and a double.

Mickey Mantle won the MVP in 1956, 1957, and in 1962.

During my time Mickey Mantle was hurt most of the time. I give him a lot of credit. I've never seen a ballplayer like Mickey Mantle. When he was hurt, he'd go out in the field and play for you. I don't think the average man could do what Mickey Mantle had the ability to play under his conditions. He would do everything. His legs were wrapped up every day. He'd go out and bust his rear every day for you. I can recall in the 1961 World Series we played the Cincinnati Reds. He had a big hole the size of a golf ball in his leg, and he played until blood ran down the back of his uniform, and Ralph had to take him out of the game. He didn't want to come out of the game.

Mickey was a leader. He gave the club inspiration. We had a lot of good ballplayers, but let's face it, Mickey Mantle truly was a big superstar. The guy could hit the ball out of the ballpark both ways, left- and right-handed, and he could fly. He had more speed than anyone I've ever seen going down to first base. He was a big man. He weighed 210 pounds. He never played a full season, and he still had outstanding years.

Mickey had a pretty good sense of humor, didn't he?

Mickey was funny all the time. He'd make you laugh. He'd always come up with something. He was just great. If you said something, he'd come back in a minute. He'd make everybody laugh. He'd keep the club in great spirit. We'd get on the bus, and he would say something to make you laugh.

Billy Martin and Mantle were great friends. They used to run around a great deal. He would always come back with something. He'd give you the funny line. Joe Pepitone loved the guy. He admired Mickey a great deal. Pepi was a kid, and Mickey was still playing. I remember when Pepitone signed. He came right from Brooklyn. He used to come out and watch us play. He wound up playing with the Yankees.

I admired Mantle for so many things. He helped me. He made us a lot of money. He helped us win a lot of pennants. I was in ten of them. I really enjoyed him. He was a great man. There was one guy who was wrong about him, and that was Jim Bouton. He said a lot of things about Mickey Mantle. In spring training Mickey Mantle let Bouton use his car and do everything for him like that. I can't see knocking a guy like Mickey Mantle who did so many things for the world of baseball. Mickey was outstanding. He was a crowd pleaser. He did a hell of a job.

The year Maris and Mickey were fighting for the home run, when Maris hit 61, he hit 54 home runs. He was outstanding. He was super.

Mickey didn't have that popularity until Maris became the person they started booing.

Mickey didn't get booed a great deal. Maris got booed as much as anybody. I understand they booed DiMaggio too a great deal. Having someone to boo was something the fans have to have. Ron Blomberg played here, and he made a couple of errors, and they got all over him. And I tried to build up Ron's confidence. I talked to him, told him to pay it no mind. I was fortunate that I never got booed so badly that it would bother me.

In the fourth game of the 1957 World Series in Milwaukee, you pinch hit in the ninth inning.

I hit a home run. I hit it off Warren Spahn. He threw me a curveball, and I hit the ball really good, hit it hard, and I was lucky enough that it went out. I never will forget it, because the whole ballpark got quiet when I hit the home run. Nobody said anything after that.

In 1958 you still had to stay in segregated quarters, in Columbia, South Carolina.

We'd be on the train, and we'd come into town. The white players would change in the hotel, but we couldn't go into the hotel. We had to go to the black section.

In July of 1958 you had played in only 18 games, but you hit .320, and Casey put you on the All Star team.

Yeah. He told me he would take me as one of his catchers. He said, "There's nobody better than you, so that's why I'm taking you. No one in the league is better. I have the two best catchers, Yogi and you." That's why he took me along.

I admired Stengel. He talked to me.

"You're my four-way man," he said.

I played left field, right field, first base and catcher. But he was tough on some guys. Fortunately, he wasn't tough on me. Right today I communicate with him. In fact, my son would like someday to go to USC, and Stengel arranged for me to talk to Ron Dedeaux, the baseball coach at USC. He used to be a scout, and he played for Stengel. I got a nice letter from him, and someday I hope my son will go to USC.

Stengel truly has done a lot of things for me. We went over and played Japanese teams in 1955. I didn't want to go. My wife was about to give birth. He told me, "I want you to start hitting the ball to right field."

I was strictly a pull hitter. In Japan I started to hit the ball out to right field, and I must have hit over .500 against the Japanese teams.

"They are going to have parties for you, but when you get out on that field, beat them," Casey said. "Don't let them beat you, because they'll play it up."

We really ran them to death. We won 21 ballgames in a row. The Japanese team didn't beat us a ballgame. They tied one game.

During that time my wife was home expecting a baby. One thing Casey told me, "I want you to call your wife and talk to her all night on the telephone if you want to."

We were staying at Sendai Air Force base in Tokyo. I got on the phone, and I talked to her while she was in labor. She said it was the best thing that ever happened to her, because she was so scared.

Casey was a nice man. He gave me a chance. Naturally I gave myself a chance. I worked hard at it, but he was the manager of the ballclub, and he did an outstanding job. He had great ballclubs. I enjoyed him. As I said, some ballplayers didn't enjoy him. He was very nice to me, and I appreciated it.

Some of the pitchers I spoke to said they preferred to have you catch than Yogi. Did Stengel catch you when specific guys were pitching?

Jim Turner liked for me to catch a lot of guys on the ballclub. I had a way—one of the most important things when you're working with a pitcher is to help him. I never did get in an argument with a pitcher. If he wanted to shake me off, okay. But the most important thing is to try to work together. You're trying to get the hitters out, so what the hell is the use of me arguing with him, because he threw a bad pitch. And I would go out and try to relax the ballplayers and try to build up his confidence. It was one of the reasons a lot of pitchers used to like to throw to me, and I enjoyed every one of them. I enjoyed working with every pitcher I ever caught, because we all got along. The relationship was outstanding—everybody—it was something I enjoyed.

I put everything I got in it, trying to get the hitters out. I studied the hitters with them. We talked the situation over, and I'd go out to the mound a lot and I would express what I think, and they would tell me what they think, and we'd put these two things together. We had two heads working instead of one, see. When he shook me off, he's thinking as well as I am. I put down a sign, and if shakes me off. If it's a young pitcher, I'd go out and tell him, "Don't throw that pitch." Because he doesn't know.

You have to go out and talk more to a young man just starting out than you would the veteran. But I never did have any problems with any rookies. I remember Sparky Lyle when I went to Boston, he shook me off, and [manager Dick] Williams said, "The next time you shake him off, it's going to cost you fifty dollars."

I worked it out. I told Sparky, "You can shake off, but don't shake your head. I'll keep flashing down signs. We got to work together. If we get along, you will be a happier pitcher than if we're arguing and having disrespect for one another. We have to get hitters out, and we're not going to get hitters out arguing with one another. Let's go out and get this hitter out. Find out what he can hit and what he can't hit."

What happened to the Yankees in 1959?

We went up to Chicago and got beat, and we went to Boston and we got beat four games. And we went right down. I couldn't believe it. It looked like a building fell on us, and I never will forget that. We should have won it in '59. We had the good ballplayers. I don't know what happened to us. Something just happened all at once, because we had a lot of talent. We had good hitters, good pitchers. That was just one of those years I couldn't believe.

I have to go out to the field right now.

CHAPTER THIRTEEN

HOT ROD KANEHL

Casey's Pet

*R*od Kanehl, an original New York Met who was beloved for his hustle *and his fearlessness, grew up in Springfield, Missouri, and was the son of the athletic director and track coach at Drury College. He played American Legion baseball, and in January 1953 he was signed by New York Yankees scout Tom Greenwade, who had signed Mickey Mantle. After he signed, in the spring of 1954 the Yankees sent him to the advanced rookie camp in St. Petersburg, Florida.*

I asked Kanehl about his early days with the Yankees.

I was born in Wichita, Kansas, and I left there when I was 9. My father was a school teacher. He went to the University of Kansas in Lawrence, Kansas during the war. I moved there in '43. For five years he worked with the Navy's V-12 program as a phys ed teacher and track coach.

In '48 we moved to Springfield, Missouri. He went to Drury College as athletic director and he coached track. I was around school teachers and athletes all my life.

I didn't play baseball in high school. I played American Legion baseball in the summer. The high school had a team, but track was my interest. I pole vaulted and high jumped. I wasn't fast. I was the Missouri State Champion in the outdoor pole vault and in the indoor high jump.

Dad was the track coach at Drury College, and I went there. As a freshman I was fifth in the decathlon in the Kansas Relays. I lost to J.W. Mashburn, who was an outstanding quarter miler at Oklahoma A&M.

He was ineligible scholastical-
ly to run for Oklahoma A&M,
so he competed as an independent, and he won. Also in that
event was Palmer Retzlaff, who
later became Pete Retzlaff from
the Philadelphia Eagles. He was
from North Dakota State. That
was 1953.

*At some point you signed with the
Yankees.*

I signed with the Yankees in the
winter of '54.

Rod Kanehl. Mets team-issued photo

How did that come about?

I became ineligible for track in the spring of '54 by failing a physics
course. I was only carrying 15 hours, and it was a four-hour course, and
so I only passed 11 hours, and you had to pass 12 hours to be eligible to
compete.

If I'm not going to be eligible for track, I thought, *I'm going to go into
baseball.*

Tom Greenwade, who signed Mickey Mantle and a lot of other guys,
lived in the Springfield area, and he scouted me in American Legion ball.
Tom knew my dad was a track coach, and he knew I was interested in
track, but he said, "If you're ever interested in baseball, let me know."

I called him in January of '53, and I signed with the Yankees. One of
the conditions of me signing was my going to the advanced rookie camp
in St. Petersburg. I signed in early February, and in mid-February I went
to St. Petersburg. My first experience with the Yankees was with Casey
Stengel and all the guys who were down there.

Who was with you?

Tony Kubek, Gus Triandos, Marv Throneberry, and Frank Leja, who had
spent a couple years with the Yankees because of that rule that kept bonus

babies on the Yankees roster for two years. Bonus baby Tommy Carroll signed a year later.

Woody Held was an outfielder. Tony Kubek had played outfield in '53. Because Phil Rizzuto was retiring, Casey took all the guys who had played centerfield and started making shortstops out of them. That's how Kubek ended up as a shortstop, Woody Held ended up as a shortstop for Cleveland for years.

There were a lot of others: Lou Berberet was a catcher. So was Gus Triandos. Elston Howard was there in '55 at the advance camp. The coaches were Frank Crosetti, Bill Dickey, Johnny Neun, and Jim Turner.

When you got to that camp, where did Casey have you play?
I was playing outfield in '54.

What was Casey like?
Casey started developing the Yankee system. He wanted everybody to learn how to take signs one way, and how to lead off first base, and how to lead off second, and how to round the bases, how to make the throws from the outfield, and how to pivot to make the throw to second. This was school with classes.

He wanted the corps of the players they expected to finally make the big leagues to be able to advance up the ladder from D ball—D, C, B, A, AA and triple A—with everybody doing the same thing. Casey had a lot of the managers at this advance camp, so they would know what he was teaching, so if you ever got a shot at the big leagues, everybody would be on the same page. That was the Yankee system.

Casey had a routine he would start the first day of spring training. He'd take you from the bench

Casey Stengel

to the on deck circle to home plate, and around the bases. This is a routine he would do every spring training, year after year after year.

I signed when I was 19. That April I turned 20.

Were you awed?

Yeah. But there were a lot of people down there in the same boat. *Everybody* was awed. Even though Bobby Richardson had played the year before—he went into it after high school, and Kubek the same thing, they were down there, but they were in awe also. But they had played half a year of minor league ball. Everybody was in the same boat.

I read that one of the things Casey remembered about you is that you had run into a wall.

No, I jumped the fence.

When did that happen?

In '54, the first camp. I'm green as a gourd from Springfield, Missouri, and Miller Huggins Field in St. Petersburg had a barbed wire fence. They didn't have chain-link in those days. Balls would run under and through the fence, and the kids would chase the ball down. There was a big lake in the back.

I was out in the outfield, and being a high jumper, I hopped this five-foot fence. It was no big deal for me. I hopped the fence and beat the kid to the ball, and then I hopped back in and threw the ball in.

I didn't hear about it until the next winter at the Hot Stove League dinner in Springfield. Tom Greenwade came over to me and he said, "You know, you really impressed Casey with that," and he told me the story. Nobody made anything of it at the time, but Stengel saw it, and he remembered it.

During that first spring training, did Casey ever sit and talk with you?

Oh yeah. Cause he was also from Missouri. That's why he was called Casey, cause he's from Kansas City. He knew my dad was a coach and a teacher, and he was a coach and a teacher at Kankakee, which is in the same area of Kansas. Casey was from Westport, out of Kansas City, and apparently I played like Casey used to play. Casey and I always hit it off. We'd sit and talk. He would point out things on the field. I was like his bobo.

Did you come to develop affection for him?

Oh, of course. We spent two weeks, and then I went back to Springfield for two weeks, and then I went to spring training with Double A Birmingham. Mayo Smith was the manager, and we trained at Ocala, Florida.

It was all new to me. It was an experience. You handle it. You're playing, but the other guys were more experienced, and experience is everything at that level.

Did you have anyone to lean on or to talk to?

No. Kenny Hunt was the only player from Birmingham to make it.

I had heard you played with the Mantle twins.

I played two years with Ray and Roy, Mickey's younger twin brothers. They signed in '54 and were at the rookie camp in '55. After Birmingham spring training in Ocala, I went to McAlister, Oklahoma, D ball. I started in D ball, and Ray and Roy, from Commerce, Oklahoma, signed and they sent them to McAlister, so I played with Ray and Roy Mantle at McAlister in '54.

What were they like?

They were guys' guys. They could run like the wind and throw, and they had great swings. But they had trouble with the curveball. They had their problems. But they were good looking guys, six foot one and two. They were not built at all like Mickey. At McAlister one played left, the other played right, and I played center.

Roy and Ray quit in '61 or '62. Mickey got them jobs in Vegas as dealers. When I got out of baseball, I was in the insurance business, and my boss was a high roller, and we would go into Vegas, and Roy would be at the Riviera, and Ray would be at Circus Circus, and every time I'd go to Vegas I'd look them up. They had been at the Aladdin, at the

Mickey Mantle with twin brothers Ray and Roy

Thunderbird. They've dealt everywhere. They became pit bosses, after ten years. Now, twenty years later, they're retired. They play golf every day and live in Las Vegas.

I went with Ray and Roy to Sunshine Park, the dog track, and we had to sneak in the back because we weren't old enough to get in through the gate. We went around to the back of the place, and we sneaked in where they were walking the dogs. That was in '55.

Russ Snyder, a player in the Yankee chain who went on to play at Baltimore, was also at that advance camp in '54. Russ had hit .432 at McAlister in '53, and I followed him in '54, and I hit in 33 consecutive games, setting a league record, drove in 100 runs, and hit 11 home runs, including three grand slams. I had a good year. I hit .313.

That got me back to the advance camp in '55. This is when they started making shortstops out of all the outfielders. Ray and Roy also were at that advance camp in '55.

In '54 we had stayed at a place called the Bahama Shores, that's out on the beach somewhere, quite of the ways out of town. Lou Skizas—Larrupin' Lou—was there in '54. I roomed with a guy named Tom Hamilton, who had come over from the A's in a trade, and in '55 we moved to the Soreno Hotel, which was an experience, because I had never eaten at a resort-like hotel, where you fill out the card on your menu. If you want, you fill out a card, like on the train, which is another story, the train.

Somebody ought to write a book about it. It's a story of the past. When you sign a contract, you sign to get first-class transportation. And first class transportation in 1954 was the train, the Pullman.

I lived in Springfield, Missouri, and this Frisco train line started in Kansas City, and it's like a tributary. All the guys from Nebraska, North and South Dakota, Iowa, and Kansas would go to Kansas City, and they'd get on this train.

It would go through Springfield, and we had a lot of ballplayers in Springfield, and then it would go to Memphis, and all the guys from up around St. Louis or Chicago would come down to Memphis and would get on this train. The train would go to Birmingham, and then all the guys from the Ohio Valley would get on in Birmingham, and then we'd go to Atlanta. It's like a river.

You then had to change trains in Jacksonville, cause then you get the Seaboard Line coming down from New York, and when it left Jacksonville, it was nothing but ballplayers, card games and crap games.

I remember one poker game. I was an observer. I never had enough money to play. Leroy Thomas was in it. We called him Leroy. He's now Lee Thomas, who later became general manager of Philly. But he was down at that first rookie camp in '54. And another guy named Jimmy Johnston, and they were in a poker game, and here comes this little guy who wants to get in the game, and Johnston said, "Hey, kid, you can't get in the game." It was Fritz Brickell. Fritzie was very short, but a great kid from Wichita. He had a baby face, but Fritzie was tough. He didn't take anything from anybody, and he got in the game.

The train just started filling up. You could see how the river ran, and by the time it left Atlanta, it was practically all baseball players from all the teams going to Florida.

It was that time of year when ballplayers started going south. It's a Paul Newman, Robert Redford type of movie. Major leaguers going to spring training because first class was the train. You didn't fly. When you fly, you don't get the camaraderie, but on the train you see guys. I knew very few guys. I knew a bunch of Yankee players: Ralph Terry, Jerry Lumpe, Fritzie Brickell. Jack Urban came from up in Nebraska. He was at that rookie camp.

The way of the train was an art form. On the train you had to learn how to tip the porters, You had to learn how to order meals on the train. You had to write it down.

Even guys from California hit this train. They would come in from San Diego. Joey Delfino was in one of those rookie camps. Deron Johnson, another big kid who never made it, was in one of them. They joined the train at Jacksonville, because they would come along the southern border states from California. They'd be on that train. Joey Delfino was down there one week, and he disappeared, and nobody knew where he went. He went home. He was awed with the deal. I later played with him at Peoria in the III League.

Everyone takes it for granted that everyone flies. In 1956 we went to first class air fare. Bob Grim was at that first rookie camp. He made the team from that first rookie camp in '54, and then Johnny Kucks made the team from that '55 rookie camp. Stengel was always filling the roster with young blood. That was his attribute.

Gil McDougald once told me, "Casey's greatest attribute was that he *loved* to sit a proven veteran on the bench and play a kid." That's why he had rookies of the year, year after year after year. He had a young pitcher coming up on every staff.

Did you work your way up the Yankee chain?
I went from D ball to C ball, when they wanted me to go to Monroe and play shortstop. They also wanted me to switch hit, because I was quick and fast and I could run bases. They wanted me to learn to bat from the left side.

We had a contending team. I tried switch-hitting for a month, and then I went to the manager and I said, "Hey, I'm hurting the team when I go left handed. I'm just an out."

Reluctantly let me quit batting left handed.

The manager was Ed Head, who had pitched a no hitter for the Dodgers. He was a left-handed pitcher, and there was a bus accident, and he learned to pitch right-handed. He was from Monroe.

I played for Ed, and we won the league and the playoffs in the Cotton States league. Jim Brodstead, Ed Dick, and Ray and Roy Mantle were with me. In the playoffs we beat Eldorado, which was a Giant team who had Jim Davenport and Jose Pagan at third and short.

I went back to Monroe, and the next year I went to Winston Salem, but I broke my hand the first week of the season. I was playing at Danville, Virginia, a New York Giants farm team that had Willie McCovey, Tony Taylor, and Leon Wagner. They had a heck of a team.

I slid into second base and broke my hand. They had always told us never to slide head first. In those days they didn't want you doing that. That's how times have changed. I slid head-first, and I broke the middle bone, so I was out a month.

I went back to Springfield, and when I came back, I went to Winston Salem and was there a month. They had a field that was wide open. I made a lot of errors at shortstop and was ready to get out of there, and Monroe wanted me back, so I went back to Monroe and finished up the '56 season there. Billy Short and Bill Stafford were there.

I finished out the year, and then in '57 I went to Peoria. The manager was Vern Hoscheit. The III League was a pretty good league. We got beat out for the league championship Saturday night, the season ended on Sunday, and on Sunday I played every position on the diamond. Because I had played as a utility man. I didn't play regular. I was just a fill in player at this point. I was no longer a prospect per se.

What are you getting paid to play B ball in 1957?

I was getting $450 a month, and you only get paid for the five months that you played. I poured concrete in the off season, so I could afford to go play baseball in the summer. I was married and had one child when I started in '54. By '57 I'm raising five kids., and I'm fighting Lee MacPhail all the way.

I'd always hold out, send back two or three contracts. So then in '58, they didn't have a place for me in their organization. I wanted $600 a month, and they said, "There is no place for you, but we'll send you down to Monterrey in the Mexican League, a Cincinnati club for their spring training in Laredo, Texas."

Which is the armpit of the world.

In 1958 I took a train from Springfield, and I go to join the Monterrey club. The Cincinnati organization is all fucked up. Gabe Paul and Mc-Kechnie Jr. were running the team. There was no organization down there.

I got down there, and Reggie Otero is the manager of Monterrey. Nobody knows who I am. I'm from the Yankee chain. They have a big hospital, a place where the teams live. Even Seattle is down there.

I go find a room and a bunk. I get in line for breakfast. Nobody knows anything. I know I'm supposed to have a Monterrey contract. It's unsigned. I take one look at the Monterrey team, and everyone speaks Spanish, and I don't.

"The hell with this," I said, and I went over and started working with Albuquerque. I start taking ground balls, and they just start assuming that I'm on the roster. I'm making the team as the shortstop, and the owners of the Albuquerque team are real rich people, and they throw a big party for us over the border in Nuevo Laredo, and the writers are writing, and I'm having a good spring, and all of sudden they come to me and say, "Rod, you're not even signed."

"Yeah, I know," I said.

"What are you asking?"

"Six hundred," I said.

Gabe Paul said, "Oh, Jesus, we can't pay you that. We just can't."

"Well, I guess that's it," I said. "You've got to pay my expenses back to Springfield, Missouri."

"Okay," Gabe said, "Come in in the morning, and we'll have your ticket back to Springfield."

I went out that night and had a few cocktails. I came in after curfew, and Gabe Paul happened to be walking in, and we started chatting. We went into his office. I started telling him my philosophies of playing baseball.

I told him I always hit behind the runner, always gave myself up, but that if I ever had a kid, I'd tell him, "Look out for yourself and forget about that team play, cause it doesn't get you anywhere."

The next morning I was in line eating, and before I could catch my train out of there, Gabe said, "Rod, are you still the ballplayer you were last night?"

I laugh and said, "Yeah, what do you mean?"

Gabe said, "I just talked to Dallas of the Texas League, and they'll sign you on a ten-day look, and if you make it they'll give you the $600 you're asking for. They are opening in Austin tomorrow. If you're interested, here's your ticket."

I joined Dallas, the last of the good old Texas League. It was an Independent, owned by a guy named J.W. Bateman, who was a big contractor. George Schepps was the general manager.

I went there, and I'm sitting on the bench, and Davey Williams from the New York Giants is the manager. Jackie Robinson had busted him up. Freddie Martin, an old-time pitcher, was on the team, and Tommy Carroll was their shortstop. Tommy was from Notre Dame, and he had size 12 feet.

I sat for two days.

I went to Davey Williams and said, "I'm on a ten-day look, and two of those days are gone. I need to play."

Davey played me for three days at shortstop, and I made the play in the hole and got some hits, and looked pretty good. And then it started raining, and it rained for five days. They had seen me for three days, and they decided to sign me, so I ended up at Dallas, and I played shortstop.

We had a centerfielder by the name of Sam Suplizio, who was supposed to take Joe DiMaggio's place in center field. Sam Suplizio had a great year at Binghamton and was dubbed "the next center fielder for the Yankees."

At Binghamton he had gone into a fence and wrecked his throwing arm. Well, Sam was playing center field for Dallas, hanging in there. He had a big family, and he got a sickness like jaundice, and so they put me in centerfield, and I ended up hitting .295, making the All Star team, and having a good year.

From that, the Yankees invited me to spring training in '59. I went from thinking I'd be going home from Laredo to going to spring training with the Yankees.

George Schepps, the Dallas general manager, thought that because they were an independent team that they owned me. But then he found out from Cincinnati that I was just on loan to Cincinnati, so I wasn't a free agent. Lee MacPhail didn't let me go. I still belonged to the Yankees.

I went to spring training in '59 and had a pretty good spring. Casey played me. He moved me to second. I went to Richmond. Steve Souchock, a big, good-looking guy, was the manager. Jack White was the general manager.

I went there, and going north, the Yankees play us in Richmond, and I got a couple hits off Jim Coates, which was good. I expected to play, but they had a second baseman named Curty Roberts, who was a great Triple A second baseman, and Deron Johnson was on the team, and Dick Sanders. We had a pretty good team.

We go on a road trip, but I'm not playing regular, and between innings in Buffalo I warm up Bob Wiesler, a lefthanded pitcher, and he throws the slider, and I split my middle finger of my right hand.

They are going from Buffalo to Havana. I missed the Havana trip. That was the last team that went into Havana. I missed the Havana trip. I didn't get to see Superman. [See the movie *The Godfather* to see Superman.]

I had this busted finger, and they sent me back to Richmond. I'm at Richmond with this knocked-down finger, and Jerry Coleman is in the front office with the Yankees, and he calls and says, "We want you to go to Binghamton."

I had hit .295 in Double A. And this is the mistake I made in the Yankee chain. I refused to go to Binghamton.

Coleman wanted me to go to Binghamton so he could teach me to be a slap hitter, and I said, "Coleman, last year at Dallas I had 165 hits and 200 total bases, and you're going to teach me to be a slap hitter?"

What's he going to teach me? But that sealed my destiny with the Yankees. Jack White said, "You just stay here. I'll make sure you get paid, and we'll see what happens."

He got me a job with Houston, which was now Triple A in the American Association. Houston was independent. Marty Marion owned the club. This was when the Continental League was going to come in, and Branch Rickey was developing it, and they thought Houston and Dallas were going to be part of the Continental League.

I went to Houston in '59 and finished up. Roy Smalley was on the team, and so were Tom Poholsky, Ray Noble, and Jim Fridley. Dick Sanders ended up there, Dick Cole. Del Wilber. Rube Walker was the manager.

They fired Rube Walker midseason. Spec Richardson was general manager. The owner was Marty Marion, and they fired Rube, and Del Wilber took over for the last month or two. They released Roy Smalley, and he went up to Minneapolis, where Gene Mauch was managing, and they are brothers in law.

Anyway, I ended up at Houston, played well but didn't hit good, so in '60 I went down to Lake Wales, and they didn't know whether I was under a Denver contract or on a Richmond contract. I ended up with the Amarillo Gold Sox, and I was there a month when Dallas/Fort Worth, managed by Jim Fanning, and he had been a coach at Fort Worth and he knew how I could hit, and I went to Dallas, and I didn't hit like I was expected, so they sent me to Nashville. Jim Turner managed Nashville, and I ended up there and hit pretty good at the end of the season. And I'm just hanging on. It's better than doing concrete in the summertime. That was in '60.

In '61 I went to spring training in Ft. Lauderdale. I had that Richmond contract, and I went down to spring training in Ft. Lauderdale. They wanted the Triple A club to go there because they knew the Yankees were going there in '62. And Cal Ermer was the manager, and I'm on the B team, which means you get on a bus and go to Homestead, Lakeland, play all the B teams. You play very few teams in the ballpark there at Ft. Lauderdale, but this was the year of the limbo, '61 in Fort Lauderdale. This was the year of "Where the Boys Are." And all the chicks from up north were coming down. This was the year that started it all. And we stayed at the old Broward Hotel, which was downtown, and my roommate was a guy by the name of George Risley, who went to Boston College and played Triple A ball, and I thought lemonade was the greatest drink in the world, but he introduced me to Cuba Libres. We would work out, and there was a liquor store next to the Broward Hotel. We'd get a pint of rum and a six-pack of cokes, and we'd go up to our room and the glass pitchers were on the dressers in those days, fill that with ice, cut the limes up, and we'd sit there and finish that pitcher of Cuba Libres.

After every workout. And after we finished that, instead of going to dinner, we'd hit the beach. Hell with dinner! We're gone. And then they had those clubs with the midnight licenses like Randy's Roost, Omar's Tent, Elbow Room, the O'Clock club, the Three O'Clock club, Four O'Clock club. I hit them all. But I would get my sleep on that bus going to Homestead or going to Lakeland or going to Vero. Playing all the B clubs. And I had a great spring.

They called me in, and I've always resisted being sent out. Cause I hit well over .300 that spring, had a great spring, and they called me in and they had all the brass there. Ermer was the manager, but they had backup, and they said, "Rod, they want you back in Nashville, and the season starts tomorrow."

I said, "Where's my ticket?"

I gave them no resistance. I needed to get out of Lauderdale! I was beat!

I caught a plane that afternoon and was in Nashville for opening day. We played in Sulphur Dell, the oldest ballpark in baseball. Lyndon B. Johnson, the vice-president, threw out the first ball. He needed a glove, and he used my glove to throw out the first ball.

CHAPTER FOURTEEN

ROD KANEHL

I Was an Original Met

*R*od Kanehl would be the only American League player taken by the New York Mets in the expansion draft before the 1962 season. That may seem odd, but there was a very good reason for that. Casey Stengel, the manager for the Amazin' Mets, knew that Kanehl knew his system of instruction from his Yankee days. He knew that Kanehl would aid him in getting his system across to the others.

⌐

In '61 you had a very good season.

There were only two players who played in every game in the Southern Association, and I was one of them. You'd drive all night to go from Little Rock to Atlanta to play the next day. It was a tough bus league. We had a lot of fun.

I had a good year, hit .305, played every game. Expansion was coming along, and you never know, and that winter I was drafted by the Mets.

The Yankees left me on a Double A roster, so the Mets triple A club, Syracuse, had a partial working agreement with Minnesota, and Minnesota was interested in me because Nashville had a partial working agreement with Minnesota, and when Syracuse drafted me, Minnesota assumed it was for them, but it was actually for the Mets. The commissioner had to make a ruling. The Yankees had put in a work order for Syracuse to draft me. I had a Syracuse contract when I went to spring training with the Mets in St. Pete in '62.

What was the Mets original training camp like?

It was great. I really enjoyed it. I was the only American Leaguer. I was the only guy out of the Yankee chain, and all the other guys were National Leaguers, because the National League expansion, the only players that were offered were National League players. American League didn't offer them any. There were a few free agents, like Wynn Hawkins, and players who they made deals for. But they didn't know anything about Stengel. There wasn't anyone else out of the Yankee chain in that first Mets camp. I was the only person out of the Yankee chain.

Needless to say, I was coming from Double A, and here were Gil Hodges and Don Zimmer and Roger Craig and Clem Labine and Joe Ginsberg, and Frank Thomas and Richie Ashburn and Gus Bell, and here I am.

Casey knows that I am the *only one* who knows what he's talking about, so when spring training started out, he went through this routine. He wanted to start with the Yankee system.

"Kanehl," he said, "show them how to lead off."

I went down to second.

"Kanehl, show them how to lead off second."

We'd go down to third.

"Kanehl, show them how you take the signs."

We'd go to bunting.

"Kanehl, show them how to bunt."

These guys were veterans I was instructing.

Who's this fucking Kanehl? they were thinking.

They didn't know me from Adam. I was rooming with a guy named Dawes Hamilt. There were some kids, and I was with that group of guys. But everyone

Casey Stengel

else was a National Leaguer. I was the only one out of the Yankee chain, and he was using me as his mouthpiece to show them things.

Back in those days, the optimum word was "Meat."

"Hey, Meat."

Roger Craig was on the mound, and he was supposed to be lobbing the ball in to me to show them how to bunt. Well, he decked me!

He turned one loose and knocked me on my ass!

I jumped up, grabbed the ball, and fired it right back to him.

"Get the ball over, Meat!" I said.

Later Richie Ashburn told me he was wondering, *Who is this brash fuck from Double A ball?*

And so I caught their eye, and then we started playing ball, and during batting practice I'd always work on my skills in the outfield, playing the ball off the bat while these other guys would be standing around, telling war stories about the National League. Ashburn and Gus Bell, Frank Thomas, and Roger Craig were standing in a little circle, and a ball was hit in their direction. I bolted over for it, and I called it, and Ashburn stepped out of the circle and said, "I got it," and he dropped it.

"If you call it, catch it," I said.

That's the way I was. Cause I was out there working, and they were just farting around. Later Ashburn told me, "Jesus Christ, I knew you were going to make it." Ashburn is just as brash as anybody. He loved it. *Loved* it.

I didn't give a shit. I was 28 years old. I either make it, or it's all over and I go home.

I made the ballclub. We broke camp and went north, and I still had a Syracuse contract. At the last minute, the Mets sent Joe Christopher to Syracuse, and that made room on the roster for me. But Ted Lepcio was penciled in for utility. They assumed he was going to be the utility man. I could also play outfield, and I could bunt better and probably hit a little bit better.

Rogers Hornsby was a coach in '62. What are your memories of Hornsby?

He didn't have much to do with slap hitters. He was just a figurehead. He sat on the bench, and he would make comments about hitting, but he didn't coach anybody. Nobody could hit like Hornsby, and Casey would tell us that.

Hornsby's theory of hitting was to hit up the middle. Casey's theory of hitting was to put the ball down the lines. Here's Casey's thinking: Where do they put the worst ballplayers? On the corners and in right and left field.

"Why hit to the best players on the diamond, which are the pitcher, catcher, shortstop, second base, and centerfield?" Casey said. "Why play with them?"

Hornsby would say, "Hit up the middle."

Casey held a meeting one time, and Hornsby wasn't there, and he said, "Hornsby preaches, hit up the middle, but Hornsby could hit up the middle because he could hit home runs hitting straight away. He could do it. If you guys show me that you can do that, you hit up the middle."

Casey was a very observant person. He was very practical. In spring training that first year in '62 I heard him tell Ray Daviault, "You were 5 and 13. You don't have a third pitch. You don't have a change-up. If you had a change up, you might have won three more games than you lost instead of being 5 and 13. You'd have been 8 and 10, and instead of making $20,000, you'd be making $30,000."

Casey put things in dollars and sense.

If you were going to go to a speaking engagement, he'd always ask, "Are you going to get paid for this? If you get paid, go. If not, tell them no."

I never saw him purposely put a player in a position where he would look bad. Cause Casey always tried to create a value. He would put marginal players, players he knew they were trying to get rid of, in positions to look good. He wanted to make them look good, never made them look bad. He always tried to increase your value.

A lot of people say, "Casey won because he had all those great players." Well, he developed those great players through the organization, and he kept young blood coming all the time.

It's not easy to sit there and deal with a catcher who can't speak English or a temperamental centerfielder in the wane of his career. He brought in young blood and platooned Hank Bauer and Gene Woodling and dealt with all those personalities. He dealt with Whitey Ford and the carousing without ruining a team. It took some talent for him to deal with all of that.

In a spring training game, late in the game you pinch hit against Sandy Koufax.
That was the hit that cinched my making the ballclub in '62.

Tell me about that day.
It was the first ballgame televised back to New York. It was between the Mets and the Dodgers. In the spring of '62. I sat down in the bullpen of Al Lang all day, and there were two outs in the last of the ninth inning and runner on second. Koufax was pitching, and there were shadows coming across between the pitcher's mound and the catcher. It was pretty tough, and he's tough anyway.

The game was about over, so I inched up going from the bullpen to the dugout, cause you want to race to get cabs back to Miller Huggins field.

I reached the dugout.

"Kanehl, get a bat," Casey said.

I get a bat and go up, and Koufax threw one right down the middle. I didn't even see it. Strike one. He threw another one. Strike two. I haven't even moved my bat.

"Butcher boy, butcher boy," Stengel starts hollering.

I knew that meant to swing down and try to hit the ball.

I was striding as the guy was releasing, and it was going to be high, so I checked my swing, and it was this big curveball, and the ball hit my bat, and I hit a line drive between Ron Fairly and the right-field line, a double. The ball was hit between the first baseman and the bag. It had eyes. I ended up on second base, and it tied the game.

Felix Mantilla was the next hitter, and he got a base hit, and I scored the winning run. And that was it.

I made the team. I became a hero in New York, and that killed George Weiss. George Weiss never did like me. He always wanted to get rid of me, and now he couldn't. Cause all of New York was asking, *Who is this guy?*

On the front page of the *Daily News* was a picture of Stengel with his hat pulling me out of it like a rabbit.

Weiss didn't like Billy Martin either.

For the same reason. Neither one of us looked like we had any talent, but we won ballgames. We did things, and we always made Casey look good.

I got a few hits, and the San Francisco Giants came to town. There are 50,000 people at the Polo Grounds, a Sunday doubleheader, and Gil Hodges has a bad knee and can't play. Billy Pierce is pitching for the Giants, so Casey comes to me and says, "Can you play first?"

You know you gotta say yes. You're a utility man, right?

I had never played first in my life, except for goofing around the infield.

So I said, "Sure."

"Get a glove," Casey said. "You're in there because Hodges can't play."

This was the first game of the doubleheader. I played first, and I hit a home run off Pierce, and we got beat 6 to 1. In the second game we faced Juan Marichal. Casey's got to play me, so he plays me in right field, and I went 2 for 3 off Marichal, and I was the toast of the town!

Who's this Kanehl? No one had ever heard of me, other than that spring training incident. He played me or pinch ran me, and I scored the tying run, and then I have to go play somewhere, and I was in the top ten hitters in the league up through June. I was hitting over .300, but I had only been up a hundred times. They were touting me for rookie of the year, and when I started reading that, then I went to hell!

Tell me about the ticker tape parade that they scheduled.

That was wonderful. See, we opened up in St. Louis, and then when we came back from St. Louis, they had that ticker tape parade, and it was great. We ended up at City Hall, and Mayor Wagner was on the steps, and he gave Casey the key to the city. It was quite an experience.

Don Zimmer was the first third baseman for the Mets.

Yes, on opening day this was in St. Louis, Zim was at third, and Mantilla was at short, and Charlie Neal was on second, and Gil Hodges was on first. In the outfield were Gus Bell, Richie Ashburn and Frank Thomas. Roger Craig pitched, and Hobie Landrith caught. Hobie was the first Met player taken in the expansion draft.

The Mets spring training record was pretty good. When the season started were you hopeful?

As a team we were full of confidence, but we had absolutely no pitching. We probably had one of the finest relief pitchers in the National League as a starter, Roger Craig. He would have set all kinds of relief records had he been able to be used as a reliever. He was a good five-inning pitcher, and he had a good pickup move. He was perfect for relief. He had a good sinker/slider. He could come in and get the ground ball, and boom, it's over. He would have been a tremendous reliever. But we had to use him as a starter. We had Vinegar Bend Mizell! We had Roadblock Jones. Clem Labine was there maybe a week. He and Joe Ginsberg left about the same time.

Don Zimmer went 0 for 34.

He couldn't buy a hit, and we traded him to Cincinnati. We got Hawk Taylor and the left-handed Bob Miller.

Talk about the skill of the infielders.

Gil Hodges couldn't cover any ground. Charlie Neal was a good second baseman. Felix could play and Elio Chacon could play. They all could play. We could all play. But then Charlie got hurt. He had a bad hand, a bone spur, so I started playing regularly at second base, and when he got well, they put Charlie at short, and I continued to play second. Charlie and I made more double plays in a six-week period than anybody who had ever made double plays before. We turned them, and we had a lot of pride and confidence in making the double play. I was hitting good and playing a regular second base, and Charlie was playing short. But we just didn't have any pitching. And we had no bullpen.

We would be in the game through the sixth or seventh inning, and then it was over. But Casey had the knack, you know the "Let's Go Mets" thing.

We were in a lot of games until the ninth inning, and he always had Hodges or Woodling or Snider to send to the plate to give the people hope. They would have to hit a home run to win it or tie it. Snider did it a couple times. Marv Throneberry hit home runs in the ninth inning to win games a couple of times.

Casey was good at having the right guy at the plate. We got Gene Woodling and Marv Throneberry from Baltimore for Hobie Landrith and Harry Chiti. A lot of people think Throneberry was one of the originals, but he arrived in May, and he didn't even play in '63. People think Throneberry was forever a Met.

Marv got to play because Hodges was in bad shape.

And because he was left-handed. We had Jim Marshall and Eddie Bouchee, but they left early.

Tell me about Gil Hodges.

Gil Hodges was a friend of mine. We were teammates just that '62 year and the first part of '63. We would sit around, because we talked baseball. I was one of those guys who would sit in the locker room and talk baseball with Zimmer, Ashburn, and the guys.

I'd refer to my father as "my old man." Gil pulled me off to the side and he said, "Ron, when you're around me, never refer to your father as your 'old man.' Always refer to him as your father." That's the kind of guy Hodges was. The phrase bothered him as being disrespectful. He just didn't like to hear it.

When we'd go to Pittsburgh, we'd leave out of Newark airport, and we'd fly the Caravelle, a short-hop plane. We were leaving out of Newark. Casey called him "Gilly," so people started calling him "Gilly."

As we were boarding, people were saying, "Good luck, Gilly," and my son Phil, who was eight or nine at the time, said, "Good luck, Gilly," and they shook hands.

We got on the plane, and we got airborne, leveled out. Hodges came over to me and said, "Don't you think your son ought to call me Mr. Hodges?"

My son could only come in the clubhouse after the game if we won, so we got back home and it was two or three weeks before we won a game again, and I watched as Phil came into the locker room at the Polo Grounds, and he walked straight to Gil, and he said, "Nice game, Mr. Hodges."

Gil looked and me and winked. Hodges loved those things.

The team started off losing the first nine games. At 0 and 9, is this a bad omen of things to come?

No. No no. We just didn't get off the ground. We were in a lot of those games.

You are still upbeat?

Oh yes.

And Stengel is still upbeat?

Oh yes. He's leading the parade down Broadway. If it wasn't for him, we would have been buried. What he did was keep the writers off our backs individually. They could write all the bad things they wanted collectively, but Casey wouldn't let them pick on individual players.

What would Casey do?

I think he must have made an agreement with them early in the season. Or it just evolved that way that,

"You can write all the bad things about the team collectively. We all know we're short-handed, that we have a lot of inexperience here," he told them.

We started with nothing but veterans, because that's what George Weiss wanted. He wanted to attract the National League crowd, and Casey didn't want that at all. Once the older players were gone, there was nothing but Dick Smith and castoffs from other clubs.

I was hitting .330, and this was in May. I went up to Casey at his office in the Polo Grounds, and I said, "I'm hitting .330, leading the team in hitting. How come I'm not playing regularly?"

Casey asked me how much I was making.

"Eight thousand," I said.

"You're not making enough to be playing regular," he said, "I'm going to give the Old Man upstairs the walking dead til he's sick of it."

Casey meant he was going to play these old guys until Weiss said, "Okay, let's start playing some young guys." This was in May.

Hodges went down, and then Zimmer was gone. We traded Bell to Milwaukee. We got Hawk Taylor, a catcher, and pitcher Carlton Willey in that deal. And we got another outfielder.

Before the season was over, Casey started playing young guys, but we didn't have any prospects. In '63 Solly Hemus had scouted Ron Hunt, and we signed Hunt. He was out of the Cardinal chain. Buddy Harrelson came in spring training. Ron Swoboda arrived in spring training.

We signed Ed Kranepool the first year. He was right out of high school. He just came up, and then he went out. He came back up at the end of the year.

Eddie was brash. He was cocky. He was a New Yorker, and he knew he was going to make it, because they gave him a lot of money.

He went to James Monroe High School and had a good high school career. He came over to take batting practice with us for a look, and he hit balls out of the park. He hit the shit out of the ball.

Everybody thought he was going to be a big home run hitter. I was in the on deck circle when he got his first base hit. We sent him out to Syracuse, and the second year it was Buffalo, and at the end of the season he came up and got a little slap hit into centerfield. And that's the way he hit. He was a slap hitter all the way. He was all right. He lasted a long time.

Tell me about Throneberry and Ashburn and their routine.

If it wasn't for Ashburn, Throneberry never would have been as famous, because they lockered next to each other, and Marv would make a boo-boo or whatever he did.

Anyway, the writers would come in, and Ashburn would say to them, "Throneberry said, 'blah blah blah blah,'" and they would quote Throneberry, but it was Ashburn's glibness that put the words in Throneberry's mouth.

Jim Hickman and Throneberry didn't talk much.

No. No no. Hilly Billy. I had played with Hickman in '60. I've known Hickman a long time. They don't talk much. Oh, Hickman was miserable in New York. His wife was miserable. His kids were miserable, and it was miserable.

He and I lived in the same apartment building in '63. It was over in Jackson Heights by the Motor Inn. I lived there with Galen Cisco, Tim Harkness, and Al Moran. We lived in this fourplex. We owned it.

We were still playing in the Polo Grounds. But Hickman couldn't stand it. And Casey couldn't get him motivated. The guy looked like he was going to sleep all the time. But when he popped it, the ball jumped off his bat. He had a live bat. But he was a straight away hitter, and the Polo Grounds was not his ballpark.

When he went to Wrigley Field, he went crazy. But before he got to Wrigley Field, he went to the Dodgers, and he couldn't hit with the Dodgers. They put him on the mound. He had a great arm. He pitched an inning or two with the Dodgers.

I was living in LA at the time, in the late 60s. He then went to the Cubs, and in '69 he had a great year. He was a country boy, and he was in the city.

So was Throneberry. At one time Marv was supposed to be the next Lou Gehrig on the Yankees.

Let me tell you. He had this brother, Faye, who played with Boston a little bit, and at that Yankees rookie camp in '54, he was there. Marv was agile, and he bounced around, and he looked good, and he wore the cuffs of his pants just like Mickey. He had power and was going to be IT.

Well, Marv spent all his time in the minor leagues. He drove in 150 runs at Denver, hit 45 home runs. He did this two or three years in a row. Look up his record. He spent his better years in the minors, and then he went to Baltimore, and for five years he sat on the bench behind Jim Gentile. When he came to the Mets, they expected him to play. He never was twinkletoes, but he always looked good in the lobby!

Marv was a country boy, but he had the taste of the big city. He loved New York.

Was he perplexed how he became the symbol of the Mets?

Ashburn schooled him on the fact.

"Accept the notoriety, good or bad," Richie told him.

I roomed with Marv in '62. He didn't take it badly. He did *not* take it badly. He was a celebrity, and he liked his celebrity, and he got along with it. He signed autographs. Mentally he was in good shape.

I heard a great story about him with the Miller beer ad. He was broadcasting games down in Memphis for the Chicks, and they said, "We want you to come to New York and make this commercial." He laughed and hung up the phone. He thought this was a prank. They had to call him *three* times before they could convince him that they weren't kidding.

Marv got a lot of his notoriety from that Miller ad. That brought him back. That's why a lot of people think he was around a long time.

The newspaper stories about Marv had to do with throwing errors and his base running errors. Once he let Stan Musial go home on a rundown.

I was involved in that. It happened. Sometimes you get caught in a situation where there's a point of no return. You have to let the guy go. Marv was unconscious that way. The things that he did were magnified, but then he won some games for us with dramatic home runs. And Marv was a great guy. He was like a teddy bear. He would laugh it off. He laughed off the criticism. He would hear the fans saying, "Raspberries, strawberries, Throneberry."

You know I hit the first grand slam in Mets history, and the first banner ever flown in the Polo Grounds said, "We love the Mets. Hot Rod Kanehl."

I was on the bench, and Richie Ashburn called me over, and he said, "What did you pay those kids?" The banner was hanging up in the deep left field upper deck in the Polo Grounds, right in the corner where it turns. It was about a month into the season.

In May, the Mets won 9 of 12 games.

We beat Cincinnati, and we beat the Braves.

Right after that you went on the road and lost 17 in a row.

We lost in the most improbable ways. We hated to go into LA. We couldn't beat LA. Maury Wills would drive us crazy. Stengel used to get up on the bench and holler at our catcher, Chris Cannizaro, "Throw it to third," meaning if Wills attempted to steal second, just throw it to third. Instead of throwing it into centerfield, so he ends up on third.

Mets fans at Shea Stadium

I don't know how many times that would happen. Cannizaro would hurry the throw. Stengel said, "Throw it to third."

It wasn't a joke. He meant it.

Solly Hemus, our coach, was great. Solly was one of the hardest working coaches I've ever seen. He never gave up. He was always helping, throwing batting practice. If you wanted to take extra batting, he'd come out in the middle of the day.

Red Kress was great. He died that winter. He and Hornsby died that winter.

On June 30, Koufax pitched the first of his no hitters.

I played in that game.

He struck out Ashburn, you and Felix on nine pitches to start the game.

But I got on base in the ninth inning. I forced somebody, who had walked. Gene Woodling was the last out. He went crazy when Casey called him up to pinch hit. They almost had a fight on the bench. His being left-handed, Gene called him every name in the book for sending him up against Koufax.

"You got young, righthanded guys, and you're sending me up, you no good . . ."

I was on first base. I could hear every word.

And he struck him out, and that was the end of it.

On August 7, the Mets were eliminated from the pennant. They were 29 and 82.

It was the first week of August. We were in LA, and Casey called a meeting and said, "Now guys, you can relax now. We're mathematically eliminated from the pennant race."

He was half joking. But he called a meeting for it.

"You can loosen up now, and start playing games."

And so we loosened up, and we won 11 more games in the last two months!

Richie Ashburn quit to take a lower paying job as a broadcaster.

He hit over .300. Richie would get on the pitchers. He'd say, "I'd be leading the league if I got to face you guys."

Richie was the greatest. His last play in the big leagues, he was the third out of a triple play. We were in Chicago, and it was a Saturday game. It wasn't even the last game of the season. He was on first, and Sammy Drake was on second, and Ken Hubbs was playing for Chicago. Joe Pignatano hit a looper over Hubbs, and he caught it running away, and he turned and threw to second and got Drake for the second out, and then they threw back to first to get Ashburn for the third out.

He had that little come-up slide. He popped right up, and our dugout was right there. He took two steps into the dugout, grabbed his glove, and he said, "That's a fine fucking finish to this year. I'll see ya next year."

He went right on up the ramp. That wasn't the ninth inning. By the time the game was over, he was packed and gone. We thought we'd see him the next spring, but we never saw him again. That was his last play in the big leagues.

All in all, when the final game ends at the end of '62, are you okay with all of this?

I was going good in the first part of August, and they were talking Rookie of the Year, but then I didn't play a whole lot after that. My knee started acting up, and that had something to do with my bat too.

It was a long season. I was worn down. We ended up playing in front of 300 people in Chicago. Bob Miller finally won a game, and all the writers had gone to the track! There was a big horse race, and this was the next to last game of the season. Miller wins it, and there are no writers.

"All year every time I'd lose a game, ten writers would want to know what went wrong," he said. "Now I win the game, and there's nobody here."

Bobby is a great guy. He took it well.

Was there anybody you could think of who didn't?

Jim Hickman, but it wasn't the losing. He wasn't doing good, and he hated New York. And he took the criticism personally. He'd get his dauber down. He'd duck writers. He hated writers.

Charlie Neal wasn't a happy camper, but I don't think he was ever happy. I played with him in '65 in Wichita, when we won the national semi-pro tournament. We won the nationals in '65. He was always grumbly.

Frank Thomas loved New York. He was happy there. Ashburn was all right. He just hated to lose, but he got a lot of notoriety and press that he never got in other places, and he survived because he was the sportsman. Roger Craig survived. And McKenzie was a winning pitcher in '62. Jay Hook didn't take it too well, and Craig Anderson, Ray Daviault, and Bob Morehead didn't survive. Jay Hook didn't survive. He had a great arm. He threw some of the longest balls I've ever seen thrown. He would throw them, and Willie Mays would hit them into the lights in left center at the Polo Grounds on the dead fly. Frank Howard would hit golf-ball-like balls. Elio Chacon jumped for a ball at the Polo Grounds one time at short, and it hit off the Listerine sign in left center!

There's only three balls ever hit into the centerfield bleachers in the Polo Grounds, and I saw two in consecutive nights. Before '62, Joe

Adcock had hit a ball into the centerfield bleachers against the Giants. The Braves were in town against us, and Hank Aaron hit one. The Braves left town the next day the Cubs come in, and Lou Brock hit one. Those are the only three ever hit, and two of them were on consecutive nights!

Brock's home run was one of the longest balls ever hit anywhere.

That ball was high and dead-center and just off from the steps and went over the green background where Mays made that catch. That was a great trade the Cubs made with the Cards.

In '63 the Mets added Duke Snider to your team. Were you impressed with having Snider on the team?

When he joined us, he came over to the club and he made the statement that he was "happy to end my career here," that he was "looking forward to playing for Stengel."

"It's a wonderful deal," he said.

And he didn't do for shit. He hit two or three home runs and struck out a lot.

I remember he won one game with a home run in the ninth.

Yes, he did. He popped it, big time. That was early, when he first got there.

We got Harkness and Burright in 1963. That's when I thought I was going to have the second base job, but I had had a knee operation in the offseason. So they got this guy Schreiber out of the Boston chain, and they got Burright, and Al Moran was at short. Felix was gone. They got Cook. He had a back operation. Team doctor Peter Lamont liked to cut on everybody. He did a lot of chopping.

Chacon was gone. It was Al Moran at short. When did Roy MacMillan come? He must have been there in '63. Our first legitimate prospect was Ron Hunt in 1963. We had a shortstop out of the Dodger chain, Chico Fernandez. He got the last hit in the Polo Grounds.

I got the last pinch hit.

Anyway. Things really disintegrated in '63.

[The Mets' record in 1963 was 51–111.]

⟳

Kanehl had a lifetime .241 average, hit six home runs, and had 47 RBIs. As Kanehl explained, he was not invited to spring training after the 1964 season, and when the Yankees offered him a coaching job, Mets general manager George Weiss refused to free him from his Mets contract. He worked in construction, sold insurance, and for a time owned a restaurant. He was the only Met to attend Stengel's funeral, and after suffering a heart attack, on December 14, 2004, he died in a hospital in Palm Springs, California, at age seventy. For Mets fans of a certain age, he will always be their first hero, Hot Rod Kanehl.

CHAPTER FIFTEEN

DOCK ELLIS

A Life on the Edge

*C*hanges in one's life can come out of the blue. In the summer of 1989, I was living in Ridgefield, Connecticut, a bucolic, lovely little town about an hour out of New York City.

I left my driveway and drove down the hill into town for breakfast. Afterward I stopped and bought a USA Today newspaper. I don't know why. I rarely read it. After I got home, I opened to the sports section, and in the middle of one of the sports pages was a small ad asking retired former major-league baseball players over the age of thirty-five who wanted to play a four-month season that winter in sunny Florida to apply. The ad included a phone number.

What a great idea, *I thought*. It'll be like senior golf. It'll also give those former major leaguers a chance to compete once again on a high level. *My other thought:* This will make for a wonderful book. *I had spent the 1985 season with Davey Johnson and the New York Mets, so I knew what the secret life of professional ballplayers was all about. It was a terrific experience, and I wanted to do it again.*

I dialed the number. A man by the name of Jim Morley answered the phone. He said the league would consist of eight Florida teams in such cities as Miami, Port St. Lucie, Winter Haven, Bradenton, Ft. Myers, Orlando, and St. Petersburg. The season was to start on November 1 and continue through the month of March.

Morley, a young real estate mogul from Denver, was excited that a journalist was showing interest in his baby.

"I'd like to pick one of the teams to hang out with and write about," I said.

"We're meeting next month at the Breakers Hotel in Palm Beach," Morley said. "Come to the meeting and pick the team you want to spend the season with."

I flew to Palm Beach and attended the meeting. The West Palm Beach Tropics were owned by John Henry, later the owner of the Boston Red Sox. The Tropics would be managed by Dick Williams, who had led Oakland to a number of pennants. On the team would be former Mets slugger Dave Kingman; pitcher Rollie Fingers, who had played under Williams in Oakland; and outfielders Ray Burris, Rodney Scott, and Jerry White, all of whom had played for Williams at Montreal in 1981.

I told the PR guy of the Tropics that I wanted to spend the season with his West Palm Beach team. I told him where I was staying in case he had any questions. I then went to see a real estate broker. Sight unseen I rented a home on Fisher Island for $2,000 a month for three months and left a deposit.

When I got back to my motel, I was handed a message at the deck.

The message was from the Tropics PR guy. It said he had changed his mind. The year before I had written Personal Fouls, a book about the unethical way basketball coach Jim Valvano ran his team at North Carolina State. Valvano was fired as both athletic director and coach after the book came out. The Tropics PR guy said he was a close friend of Valvano's. He said he wanted nothing to do with me.

In a state of panic I immediately called Jim Morley to tell him what had happened.

"Is there another team I can spend the season with?" I asked.

"Why don't you spend it with my team, the St. Petersburg Pelicans?" he said.

On such shifts of fortune are lives (mine) changed irrevocably.

My wife and I, along with our two-year-old son Charlie (named after Casey Stengel), and our two dogs, German shepherd Sparky (named after Sparky Lyle) and our Great Dane Mickey (named after Mickey Mantle), drove from Ridgefield, Connecticut, to St. Petersburg, which is on the west coast of Florida. I had never been to that coast. Whenever my family would go to Florida for a winter vacation, we would go to Miami. One year I took tennis lessons *from tennis great Fred Perry at the Diplomat hotel. I loved eating breakfast at Wolfie's on Lincoln Road in Miami Beach.*

To get to St. Petersburg from Connecticut, I drove down I-95 and cut across the state of Florida on I-4 after reaching Daytona Beach. As I drove onto I-275 from Tampa across the Howard Frankland Bridge to St. Petersburg, I had no idea where I was going, but when I saw a sign saying the next exit would be the last one before the Sunshine Skyway Bridge, I got off and found I was headed toward St. Pete Beach.

As I approached St. Pete Beach, a bridge rose to allow sailboats to pass underneath, and from that lofty vantage point I could see the beautiful pink Don Cesar Hotel. The blue of Tampa Bay sparkled in the background. It was October 31, 1989, and it was seventy-eight degrees out.

I'm in paradise, *I thought.*

I booked a room in one of the many motels on Gulf Boulevard. I was scheduled to meet Pelicans owner Jim Morley at nine the next morning at Stengel-Huggins Field before a Pelicans practice. The Pelicans were scheduled the next day to go by bus to Winter Haven to play their first game against the Winter Haven Super Sox, a team mostly of former Red Sox players.

GPS didn't exist, but I was nevertheless able to read my Texaco map to find the Pelicans clubhouse adjacent to the practice field. I sought out Morley and found him talking with manager Bobby Tolan, who had played on five teams but was best known for playing centerfield for the Cincinnati Reds.

"I think we have a problem," Morley said to me. "Have a seat. Bobby wants to talk to you."

Bobby Tolan, who was best known for the bitter fight he had with the Reds front office, proceeded to explain to me in a roundabout way that some of his players were nervous to have a writer who they didn't know in their midst watching their every move. As Tolan was explaining all this to me, his star relief pitcher and pitching coach, Dock Ellis kept circling around me, whispering, "Loser writer. Loser writer." He had a big grin on his face. Ellis, who was famous for having once pitched a no-hitter while on acid, was trying to rattle me. He was succeeding.

"Bobby," I said. "Let me talk to the players. The purpose of this book is to let the world know how wonderful it is to be playing major-league baseball again after being forced to leave the game."

"Come with me," said Tolan.

He led me into the clubhouse, where the players were standing around and sitting in their lockers.

"Men," he said. "This is the guy who wants to spend the season with us. I told him he could talk to you and tell you want he wants to do."

Not a lot was riding on what I was about to say, only the substantial contract offered to me by Birch Lane Press. Like most writers, I wasn't keen about having to give back the money. My heart was thumping, but I was not flustered.

"Gentlemen," I said, looking around the room at the former major leaguers, many of whom I recognized, "This is a book about your love of baseball. It's about your having to leave the game you love and about coming back a second time to play. My intention is for this to be a very positive book about each of you. My promise to you is that after I write the book, if any of you want to see what I wrote, I will show it to you, and I will take out anything you object to."

There wasn't any more to say. I could see a few of the players nodding, but no one said anything to me. One by one the players left the clubhouse, got in their cars, and drove off. Would the players allow me to travel and spend the season with the team?

I had no idea.

The next morning I drove to Al Lang Stadium to meet the team bus going to Winter Haven. I brought my briefcase with my tape recorder and notepad. No one said a word to me. I walked to the back to be as far away from the front door as I could so it would be harder for them to throw me out. The bus drove off. I was on my way.

I spent the first season with the Pelicans team and was befriended by a number of the Pelican ballplayers including Ron LeFlore, who had been rescued from a Michigan prison by Billy Martin; pitchers Milt Wilcox, Jon Matlack, Dick Bosman, and Randy Lerch; and most memorably by Lenny Randle, a colorful team leader who had been tossed from the Texas Rangers for punching manager Frank Lucchese in the face after he called Lenny a disparaging slur.

In 1981 I had had a sports talk program on WOR in New York, and as a favor to Jim Morley, I became the color commentator for the Pelicans on WDCR radio. I was the sidekick of Jack Wiers, who had been the play-by-play announcer for the Baltimore Orioles. Wiers and I had the highest-rated radio program during Pelicans games.

The Pelicans won the league championship in the league's only full season. The team they beat for the championship: the West Palm Beach Tropics.

Midway through the season, the Pelicans were playing in West Palm Beach when the PR guy who had rejected me came over and asked if I wished to switch teams in the middle of the season. By then my loyalties to Morley, Tolan, and the Pelicans had been set in stone. I politely declined.

We won the championship on a fine spring evening in Ft. Myers. In the clubhouse we drank champagne and hugged and celebrated. An hour later the players dispersed, leaving a void in the room that left me saddened. Suddenly, the season was over. The camaraderie was over. Only the memories remained.

My family and I drove back to Ridgefield, Connecticut. In June I put our home up for sale, returned to St. Petersburg, and rented the home I am living in today, thirty-three years later.

The Senior Professional Baseball League played a second season in 1990. The owners decided what the league needed to survive were teams in California and Arizona. The cost of the airfare was too much, and on Christmas Day the league folded. Jack Wiers and I hugged, a sad goodbye to what had been a wonderful experience.

You can find some of this material in my book about the Senior League titled The Forever Boys. *The book was my paean to the players of the St. Petersburg Pelicans. Just as I envisioned, each player had a great love of the game and felt privileged to be able to play again. For me, each one of them—every single one of them— was unforgettable, Dock most of all.*

Dock Ellis

Dock was diagnosed with cirrhosis of the liver in 2007. He was on a list for a liver transplant. He suffered from heart damage the last weeks of his life, which ruled out a liver transplant. The great irony was that one of my closest friends on the team turned out to be Dock Ellis. We remained friends until the day he died of heart failure on December 19, 2008, at the age of sixty-three.

I couldn't believe how honest Dock was about his life.

Dock Ellis: Dock was my given name. I don't know where it came from. My father was named Dock. My son is a third. The closest my father came to being a doctor was when he was an orderly in Louisiana. That's where he met my mother. My mother was four-months pregnant with me when they got married, and I was born on March 11 of 1945.

I grew up in Los Angeles. I had just turned seven when I started to play in Little League. We played on the El Segundo playground right behind Centennial High, where Lenny Randle went to school. I played centerfield, and I could throw the ball over the backstop, so they put me on the mound and let me pitch.

The way I am now is the way I was then. I was more excitable when I was younger. Everything about the game was new. It was all new.

I reacted badly when I didn't win, just like I do now. We were taught that you kick ass and take names no matter what. If you kick ass and take names today, you're going to kick ass and take names tomorrow. That's the way we were taught.

I had a lot of confidence in my ability. I always played with the older kids, because I was better than the kids my age.

I was not on the neighborhood team. The guys from my neighborhood told the coach, Mr. Brewer, "You don't want Dock. Dock is a troublemaker." And so he didn't come down the street to get me, the way he went and got Bobby Tolan. Then too, I was always fighting, so I was not on the neighborhood teams. The other guys would always say, "All Dock wants to do is fight and argue."

My attitude was, *Fuck the guys in the neighborhood. I didn't give a shit about them.* I would have to go to other cities to play. It's too bad, because my best friend, Floyd Hoffman, who we called Big Daddy, had to pitch all the time because I wasn't there, and he blew out his arm. Floyd had a better arm than me. He could hit better than me. He could run faster than me. If I had played on that team, you wouldn't be talking to me. Floyd would be the guy you'd be talking to.

When I was 14 I played on a team in Compton, California. I lived in Compton because my mother had a cleaners there and a shop. When I was little I had to live there. It's where I met all the guys on the team.

Our team was 0 and 15. I pitched and lost every game. The team didn't have much talent, but they were friends of mine. They were big guys who wanted to play baseball, but they couldn't play. Only one could play, but he was more or less a gangster, but he could really hit. I'll never forget him. His name was Clyde Gun.

I led the league in ERA. I led the league in home runs and RBIs. In the fifteenth game I got hit in the elbow with a pitched ball. It was the last time I hit right-handed against a right-handed pitcher.

We played outside the stadium at Cressy Park. It's now called Jackie Robinson Stadium. One of my rival players was Don Wilson, who later pitched for the Houston Astros. We both have the same cousin. There were times Don and I almost fought on the field when I was pitching for Pittsburgh. We had a rivalry stemming from childhood. The other kids were always trying to lure me from Mr. Brewer's team to Mr. Wilson's team, because Mr. Wilson had a good team. But Don didn't want me playing on his father's team. But again, all I wanted to do was fight. I fought a lot.

I'd fight over any damn thing.

I was 15 when I played for Mr. Brewer. He had a team made up of teenagers and men, and those men taught us how to play baseball. No matter how hard I threw the fucking ball, they hit it over the fucking fence. We had to come to our senses and say, "Hey, we gotta throw something else." That taught us to throw different things. I faced hitters like Reggie Smith and Willie Crawford and Bobby Tolan. Every time I threw them a fucking fastball, they hit it over the fucking fence.

We had guys who pitched in Triple A. Some who threw against us could have pitched in the major leagues, and we were kicking their ass. Here comes Mr. Brewer and all these little fucking kids. Mr. Brewer was just laying back laughing. We were whipping their ass.

We were a traveling team. We didn't have a home park. We'd go to towns, and we'd start kicking their ass, and they'd turn the lights off. Oh yeah. And white teams wouldn't play us, so Mr. Brewer fixed their ass. Mr. Brewer started getting white players. Bill Rourke, who used to play for Boston, was on our team. We had a dude named Littlewhite, from Arkansas. He should have signed. He never did. He could play some baseball. Willie Crawford and Bobby Tolan were on our team. He has toned down, because he's a manager. But Tolan can be a chickenshit, arrogant motherfucker, a cocky arrogant motherfucker. Like me, but you don't see it as much because of the position he holds. To me he hasn't changed. You don't see that part of him like I do. Sometimes I hear it come out and I say to him, "Man, that shit is coming out now."

He says, "No no no no. I'm being diplomatic."

"I don't know about that," I tell him.

I got my first chance to start when Wendell Jackson got killed. He had signed with the Pittsburgh Pirate organization, went into a restaurant, and a guy from across the street shot him in the head. He sat down at the counter, ordered, and he died. That's when I got the chance to start for Mr. Brewer. The following day I started the game.

Mr. Brewer yelled at me, not like the way the parents yelled at the Little League kids. It was more like, "You gotta know better." Because he talked pitching to me all the time. What he saw in me, more so even than Floyd Hoffman, was himself. He saw him in me and what he could have been had he been as big as Floyd Hoffman. Not as big as me, because I was a little bitty thing. I was five seven. The next year I went to six three.

With Mr. Brewer every game was a championship game, because that's the way he billed it. That's the way he pumped us. I don't remember any regular games.

I pitched for Mr. Brewer many years. I pitched for him when I was in professional ball.

Mr. Brewer worked for Hughes Aircraft. He was a quality control guy. It didn't dawn on me until ten years ago that he quality controlled us the same way.

Chet Brewer

I only played three or four games of baseball in high school. My thing was basketball in high school. I don't know how good I was. I don't know how good I could have been, but I knew I was good. I was the MVP on the team, even though our leading scorer averaged 35 points a game. He couldn't figure out why he wasn't the MVP. But I passed him the ball twenty times a game.

I used to try to make people look like an ass, like Magic Johnson. One of my friends tells me now, "That shit Magic Johnson does, you did that shit when we played."

"Come on, Lenoius," I said, "I don't remember doing that."

"You don't remember it," he said, "because it was natural. The only thing you wouldn't do, you wouldn't shoot the damn ball." Even the guys who used to tell everyone I was a troublemaker begged me to shoot the basketball.

I ended up becoming a baseball player instead of a basketball player. What happened was, when I got ready to graduate from Gardena High School, I had a hell of an era. If I was in the eleventh grade today, I would take college preparatory courses. I know this now. My family didn't know it. No one was counseling me. I have a cousin who became a journalist. He was told this by his instructors in high school. So he knew this, but he didn't pass it on to me. My nieces and nephews today are taking these courses, and they are going on to college. I was not told this.

I went to college, and I got pissed off because they wouldn't give me the courses I wanted to take. I loved history. I was curious about history, because the only black people in books were hanging in trees, and I said, "What the fuck is this?"

I was disrupting the class, and I had to be put out of the class.

I played basketball in college. I saw a couple of the baseball players on the college team had signed minor league contracts. They were going to school, but they weren't going to class. I said, "If you ain't going to class, I ain't going to class."

They got Bs and I failed. So as far as basketball in college, that was that.

I had only played three or four games of baseball in high school, but the scouts had been looking at me since I was 10 and 11 years old. Scouts in California went to Little League games. The community talked, and they'd say, "Let's go check these kids out," and I was one of those kids. We had a kid, John Turok, who threw BBs. He later went to Arizona State. I caught him. The scouts would come to see him, and the following year it was me, and then Don Horn and then Neil Banami and Skip Grafton-reed, and Larry Chastain, a pitcher. Scouts were everywhere.

I played in Gardenia, a white community. The team had two managers, Mr. Abercromby and Mr. Nicholson, Dave Nicholson's father. Kids were calling me "Nigger this," and "Nigger that." The coaches went and got some white thugs, and they said, "We'll give you ten dollars. Go and whip everybody's ass." And they ran them away.

I grew up with the racist shit. It was like Mississippi, only they weren't going to hang me. I found racism in the classroom too. I broke into a teacher's desk and found the IQ scores. My friend Horace Met said, "Look man, we're in the 130s. Look. Look."

"Why didn't she tell us?" I said.

Instead she'd say, "You must study harder. I want you to stay after class. You don't have to, but I want you to."

"Fuck that."

She wanted me to be a writer.

"Nah, nah," I said, "I don't want to be a writer."

Because that's what I was. In the tenth grade I wrote a story about a player who went to USC and the San Francisco Giants. She put that article in something. She was the only teacher who tried to encourage me and my friend Horace Met. We didn't respond because we didn't understand. She didn't sit down and explain it to us. I guess she thought we would comprehend what she was saying. But we didn't. She was the only one. I have a lot of resentments. I deal with that every day.

If I had understood maybe my life would have turned out differently. I can't say no. Maybe. Could have. When I was 35 years old I went back to school. I went to the University of California at Irvine. I was leery about going back to school because I had had so many bad experiences, especially when I went to junior college. I went to lab class, and the first thing I did was look for the housewives, the ones who were there to fuck. I knew what they were there for.

After I took my first couple of tests at UC Irvine, I waited and waited to get the results, and I got A's. What the fuck? So then I just started driving the professors crazy because I wanted to know what the tests were going to be about, what we were going to be graded on, and they said, "The reading."

"How much of this do we have to cover or how much is bullshit?"

I enjoyed it. Then I tried to transfer credits from my continuing education courses at Cal State Dominguez, and they would only transfer a few of them because it was not a Cal State school. I told the lady, "You better get out of here, because I'm going to start throwing chairs."

"Why? Why?" they said.

"Because I'm trying to get into fucking school. Everyone is pushing me into school to take psychology, to make it in psychology, because I'm working for a psychologist. He begging me to train these motherfucking people, to get certified in confrontation, and I'm telling him, 'If you don't give me $5,000 a month, it's your ass.'"

"Okay," she said.

I didn't throw no chairs. I just stood there and cried.

They didn't let me in. I didn't get my degree in psychology. But I don't give a shit. Fuck it.

So many baseball players came from California, guys like Willie Stargell, Frank Robinson, and Bill Russell, guys from northern California who came before us. They had them guys like Vada Pinson who knew how to be quiet. Guys like Rudy May, Curt Motton, and Jerry Royster weren't arrogant like the guys from my era.

We were arrogant and cocky. Even the guys who came after us were cocky. Reggie Smith came from my neighborhood. If we'd have been more like them quiet guys, a lot more guys from our era would have gone into the Hall of Fame. We were all known for being troublemakers, because we didn't take no shit, and we were taught that because of what we saw going on around us. Which was the prejudice. The racism. It was subtle, but it was going on. And so we went into baseball with a chip on our shoulders, and we would dare somebody to touch it.

Every one of us except one. That was Bob Watson. I believe the reason he didn't do it was because he was raised by his grandparents, so he wasn't exposed to street life as much as we were.

I was sheltered but I was wild. There weren't a whole lot of things I could do outside. When the sun was going down and my father drove by when I was growing up, I knew to go home. Even so, I got out and about. How that happened, I don't know. I think it was because I had relatives all over the city, and the gangs knew me from being over there, although I wasn't from there. I was known over here and over there. I was known everywhere. I crossed all turf. Because I had relatives and friends everywhere, no one really knew where I was from.

They still don't know where I was from, even the gangs that I now work with. When they question me about where I grew up, I say, "Well, I was everywhere." They can't believe that. But I was.

I ended up signing with the Pirates from being with Mr. Brewer. Mr. Brewer was a bird dog. He sent in reports about the kids he handled and projected their progress for when they would be ready.

I haven't seen Mr. Brewer in a long time. He's sick, but I don't like the wife he has now, because she's so fucking smart ass. I could be prejudiced because I was in love with his first wife. When I threw my no-hitter, they made me a big plaque, and I presented it to Mr. Brewer. And the next day his wife died.

Mr. Brewer recruited players for the Pittsburgh Pirates, and they didn't compensate him for maybe two or three hundred dollars a month. I remember when we won the World Series, and I saw some motherfuck-er wearing a World Series ring, and I said, "Who the fuck are you?"

He said he was a scout in California.

"A scout in what?" I asked.

"Scouting ballplayers."

"You ain't scouting no ballplayers," I said.

"I know you," he said.

"You don't know me. I ain't seen your fucking face."

"Where is your ring?" I asked Mr. Brewer.

"What ring?" he said.

"Your fucking World Series ring."

I went off right there in our dugout, right there in Dodger Stadium.

"I am not pitching," I said, "until I get back to Pittsburgh, and I don't give a fuck, unless Mr. Brewer gets a ring."

They didn't give him a ring, and I didn't pitch.

When we got back to Pittsburgh, I went to see Joe Brown, our general manager, and I said, "How did all these motherfuckers get World Series rings and Mr. Brewer didn't get one? Take it out of my pay, and buy him a fucking ring."

So he got a ring, but Mr. Brewer was crying, because he said I was jeopardizing the chump change they were giving him.

I was ready to sign when I was coming out of high school. I didn't play in high school because of bullshit. I tried out for the team in the tenth grade. I knew I could play. A kid in the twelfth grade used the word "spear-chucker," and I didn't know what that meant so I asked the kid. I didn't know who he was. He was one of the pitchers on the team. I quit. Then they caught me getting loaded, and they told me they wouldn't kick me out of school if I played baseball.

I played three games in the league and one in the city tournament. After that game the Dodgers signed Rene Lachman and Jim Lefebvre, who I played against, and Dodger scout King Marr came to sign me.

"I'm not signing shit," I told him.

I wasn't leaving home to go to Vero Beach. I didn't even know where the fuck Vero Beach was.

I could have signed with the Dodgers, but I don't know if they could have dealt with me. I wouldn't have fitted their mold. They would have molded me pitching-wise, but they couldn't have controlled me as a person. The way they taught baseball would have been perfect for me, because I would have been easy to teach. But I wouldn't sign with them, and I wouldn't sign with the Cleveland Indians. My friends ran them out of the house when they offered me $12,000.

Mr. Brewer had gotten Ronnie Woods $65,000. We had played against Bob Bailey, and he got $200,000 from the Pirates, and Bob Bailey couldn't hit me with a banjo. So when Cleveland offered me $12,000, to my friends that was an insult. They said, "All right, get the fuck out of here."

Then my father died. He died of a heart attack. Then I got it into my head that I must play baseball because that's what my father wanted me to do. The Pirates came to me knowing this, and they signed me for $2,500.

"Go ahead and sign no matter what," Mr. Brewer said. "That's an opportunity. You can pitch. You say you can pitch. I know you can pitch. You're going to the big leagues, so don't worry about it. Just make them pay later."

I signed a progressive bonus, but he didn't give a shit about that because he knew I was going to progress, and as I progressed, I got more
money and he got more money. And when I got to training camp, I saw
those motherfuckers in camp who couldn't do shit, guys they had given
all that fucking money to, and I went crazy. I cussed those motherfuckers
out.

"Get the fuck out of here. You can't pitch. Go back to Ohio and buy
yourself some popcorn, because you're not going to make any money
playing baseball."

And these hundred-thousand-dollar bonus babies were gone in a year.

I was sent to Batavia, New York, and that was cool. I had seen snow on
the mountains of California, but I had never seen it falling. In the town
there were no more than fifty black people. It wasn't that bad, but I got
into drinking. I really got into drinking. The legal age was 19, and I was
19. When I found that out, I said, "I don't want this beer. I want what
they are drinking at the bar, that green shit." That was crème de mint. Or
a stinger. That's what I started drinking. I really got into drinking.

I really enjoyed it. It just fucked me up.

I was supposed to go to Kinston, North Carolina, but they wouldn't
send me there because it was in the south. They knew if I went there,
somebody was going to kill me. Because during spring training with the
Pirates I had cut a heart into a boy named Shoemaker because he had
called me a nigger. He was a year ahead of me, and I went crazy. He was
almost knocked out, and I cut a heart in him with a knife. I dug into him
and made a heart, and I told him, "The next time it's going deeper."

So they knew not to send me to the South, because they knew what
would happen. When they called me in, I said, "Don't you call me into
no fucking office. Don't say shit to me."

At Batavia, my manager was Gene Baker. I was on a team with a lot of
older guys. I was 19, and they were 25 and 26. I was told the guys in the
league were college All Americans.

One was Jerry Moses.

"Jerry Moses," I said, "you're from Yazoo, Mississippi."

"How did you remember where I'm from?" he asked.

It was because a teammate said to me, "Dock, he's from Yazoo, Mississippi. Do you know where that is?"

"From Mississippi."

The guy who told me that said he was 26 years old.

"He's 26 years old and he's playing D ball?"

"Yes, Dock."

They sent home a player by the name of Melwood Civil after he hit three home runs. He had gotten a large bonus to sign. I said to him, "Man, you may not have a chance to play in the big leagues, but you got more money than the motherfuckers who played in the big leagues."

They sent him home because the Pirates didn't want anyone to draft him. Then they sent me home and told me to tell people my arm hurt from my wrist to my shoulder. They did this to protect me from the draft. So I went home and told everyone I had hurt my arm. When I ran up to Santa Barbara to watch Willie Crawford play, scouts wanted to know what was wrong with my arm.

"I hurt from here to here," I told them, tee hee.

The next year I went to Kinston, North Carolina, high class A ball. They sent a catcher, Elmo Plaskett, to go with me. They told him he was going to catch me and watch me. The first night I was in town I cussed out the police. They wanted to know, "Where are you going?"

"None of your motherfucking business," I said.

"Let me see your ID?"

"For what, motherfucker."

"Boy, where are you from?" they asked.

"California."

"You one of them ballplayers?" they asked.

"Damn right."

He shook his head and called the chief, and when the chief got there, it turned out the chief was the guy who drove the team bus. He drove us from Daytona Beach to Kinston, North Carolina.

There was a lot of name-calling in the stands. One night Charlie Manuel was hitting. We were playing Minnesota in Wilson, North Carolina, and a guy was calling Ronnie Woods "Onionhead." Elmo Plaskett was catching, and he called him "Black Norwegian." And me he called "Step n Fetchit."

I struck Charlie Manuel out, and I dropped my glove, and I gave the guy both middle fingers. The guy who called us names had an arm that was all twisted up. Elmo said to him, "You talking about me, because the nigger almost tore your arm off."

The guy was insulted, and the cops were going to arrest Elmo.

Bob Clear, our manager, told us, "Hurry up and get out of here."

One time Clear called the Pirates on me because I refused to pitch. I had warmed up for the game, and the game was rained out. The next day he wanted me to pitch, and I told him, "I'm not going to pitch. I warmed up yesterday."

"Oh, yeah, you'll pitch."

So I went on the mound and I was throwing meatballs, and he got me out of the game and called the Pirates, saying I was throwing the game.

That year I was 11 and 1. They moved guys like Fritz Peterson up to Triple A, and I didn't get moved, and I went crazy. They then called me to pitch in a charity game for polio in Cleveland—what we called a hypo game—between the Pirates and the Cleveland Indians.

The Indians hitters were saying, "The motherfucker has control. Let's get his ass."

But they couldn't get me, and I knew this. I pitched well for seven innings, won the game, and for three weeks they made me stay in the big leagues just to have me around. They were trying to do shock therapy on me, trying to make me a better ballplayer. They wouldn't let me move up, and they wouldn't send me back to Kinston.

The Pirate hitters didn't want me there, because I had to throw batting practice to them.

"Fuck it," I said, "This is like a game for me. Get in there, mother-fucker, and grab a bat." I said, "There it is, motherfucker. Try to hit it."

"Get that motherfucker off the mound," they were saying after ten minutes. "We want to take batting practice."

They didn't let me pitch. They wouldn't put me on the roster.

"Get me the fuck out of here," I told them. "What the fuck am I here for?"

Finally Harry the Hat Walker, the Pirates manager, said, "Get him out of here." And after three weeks with the Pirates, they sent me back to A ball.

I didn't win two or three games after that. That was disappointing, because I was supposed to move up, but then they called me up to Triple A for the playoffs, and I was pissed.

The following year the same shit happened. I broke out and won eight or nine games in a row for Double A Asheville, and when they wouldn't move me up, I flipped out. I knew the guys in the organization, and I saw who they were moving up ahead of me. I *always* knew who was ahead of me. I always knew who the Pirates had who I could outpitch. They were hoping. I'd tell them, "You can hope all you want. You motherfuckers are going nowhere."

At Asheville I learned the word "jake." Management said I didn't take the game seriously. They said I didn't get mad enough when I lost. That was the way I was taught to play baseball.

In my next game I got beat 1 to nothing, so I thought, *They want me to get mad,* so I kicked the gate down.

They fined me fifty dollars.

"You motherfuckers," I said, "You ain't fining me fifty dollars."

I put the gate back up, and I said, "Put the money back in my check."

Before the season was over, they ordered me to Triple A, but I was in hiding. I was locked in an apartment in Asheville with a woman. I was locked up with her for three days before they could find me, and I didn't give a shit because I had sent my wife to Puerto Rico. I wanted to live there. I had met a lot of Puerto Rican ballplayers, and I wanted to see what the fuck they were talking about. Later on I was called on to play Winter Ball in the Dominican Republic, which was unheard of for a Double A ballplayer. The Pirates sent five Double A players.

So they called me up to Triple A. I had a 42-ounce bat, and I was asked, "What are you going to do with that bat?"

"I'm going to hit with it," I said.

I couldn't hit. I started against the Atlanta Crackers, and in the first game in the first inning, I walked the bases loaded. Larry Shepard, the Columbus Jets manager, came out to the mound.

"When the fuck did you learn how to pitch?" he said.

He made me mad.

"Get the fuck off the mound and watch me pitch, motherfucker," I said.

I struck out the side. One of the batters was Adrian Garrett. I walked in, and Shepard said, "That's it, rookie. Go take a fucking shower."

That was 1966, and I won a game in the playoffs. Toronto won that year. In 1967 Pete Peterson became the Columbus manager.

Columbus wasn't too cool. We had a white dude, Bob Robertson. We had camaraderie from Asheville. If you looked at him, you'd think he was black, and they would not let him and I room together. In the minor leagues management didn't want that shit. They especially didn't want me rooming with Bob Robertson. Bob Robertson was the Great White Hope. He was a power hitter built like Mickey Mantle.

I went cookoo. I went crazy. I wouldn't let anybody near my locker. I watched my own shit. I wouldn't talk to nobody. They sent me back to Double A because my hair was an afro about a foot high.

I couldn't believe these motherfuckers sent me down because of my hair, and when I got to Macon, Georgia, I shaved it off, and right away they told me to come back to Columbus. I told them they could kiss my motherfucking ass, so they said they would fine me every day I wasn't there after two days.

"I'll be there on the third day," I said.

I went back. You are scaring up a lot of shit. On the team I was on at Columbus there were a lot of old motherfuckers coming out of the big leagues who didn't like the shit I was doing or what I was talking about or what I stood for.

Toward the end of the season I was hit by a line drive on my left leg. They didn't do nothing to it. No trainer put ice on it. The doctor didn't look at it, and after about a week's time, I was complaining because it was hurting. When they cut it open, jelly came out. So now we were getting ready for the playoffs. They were trying to get me to pitch, and I said, "No. I can't pitch. My leg is fucked up. But I'll try."

I went to the bullpen and I was throwing BBs.

"Oh, you can pitch," said Ed Hobaugh, one of our pitchers.

"You want me to pitch because you can't pitch, you motherfucker," I said. "You can't pitch, and I ain't gonna pitch."

That was when the Columbus team signed a petition against me. One was Ed Hobaugh. There was a dude named Aker. Ernie Bowman was another one. Freddie Patek was our shortstop. Most of those guys were old. Pedro Ramos was on that team, and he was the one who said to me, "They have signed a petition to get you off the team."

They took me off the team. I just stayed home in Columbus. They went on the road and played and won in the playoffs, and I didn't get my share of the money or nothing. The team then tried to charge me for my hotel bill. That's when I threatened to hurt somebody. They paid the bill, and I got the fuck out of there. And I swore I would get even with every one of those motherfuckers. I told them I would kill them, and in the next few years I got everyone who had played ball on that team with me except Freddie Patek. One time I almost killed Bobby Cox because I thought he was Ernie Bowman. We were playing Richmond, and Cox was the third baseman, and I thought it was Bowman, the shortstop, coming up, and I tried to kill him. I hit his helmet, and I thought I had hit him in the head.

I got everyone on that team except Freddie Patek, and the only reason I didn't get him was that Hal McRae begged me. Patek was with Kansas City. Every time I pitched against Kansas City, he would scratch himself. He knew I was going to try to kill him. Freddie knew me. He knew I wasn't bullshitting.

"Dock," Hal said, "you're a man. That man is scared of you. He is frightened to death. He will not play against you. Let's think about this. This is a man who plays baseball, and at one time you liked him."

Hal went back to Patek and told him, "Dock said to forget that shit." And he was in the lineup. He didn't duck or nothing because he knew if I said it was over, it was over. And he hit two doubles off me. Because he could hit. He could play ball. He was small, but that didn't mean nothing. He was the only one I didn't hit.

Yeah, I broke one guy's arm. I broke another guy's leg. They were in the Baltimore organization. I was with Columbus, and I got them.

Even so, the Pirates knew talent. And I knew my talent. I came to the Pirates in 1968. I knew as long as I could throw, I'd be around, and then that would be that. I told them, "When I can't throw, when this arm can no longer do what you think I can do, I'm gone, and you're going to tell me to kiss my ass. So you can kiss my ass now."

But all those years I was a sick person. I was an alcoholic. All those years I was in Pittsburgh, when I was really the sickest, the only one who could have helped me was Bob Skinner, and he didn't know it.

All players relate to one coach or the manager. Skinner was the coach I related to. Not to say I would have done anything he told me to do, but I would have listened. He could have coerced me into getting some treatment. But again, he didn't know that. He was just a coach. He didn't know I respected him as a coach and as a man. He didn't know I related to him. Today teams have people who try to help players. They instruct them to watch for certain behaviors and know what to say to these guys. He would have been the one who could have gotten to me.

In 1968 the Pirates had to take me. That was because Lord Wick—Dave Wickersham—was gone. We called him Lord Wick because he was a preacher. What happened was, Johnny Pesky was the manager at Columbus, and he asked me to be his big dog every day so I would get to the big leagues.

"What do you mean?" I asked him.

"Be ready to pitch every fucking day," Pesky said.

"All right," I said.

"Take two weeks off," he said. "All I want you to do is pitch batting practice."

So I did. At the start of the season I had a 2 and 1 record and 12 saves. That's fifteen games. We had played nineteen games. And I was called up to the big leagues.

Pesky saw the coming of a new era. He knew the kind of guys us kids were. He knew we were together as a team. He knew what had happened to me and what happened to other players, and he would talk about that.

"That shit will not go on here," he said. "We are going to kick ass and take names."

And that's what we did. In two years he lost his whole team. Everyone was in the big leagues.

And they never brought him up. I don't think Johnny fit the Pirate mold. He could have taken those guys to a championship, but he couldn't because Danny Murtaugh had them. Murtaugh saw a world championship, and he wanted to be part of it. He had served his time to get that. He had been a special assistant who had said, "Send Dock here, and send Al Oliver, and send Dave Parker, and send Freddie Patek." He had a lot of input, and he said, "I'm going to manage."

My first year in Pittsburgh was 1968. The Pirates finished sixth. It was an old team, and I said to anybody in the clubhouse, "You motherfuckers are not going to be around here. You motherfuckers are gone." Because I knew what was behind me. I knew what was coming. Guys like Donn Clendenon, with his intellectual way, would say, "The kid knows what he's talking about, but he's still a motherfucking asshole."

Clendenon was another one who tried to keep me down. He'd say, "You can do all that shit, but you have to be diplomatic."

I'd say, "Man, get the fuck away from me."

I didn't know what guys like Elroy Face and Jim Bunning were thinking. Bunning was still a good pitcher, but he was high-handed.

When I met him, he told me, "You can't make the club."

"Man, fuck you," I said. "Who the fuck are you anyway?"

I didn't give a shit.

He still thought he was 19.

I said to him, "Man, when I get to be your age, I'm not going to pitch like I was 19."

I used to keep an eye on the other players. I had some women, white women, who would tell me what the guys would say when they were around them. That's how I knew what was going on. I'd send these women over to find out. I said, "Let them think they're going to get some pussy. Get them talking so I know what's going on."

Steve Blass appreciated my talent. Blass also could see what was happening. He was a little ahead of us. He had some experience, and he would share that.

Bill Mazeroski sat on the fence. He saw shit happen, but Maz was the type of guy who didn't say much, but whatever he had to say, he would tell you straight up. He wasn't one to talk behind your back.

Maury Wills was in another world. You never saw him except at the ballpark, and then he wasn't there. He used to try to keep me down. He and Willie Stargell, but it was useless. Roberto Clemente just cussed me. He used to try to explain to me how I could get things done, to do it through the Galbreaths, who owned the team, but I would tell him, "I'm not Roberto Clemente. I'm not going to talk to them like you or listen to them like you."

"Fuck you," he'd say, "you motherfucking rookie. You know what I'm talking about."

"Yeah," I'd say, "I know what you're talking about, but I ain't going to do it."

I don't talk about him, because I have it here [his head] and here [his heart], where it stays.

Roberto Clemente

The Pirates got rid of Al Mc-Bean because they thought he was a bad influence on me. Which was nonsense, and they got rid of him. I go see McBean every year.

I got really pissed when they brought Bob Moose up. He was only 19. I was supposed to come up when I was 19, but they said they had a policy not to bring up 19 year olds. They had two kids, Moose and Larry Killingsworth. That was the only time I went crazy.

Larry Shepard was another one who tried to understand interracial ballplayers. The Pirates made a sincere effort to find out what blacks were doing. Joe Brown, the general manager, knew what was happening. He wanted to know who was doing what and who was saying what. Who was making things uncomfortable and who was all right. He made a sincere effort to know what was going on on the team, black and white.

That was when he got some of the veterans out of there, because he knew these kids had a camaraderie like he had never seen. And yet there were still people in the organization trying to undercut that. One was Bob Robertson. They had to stop Bob Robertson right away. Robertson would be on the bus, pounding on the seat to the tune of Aretha Franklin. Why was this big old white dude beating on the drums to Aretha Franklin's black music?

That was unheard of. I don't know if Bob Robertson would admit it, but he was bought. He might not have seen it at first, but he was bought. He stopped doing a lot of shit. He was no longer one of the brothers. The Pirates created an animosity between him and Al Oliver. Ask Al how he became an outfielder. Al Oliver was a hell of a first baseman. That's why they called him Scoop. He didn't want to be an outfielder.

The Pirates had so much talent. Richie Zisk should have been in the big leagues two years before he got there, but for those rabbits in front of him. I used to tell him, "The writing is on the wall. You have to get the fuck out of here." He could not outrun the brothers. He could hit, but they wanted rabbits, and they didn't have the DH.

I told him, "Richie, you are supposed to be in the big leagues. They ain't gonna bring you. Make the motherfuckers give you $25,000."

He was so competitive he still felt he had a chance.

"No man," I said. "Un uh."

He was still down in Triple A, but at least he got paid, way more than you're supposed to get in Triple A. They paid him just to be quiet. They were holding onto him just in case somebody got hurt. The Pirates had *so much* talent. He said the Pirates had too many blacks, so they got rid of him. The Pirates didn't give a shit about how many blacks there were. That was Joe Brown's policy. He didn't care how many black motherfuckers were out there. He wanted us to kick ass and take names.

Danny Murtaugh took over the Pirates in 1970. Murtaugh was cool. His thing was to kick ass and take names too, at all costs. That was the name of his game. What I remember most about Murtaugh was that he loved to win. When we were winning, he wasn't even walking on the ground. He was walking with his bow-legged ass on cloud nine with a big fucking cigar.

We'd be going through the airport, and no one would pass

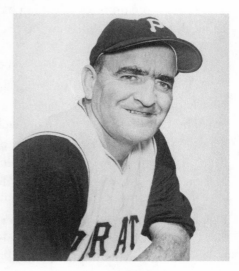

Danny Murtaugh

him. We let him lead the troops. Everyone would stand back behind him wearing those little suits—black pants, gray blazers, black and gold ties with the Pirates logo. I know he wanted to be seen as we walked through the airport.

"What is that?"

"There goes Murtaugh and the Pirates."

It was all you heard people say. He had on those white patent-leather shoes. He was stylin'.

Murtaugh taught the game of baseball. He walked us through fundamentals. There were guys in the big leagues who I played with and against who didn't know fundamentals. We hit the cut-off man. We knew how to run the bases. The pitcher covered first base on a ball hit to the right side. They did that, because Danny taught us. He walked us through it. They didn't throw the ball from the outfield. They walked from where the ball was supposed to be thrown. The cutoff man walked the ball to the base.

And if you fucked up, Danny didn't get over him, because humans make errors. Not everyone is mentally prepared every day. You'll never see me kicking dirt or cuss at a guy who makes an error. We were *taught* not to do that. Because a guy doesn't make an error on purpose.

You very seldom saw our Pirates pitchers argue with umpires about anything. The only one was Steve Blass. If he threw what he thought was a strike, and the umpires called it a ball, he'd throw his arms back. It was comical, but it wasn't showing up the umpire. It was like he was falling back from a line drive.

One time I was doing an article with the press.

"These fucking orphans coming here," I said, talking about players who had just been traded over to the Pirates, "are starting all this shit." You'll hear [St. Pete Pelican pitcher Milt] Wilcox in the clubhouse talking about, "Save me some runs for tomorrow." With the Pirates we'd have been all over him. He couldn't say that shit, because we had a guy named Nelson Briles who used to try to do that shit, and I'd beat his ass up.

One time Briles made a comment about Dave Parker not getting a ball, and I ate him up. Because Parker was a young outfielder.

"Okay, motherfucker," I said, "from now on Parker is not going to be in the lineup when you pitch. You like that, motherfucker?"

I overheard pitcher Jim Rooker one time talking about John Candelaria, saying he was a "stupid ass."

Candelaria was a young kid.

"You call him a stupid ass," I said, "and he's going to take your motherfucking job, because he'll be here tonight."

I used to hang out in the office, and I heard he was coming up.

"You think I'm bullshitting," I said. "That's why you don't like him. Now watch."

I knew the talent in the organization and when it was supposed to be delivered. And there he was.

In 1970 Dave Giusti won nine games and saved 26. I made that motherfucker. He just about saved all my games. Giusti was a good dude. He was from another organization [the Cardinals], and he had the intelligence to know he had to mix. He was a guy who was well-travelled, and he knew the groups, the black, the Latin, the white. He knew how the groups go. He knew how it was supposed to go.

There was supposed to be camaraderie all the way around. You have to make a concerted effort to try to understand the other. If you don't, you don't have camaraderie. You see it as fake. You can tell when it's fake. You can honestly tell when it's fake. Because some guys try to fake it. You can't fake it. It's either genuine or it's not. If it's not genuine, you can forget it.

I was over in the Bradenton clubhouse the other day, and I asked Graig Nettles, "Do you think this little butterball could have played on our team?"

I was talking about the 1976 Yankees when I was there. I was talking about Ron LeFlore.

"No," he said.

The question came up, "Dock, which was the better team as far as camaraderie, the Pirates or the Yankees?"

"All those years with the Pirates," I said, "there was never a team that I could say had the camaraderie the Yankees had that one year."

The Yankees had it that one year. The Pirates didn't have it every year I was there.

The difference was that all the white boys on the Yankees got loaded. They got high. We all got high together. That team drank, smoked dope, coke, everything. Poppers, you name it, parties, dissing, they didn't give a fuck. It was kick ass and take names. Because of Billy Martin. If you say partying, that's the white man's term for saying high. *All* the Yankees partied together.

Billy said, "Do whatever the fuck you want to do, but give me 125 percent." Murtaugh said the same thing. We had some sneaky dudes on the Pirates. They did it, but they were sneaky. I was out in the open doing my shit. Sometimes Murtaugh would tell the bus driver to get lost on purpose so we wouldn't be at the airport bar too long. We rushed that bar. They were ready to get drunk and then sleep all the way from L.A. to Pittsburgh.

I said, "Bussy, where the fuck do you live, motherfucker? This is L.A. You don't take the freeway at this time to get to the airport. We've been riding around for an hour."

Murtaugh just sat there. He knew the only thing we were going to do was drink what they had in the cases. But we carried whiskey with us. They had little pints. Some of them had a fifth, and they weren't going to let nobody get to it.

"Get the fuck away from me. You can't have any."

I'd be drunk when we got to the airport.

Murtaugh knew all the tricks. Way back he gave the elevator guy a ball and told him to have the ballplayers sign it after three o'clock in the morning.

"Would you sign the ball?"

"Sure."

Murtaugh would have a meeting the next day and ask, "How many of you guys were out last night?"

Nobody would raise their hand. Then he'd say, "I'm going to give you one more chance. I got an autographed ball from the elevator operator. Anybody's name on there will be fined $1,000 if they don't raise their hands now."

Hands would shoot up.

He tricked them. Murtaugh knew all the tricks.

The only time we partied hard, it was planned. We might have lost four or five games in a row, and Willie Stargell would say, "It's time to pull back together now. The motherfuckers are getting away from each other." He threw them big fucking parties, with a mix of gin, vodka, red wine, and grape juice. They called it purple passion.

Manny Sanguillen and I grew up in the organization together. When I say grew up, we weren't always on the same team, but I was always throwing to Sangy. If it wasn't in spring training, it was the next year or the following year, and we were roommates at Triple A. Yeah, Sangy was my catcher. I turned my game over to Sanguillen.

I only had two catchers, Sanguillen and Thurman Munson. I didn't really get to know Thurman that well. I had to turn the thing over to Munson because I didn't know anything about the American League. He made me throw balls I never wanted to pitch, but it was up to him.

In 1972 Bill Virdon replaced Danny Murtaugh as manager. Virdon was Murtaugh's lieutenant. Everyone knew he was Murtaugh's lieutenant. He was a disciplinarian. He wanted to treat everyone the same. I told him, "You can't do that, especially with me. I'm not like those mother-fuckers. I'm different."

"On no," he said.

I said, "Oh yeah," and I found out I wasn't bullshitting. He had to fine me a lot. He was going to fine me because I was going to do what I wanted to do.

The team was riding the bus to go to Miami. Clemente, Stargell, Justine, and Blass went on the plane with the Galbreaths. They were representing the team and talking to the Galbreaths, trying to do something about a possible strike.

That was my excuse to fly. I didn't want to ride the bus, because I told them I was through riding fucking busses.

I said, "If they're going to fly, I'm going to fly."

"That's going to cost you a hundred dollars," Virdon said.

"Here's a hundred," I said, "and here's another hundred, because I'm going to fly back."

He then had to fine me in Philadelphia because I didn't ride the bus from New York to Philadelphia.

I told Virdon, "You will not make a good manager until you cannot run to first base like you used to and you cannot swing the bat like you used to and cannot throw the ball like you used to."

Because it was in him to play ball.

I told him, "When you fine all twenty-five of us, let me know, because I want to be one of your coaches."

He was 60 years old, but he tried to relate to some of the things the young guys did. Al Oliver got him to show his guns, because he was muscular.

"Show 'em," Al said. "Show 'em your guns, Bill."

"Hmmmmmmm."

But Virdon was a good dude. They said I got him fired. I didn't get him fired. Richard Hebner got him fired. Richard was going to beat his ass. I don't know why.

"Richard," I said, "don't fight Virdon. Let it go."

Because Virdon would challenge the players. If I'm not mistaken, he got hurt in Houston when Cesar Cedeno tried to kill him. He locked up with Cedeno. That didn't make any sense. And he wanted to do that with Hebner. Hebner wanted to kill him. Hebner was that type of guy. Just leave Hebner alone.

Murtaugh saw what was happening, and they asked him to come back [in the middle of the 1973 season]. We won again under Murtaugh in 1974. That was the year I got my hand broke. I got hit by a line drive on September 16.

We went to the World Series. I could have pitched. They didn't want me to pitch. They pitched Larry Demery instead. He was young, and they figured I was bullshitting. They figured I just wanted to go get 'em even though I was hurting.

I could have pitched. They said the bone was still cracked, but I was so high, I couldn't feel it.

I was doing a lot of dope. I'm sure the organization had some idea I was into drugs heavily. We had another white dude on the team, and Murtaugh stopped us from rooming together. This dude and I went heavy into acid and mescaline and all that shit, and they knew it.

One time in Montreal we got bumped and couldn't leave. Airplanes couldn't leave Canada. We had to stay the night, and they took us to a motel, and I told them to put this guy and me in the same room. We were getting ready to get loaded, and they stopped that. We were in the heat of the race, and what happened was, one of the players got loaded, and though we needed his bat, he couldn't play a doubleheader.

He was scared. We brought it up to him that he need not be afraid, because one of the motherfuckers who was not afraid would pick up the slack. We told him, "We scared, but be there."

And after that he was.

I won five pennants with the Pirates, and after the 1975 season I was traded to the Yankees because I refused to go to the bullpen. Murtaugh tried to get me to go there, but I told him, "I ain't going nowhere."

He told me to get off the team. I told him, "Bye."

And that was that.

They fined me $25,000.

I told them, "You motherfuckers are going to look stupid going into the playoffs with only 24 players, especially without a pitcher of my experience."

They showcased me. I pitched two innings in the last game of the season.

I let it be known where I wanted to go.

Maury Wills was doing the telecast, and he made mention that "Dock Ellis is being showcased. He's going to be somewhere else next year, and he wants the message to go to Billy Martin that he wants to play for him."

The thing the Pirates was overlooking was the fact that I was a black pitcher, and I had seen what they had done to black pitchers in the past. Bob Veale went to the bullpen, and that was it. He was gone.

I told Veale, "If you had stayed in Pittsburgh, you could have broken all the motherfucking records."

He was gone, and that wasn't going to happen to me.

CHAPTER SIXTEEN

DOCK ELLIS

Cocaine and Yankee Turbulence

In December 1975 the Pirates traded Dock Ellis along with Willie Randolph and Ken Brett to the Yankees for pitcher Doc Medich. The year 1976 was a historic year for the Yankees, who won their first pennant since 1964. With George Steinbrenner as owner and Billy Martin as manager, the Yankees drove in high gear to finish the season with a 97–62 record and then defeat the Kansas City Royals in the playoffs. Catcher Thurman Munson was named the MVP of the league. Graig Nettles hit 32 home runs, and pitchers Catfish Hunter, Ed Figueroa, and Dock Ellis led the pitching staff. This was a hard-nosed bunch of players under hard-nosed manager Billy Martin.

Dock Ellis may well have been the hardest nose of them all.

Dock Ellis: The Yankees didn't have much of a spring training in 1976, because we were locked out. I came to camp, and one time I was so drunk I was puking while we were doing calisthenics.

Billy said, "Dock, Dock. Go in the clubhouse. Go to sleep. Go home. Go back to the hotel. Do what you gotta do."

It was a hard spring training for me because they were all new to me, and I had to have my time to check them out. What they were telling me was, "We're cool. We're all cool. We know you're cool. We found out about you. Come on."

I'm saying, "I don't do that." Because I didn't know them. I thought, *I don't know you guys. I heard of you. I've seen you in passing, but I don't know you.*

The first night of the season, opening night, we were in Milwaukee, and they came and got me.

The first fucking day the season opened. In the clubhouse them motherfuckers were fighting.

"Who are these crazy motherfuckers?" I said. "What are they doing? Why are they fighting?"

It was Lou Piniella and Rick Dempsey.

Who knows what they were fighting about. They were always arguing over baseball.

"You should have caught that ball."

"You should have called that pitch."

That was baseball. They talked baseball all the time.

Dick Tidrow, who they called Dirt, talked baseball all the time.

Catfish Hunter was cool. I used to tease Billy. I'd say, "You don't run this fucking team. Catfish runs this fucking team."

"What do you mean?"

"Everyone respects Catfish," I'd say. "Not everyone respects you."

I used to fuck with Billy all the time. We'd get drunk, and I'd be talking, and he'd say, "It's my fucking team."

One time we ran out of a bar, and I said, "Don't you forget. Catfish runs this fucking team. If it wasn't for Catfish, you wouldn't be where you are today."

Billy got to the door, and he said, "I run this fucking team."

And he took off.

Billy was cool.

Billy Martin

I saw Billy win five games the year I was there. I saw him win five fucking games by intimidating the umpires. Where they owed him. Where they owed him a call. When the ball was down the cock, and he called it a ball, and on the next pitch our hitter hit a home run to win the game.

They remembered. Why would the umpire call a ball down the middle a ball? And then he looks over to the dugout, and Billy kind of goes, "See that. Hee hee hee hee."

Billy was cool. You could see him work, especially with umpires and other managers. He would fuck with the other managers. He'd be out there arguing with the other manager when the lineup card was handed out.

One time Billy and Earl Weaver got into it. Both of them were crazy. Earl was just as crazy as Billy.

Billy ruled through intimidation, and that's what he wanted the team to do, to intimidate the other team, just like the Pirates. We are coming to kick your ass. Here come the fucking badass Yankees. They are coming to kick your ass.

We were a kick-ass team, and Billy wanted to be in charge. He wanted us to do things his way. But he had too many veterans, especially on the pitching staff, and what happened was, we said, "All right, motherfucker. We'll do it your way." And when we broke out into the lead, you might as well have called it Billyball. Because we were playing ball like Billy wanted us to play ball. Take them fucking bases. Mickey Rivers took bases. Billy said, "Run, run, run, run, run, run." Thurman Munson hit, and he never stopped at first base. He kept going, because he could run. And if he ducked his head at second, he'd go to third.

Most of the Yankees played hurt. Only one player was not like that, Willie Randolph. Willie came from the Pirates organization, and I explained to Sparky Lyle that in the Pirates organization you don't play hurt. Murtaugh didn't want you out there if he couldn't get one hundred percent out of you, no matter who you were.

Willie would sit out a few games every once in a while. We called him "The Glass Man." Some of the players felt Willie could have played some of the games he sat out, but then Willie would not still be in the game today if he had played. He understood that, but the others didn't. He was just a kid.

That year Ed Figueroa won 19 games. Figgie was crazy. He's nuts. Have you ever seen his little grin? What kind of grin is that? A sneaky-ass fucking grin. He's a sneaky motherfucker. He's nuts, but he can pitch his ass off. Figgie never got the credit he deserved, because he never got vocal with the press. For instance, when he had 16 wins, they were projecting that he'd be the first Puerto Rican to win 20 games. I started screaming about that, and I think I might have put him under a lot of pressure. He was determined to do it, and he did it the next year. But I had come upon him too quick.

Ken Holtzman was a crazy motherfucker. We got along. Doyle Alexander was another one. I had known Doyle when he was with the Dodgers and didn't throw sidearm. Doyle was another arrogant dude. A nice guy, but a mean dude. Doyle was cold-blooded. He didn't give a shit about anybody. Doyle and Billy almost got into it. I don't know what happened. I wasn't in the dugout that day, but they were getting ready to go to blows. Sparky and Billy too.

Billy didn't get along with some of the ballplayers, but I got along with him because I didn't give a shit about what Billy did or what Billy said. The name of his game was intimidation. He could intimidate just about anyone else, but he couldn't intimidate me.

He'd get them going. See, he couldn't get me going. I told him one time I'd whoop his little ass.

I said, "Get the fuck away from me with that shit. You're not going to slip up and hit me in the back of the head. I'll kill you, motherfucker."

Me, Holtzman, and Billy lived in New Jersey, and Steinbrenner sent a limo to pick us up. We were late, and he wanted his boys to get back home so they could get some sleep. Billy and I were drunk in the limousine. Billy said, "I'm going to get rid of that Rudy May, that gutless motherfucker."

"Man," I said, "why do you want to talk about Rudy that way."

"He's a gutless motherfucker, and you know it," Billy said.

"What the fuck are you talking about," I said.

"And you can go with him," he said.

"Send me to Mexico, you motherfucker," I said. "They play baseball in Mexico, don't they?"

Holtzman stopped us.

When we got to the playoffs in 1976, for a lot of the Yankee players it was like a dream, because not many of them had been on winners. [It was the first time the Yankees were in the playoffs since 1964.] We opened in Kansas City, and when I came into the clubhouse, I saw that guys had packed their shit to go home, and that pissed me off. It was like, "The dream is over. Kansas City is going to kick our ass."

I blew my top.

I was cussing the whole team out for not having confidence that we were going to the World Series.

[Dock Ellis pitched Game 3 of the series, the first postseason home game for the Yankees since 1964. Dock gave up three runs in the first inning, but settled down. He pitched eight solid innings. A two-run Chris Chambliss home run in the fourth narrowed the gap, and the Yankees added three more in the sixth. Dock won, and Sparky Lyle got the save, pitching a scoreless ninth. The Yankees took a 2–1 lead in the series.]

After the game I was in this big room answering questions. I was so high, and my pointer finger was jumping. It was why I had to leave the game. I threw the whole game like that, and nobody knew. I had to do the best I could with it. I remember striking out my cousin, Al Cowens.

That's all I remember, and that fucking Dick Young, the motherfucker. I couldn't stand that motherfucker. He's dead, and I would spit on his fucking grave today. He was full of shit, and not just about me. He should never have been allowed to write about the fucking game.

He was always talking about people in recovery, talking about putting them out of the game never to be brought back. He didn't talk about the owners who were drunks. He was a fucking drunk.

The rest of the writers tried to fire me up. Here I was coming over to the American League, and you know, they didn't pick me for the All Star team when I had a 10 and 4 record.

Our agreement was that Billy would keep them away from me so there would be no controversy. Controversy surrounded me. New York was a prime area for it. It was a playground for me, and he knew it. All I had to do was smoke a joint and stand on a stool talking shit, and it would have been headlines in two or three newspapers. I'd have had the back page, the front page, everywhere. Billy knew it, and I knew it.

"Billy," I said, "those motherfuckers are trying to fire me up," and he made them get away from me.

I didn't say shit. I took off.

The next day the headline said, "Ellis had nothing to say. He was supposed to be picked for the All-Star game."

"I don't want that shit," I had told Billy. "I like New York. Let's play baseball."

Billy said, "I want the press."

"You can have the press," I said. "Fuck 'em. I don't want it."

Billy loved being in the newspapers, and I can understand why. He wanted to be the Little General. So let him be the Little General, but keep the motherfuckers away from me.

The only time the press got a hold of me was when I got traded.

[On April 27, 1977, Dock was traded by the Yankees along with Marty Perez and Larry Murray for Mike Torrez.]

I was traded because of Steinbrenner. He was traveling with the team when Graig Nettles made a statement. He said, "If we keep on losing, he's going to follow us all the time, and we'll have a better chance of losing Steinbrenner in a plane crash." Nettles said it, but Steinbrenner thought I said it. But I never denied I said it. I let them think I said it, and that had a lot to do with me getting traded. Plus he wouldn't give me the money I wanted. It was not a lot of money.

Gabe Paul said to me, "Well Dock, we don't have to look at just the hole in the doughnut. We have to look at the whole doughnut."

"Fuck you and the doughnut too, motherfucker," I said. "I'll slap you upside your head, you motherfucker. Get me the fuck out of here."

George Steinbrenner

And they traded me.

Billy couldn't stop them. Steinbrenner had made up his mind. He said to himself, *Who does this motherfucker think he is? I'm going to get his ass out of here.*

Reggie Jackson might have had something to do with me going too. Reggie came to the Yankees trying to run the clubhouse. I told him, "This is my fucking clubhouse. You don't run this motherfucker. Shut the fuck up."

One day Reggie was getting on Baby Dome—we called Dick Howser that because he had a bald head. They were talking about Dick's clothes, the way he dressed, and Dick looked at me for help. I attacked Reggie. I let him know. I said, "You wear one pair of pants, one pair of shoes, so shut the fuck up. That's all you bring, you motherfucker. I've been watching you."

"Get him, Dock," Howser said. "Get him."

Reggie was a good dude, but he would stir people up talking shit, and they didn't know how to talk back to Reggie.

Reggie was a great talker. Reggie didn't destroy that group of guys. He fueled them, but he got under their skin. The one guy who I thought he would never get under his skin was Graig Nettles, because Nettles could fire back shit too. Graig could fire you up with some shit. Lou Piniella could too, but Reggie seems to know how to get the upper hand on both of them. He knew where to go with them, and they didn't know how to deal with him. I saw that. Nettles would say to Reggie, "Shut the fuck up and put up," and Reggie would put up. He'd keep talking. He could talk all the shit as long as he was doing his thing. If you ain't doing nothing, you had best shut the fuck up. But if you're a talker, you've been talking all your life. It's as simple as that.

See, the previous year, I almost killed Reggie. I hit Reggie in the face because he was talking shit. [Reggie was with Baltimore.] I was pitching against Cry or Cy Palmer. If Jim Palmer doesn't get the Cy Young award he cries. I was losing the game 3 to 1 going into the eighth inning. This motherfucker wasn't giving up anything more. Mark Belanger was at the plate, and he had his head down, and I threw the ball, and the ball tailed, and I yelled, "Duck."

Belanger ducked and when he ducked, Reggie was coming up the steps of the dugout. Reggie assumed I had thrown a pitch at him, so Reggie stood up on the steps and screamed. It was September, and there were only about 800 fans in the [Baltimore] ballpark.

It was September of 1976, and we were leading the league. We won 100 games.

I was way out on cloud 9.

Reggie called me a "motherfucker," and Thurman came out and said to me, "Ah, Bugman, did you hit your bugboy over there?"

"Man, what the fuck are you talking about?" I said.

"Well Bugman," Thurman said, "you ought to hit the big man right here. What are you going to do, Babe?"

"Get the fuck back there and watch," I said to him.

I pitched Reggie in and out until I got him leaning, and then I hit him.

"Is he dead?" I said.

After I hit him, I called out to see how he was. I was embarrassed. All I did was break his glasses, and his jaw was sore. I didn't break no bones, so I was embarrassed.

Jim Palmer said something to me just before we left Baltimore.

"Dock," he said, "you got me fined $500."

"What are you talking about," I said.

"When you hit Reggie in the face," Palmer said, "Earl Weaver

Thurman Munson

fined me $500 because I hit Mickey Rivers with a change-up."

After the game I went back to the locker room, and I found three one-hundred-dollar bills. I never had to buy another drink for the guys for the rest of the year, until the last day, when I had to pay a big team tab.

That was because I bummed drinks all the time. I'd go into the bar with the boys.

"Dock, what do you want?"

I'd mosey on down, have a drink, and then I'd be gone.

One day Steinbrenner made us stay in Detroit to see if Baltimore was going to beat Boston, because he wanted us to go back to New York before we went to Boston, so the fans could see us. That meant we were clinching on the road, but he wanted us to go home.

We had to stay in this bar in Detroit, and when we found out that Boston had won, everybody was ready to go. I was half drunk, and Piniella said, "Give the bill to that motherfucker over there. He owes everybody."

Munson stuck me with the tab, and I had to pay it, though after I hit Reggie, I never had to pay another. I didn't know Reggie was disliked like that. He woofed.

Then Reggie walked around during the playoffs trying to find out why I hit him.

I said, "Reggie, shut the fuck up. You know why the fuck you got hit. I'd have popped you with my motherfucking fists."

Reggie Jackson

Then he got traded to us when I was in Hawaii announcing for ABC.

"Reggie," I said, "you're on my team now. I want you to swing for the fucking fences every time you hit, and if you think somebody is throwing at you, just let me know. I'll hit everybody on that motherfucking team."

At the end of April of 1977 my hand was bothering me. It was cold in April, and Billy only wanted me to miss two starts, but Steinbrenner traded me to the funny farm in Oakland. [A's owner Charley] Finley wanted me to pitch right away. I wanted to stay in Oakland and pitch good, so maybe I'd ask him for more money. But I had no business pitching because of my hand.

[Dock with Oakland started seven games and had a 0–1 record with a 9.69 ERA.]

When I got to Texas and started winning [he had a 10–6 record with a 2.90 ERA] Finley said I tricked him.

I had missed a start in Oakland, and when I got to Texas, I told Frank Lucchesi I was ready to pitch. I then started winning.

My career came to an end when I got with that fool Billy Hunter. He was a drunk. When I finally made amends to the last person with Cocaine Anonymous, Hunter was one of the last three. I did it at an Old Timers game in Texas. With Hank Aaron and Willie Mays looking on, I made amends to Billy Hunter right there. I told him about all the chaos I was causing when he was managing me. I said, "If that was detrimental in any way, that wasn't me. I was a drug addict and an alcoholic, and what I am doing is making amends to you. Whether you accept it or not, I don't give a fuck, but I'm doing it right now, making amends to you right now."

The motherfucker drove me crazy the rest of the day.

"It took a mighty man to do that, Dock," he said.

But during the time we were together in Texas, he was a drunk, and I was a drunk. I knew he was a drunk, and he knew I was a drunk, but he thought he had some power, and I told him he didn't have no power, that I had the power.

And Hunter was the one who got fired. Because he was a drunk. And since I was one of [Texas owner] Brad Corbett's bobos, I wasn't going anywhere anyway.

When Brad sold the team, I left during spring training.

I was passing him by when he said to me, "Dock, I just sold the team."

"Man, you fucked up," I said. "I have to go home now."

I wasn't going to be on the team if he sold it. No other owner was going to have me, and I knew no other owner would have me.

"I know," he said. "Come by the office. We've got to work on a job for you."

"I'll be back in May," I said to him.

I came back to his company, which sold PVC pipe, and he hired me as a sales promotion manager. It was money. He knew I was no-nonsense, that I would tell him the truth, wouldn't lie to him. He liked my arrogance. I don't keep in contact with him like I should, but we're like family.

I worked there for a couple of years, and then he lost control of his company, and it was hard for him to justify my position. That's when he bellied up. He's a shrewd businessman, and he's back on top now. He wanted me to work for him again, but I wouldn't do it. He's a high-roller, and I'm through with that.

When he was a high-roller I was with him everywhere, even to Europe. He took me to all these fancy players, and I was told, "Man, you're the first black dude who's been in this place. And you're drinking out of the bottle."

This was Dom Perignon, rich man's stuff.

"Corbett, man," I said, "what the fuck are you bringing me into a place like this? No black has ever been here?"

"Fuck it," Corbett said. "You don't need to know. Who gives a shit?"

I said to myself, *This dude is crazy.*

We'd run through airports like O.J.

"Did you know I could run?" he said.

"No, I didn't."

Corbett was a big old dude who they mistook for a dummy, but he was signing players to contracts, locking them up to when it came time for them to get the big money, but they couldn't get it because he had locked them up. Other teams were ready to trade for them. Before they were saying he was stupid, and now they were saying he was so shrewd. The club was easy for him to sell because he had players locked into contracts.

I finally decided to go for alcohol and drug counseling. Why I did it was sort of silly, but not silly. It's like when I swore I would never drink scotch. But I had started drinking scotch, Chivas Regal, at Corbett's office. I would drink all the scotch off the top shelf. He was trying to figure out where all the scotch was going.

"You gave the sons a bitches two bottles the other day," I said.

"I gave them two bottles?" Corbett said.

"Somebody is stealing the shit too," I told him.

He'd lock it up, and I would get the key

Subconsciously I was telling myself, *This is brandy.*

I would drink that Chivas Regal at the office with orange juice or coffee—it didn't make any difference—but then when I went to lunch I would eat the olives from the martinis, and then I would come back to the office and slip out, and I was gone to a local bar, drinking vodka.

I am killing myself, I said. *Something is going on. Let me make a call.*

I was doing a lot of cocaine, but not as much as I was doing when I was playing ball, because I wasn't in the cities where people would give it to me.

So I called Don Newcombe. He wasn't there. His wife was there.

"Tell him I'll be in L.A. tomorrow," I said. "I will give him a call."

I went to L.A., and I called. I thought the rehab was in L.A., but it was in Arizona. Newcombe told me he didn't know if they had a bed, but hold on.

"I ain't holding on to shit," I said. "Fuck you then."

"No," he said, "I'll call you back in an hour."

"No, I'm going over to my sister's house."

"Let me call you back in four hours," Don said.

"Okay," I said, "I'll be back over here in four hours."

At 11 my sister took the kids to McDonalds for a hamburger, and I went with her. I saw this liquor store down the street, so I said, "Wait a minute. I'm going to get me a bottle."

I went and got some Chivas Regal.

That's when I said to myself, *This really is scotch, isn't it?*

I know I have to go to rehab now, I said to myself.

So I went to my sister's house, and by the time I got to my mother's house, I had drunk almost all of that scotch.

I was down the street from my mother's drinking rum, when she sent one of my nieces to get me to tell me that Don Newcombe had called.

"You have a bed in Arizona," he said, "but you have to catch a plane now."

"I'm gone," I said.

It was 1980, and I stayed for thirty-five days. I stayed almost two weeks longer than the insurance.

"Your insurance is up in twenty days," they said.

"I don't give a fuck," I said. "I ain't going out of here."

Because I was afraid. I was in a protective community, and I knew if I got out of there right away, I couldn't deal with it. I would go back and use drugs again. Because there was something I was missing. I didn't have the six bullets in my gun, and I knew it. Wherever I was, I was going to stay until I got the treatment I needed. I was looking for the okay of my counselor, when I knew he knew what to do once I got out. I came from him telling me to drink Catawba Pink, a drink that resembled alcohol. It sounded like whiskey, but it was grape juice.

That was all I had to hear.

[When Bobby Tolan was named manager of the St. Petersburg Pelicans in the Senior Professional Baseball League in the fall of 1989, he brought with him Dock Ellis, who became his pitching coach and one of his pitchers. For the first time in his professional career, Dock Ellis walked onto the mound perfectly straight.]

What happened was during our spring training I was more worried about the pitchers than about myself. It was hard for Bobby to put me in situations because I had already made the team. I was the pitching coach. I was more concerned with who we were going to start the season with. And then when the season started, the question arose, *When was I going to pitch?*

The thought was always on my mind was that I was going to pitch and I wasn't going to be high, and when I first went into a game, I didn't know what was going on. I saw the guys. I knew the guys. But the adrenaline was flowing. My mouth was dry like when I was high and I was zeroed in on the game.

I saw guys. Before when I was high, I didn't see guys. But my whole system was like I was high. It was like a high again. It felt like I was high, but I knew I was not high. My body was responding like I was high. I don't wipe my lips because my lips are dry like I'm high. That's the adrenaline. Again, my body reacted like I was high. I know I'm not high, but I act like I'm high. I did. Yeah.

Guys remember my mannerisms on the mound, when I walk around the mound not doing nothing, looking over here and looking over there. I used to step off the mound and just look.

But I remembered doing those things, so when I got out there, it was strange.

I went to a narcotics anonymous meeting. I talked about what was bothering me, that I was pitching and I was afraid.

At the meeting they didn't know what the fuck I was talking about.

"Don't look like anyone here knows anything about baseball," I said, "but I play baseball. I used to, and I'm back at it again."

And I talked about my fear.

That fear is okay. That fear was only because I was remembering the old times. That's all that was, the old times. That was like saying, *I'm going into the room where they're doing cocaine.*

I can go into the room, but I'm frightened because of the old times.

When the season ends there are several things I want to do with substance abuse. I don't think I'm going to go back and work with kids, because no one wants to help the kids. The politics is all about money. It's no different than baseball to me. I get pissed off and tell them to kiss my ass.

I know I cannot cure the world, but I can help somebody, but I refuse to stay to help someone when I have to put up with shit. I'm not going to harm me to help someone else. That's bad when you do that, even in baseball. I'm not into the politics. I was working with the Yankees, and the Yankees had a motherfucker who didn't know anything about drugs and alcohol, and he's going to tell me what he knows? He didn't know shit. They're not going to tell me I have to answer to somebody. I told them, "I'm not going to answer to no motherfucker."

I don't work for the Yankees. I ain't gonna work for the Yankees. There's nothing wrong with working for the Yankees as long as George Steinbrenner is the person I answer to. Anyone else, they don't know shit. You see, I was answering to someone who didn't know a damn thing, who didn't have nothing to do with even hiring me. Politics. I'm not into the politics. I want to pick up the phone and call George Steinbrenner and say, "George, I have learned this shit down here in this old time Seniors League. Baseball is a motherfucker. You got motherfuckers in your organization that are fucking you, and you don't even know it. You're getting fucked at the major league level, which is why you're not winning, because they are fucking you at the lower level," meaning they are fucking ballplayers up, and when they get to the big leagues, they are so fucked up, they get the fuck out of the Yankee organization.

I can pick up the phone right now and do that. I *wish* I would do it, but I'm not yet ready to go through the bullshit. I'm just not ready to do it right now. I *wish* I could do it. I *can* do it, but I'm just not ready to do it.

When I do that I want to be able to tell George why and how it can be changed. I can't change it alone. He's going to have some input how to do it. He has to know what I'm talking about when I tell him.

George is not the problem. George wants to win so fucking bad that he is manipulated by people who claim to know so motherfucking much about baseball. George doesn't know that much about baseball. George is a front-runner. George is a businessman. If I say to George, "We need this and we need that," he will go out and get it. But guys are blowing smoke up his ass to keep jobs. He trusts them. In that respect, he has a problem because he trusts people.

I just hate I was not sober when I played for the Yankees. I can only remember some of that. But it was an honor to have played for the Yankees, because I wore pinstripes. It's tradition, and the kids today are not taught that. They see that when he speaks to the team, but after that it's gone. The Yankees are just like any other organization. It's not like they used to be.

CHAPTER SEVENTEEN

GARY CARTER

The Missing Ingredient

*I*n 1985 Mets manager Davey Johnson and I agreed to work together to write his autobiography, Bats. *Part of the joy of writing it was that I was allowed to travel with the Mets toward the end of the season. I spent two weeks on the road, as the Mets finished just two games short of the St. Louis Cardinals. Davey and I were heartbroken, and not just because the Mets weren't going to the World Series.*

I rode the planes and buses with the likes of Darryl Strawberry, Doc Gooden, Keith Hernandez, and Lenny Dykstra. After games they went their separate ways, while I hung out mostly with Sid Fernandez, Rusty Staub, and one of the finest people I have ever known, Gary Carter. While the partiers partied, we went out for dinner or we went to the movies. Some of the players were reluctant to talk to me because of my writer status. Sid, Rusty, and Gary welcomed me to join them during their downtime.

When in 2002 I got a contract to write Amazin', *a book on the history of the New York Mets, I called Gary for an interview. He was playing in a golf tournament in Ft. Myers, Florida, and I drove from my home in St. Petersburg to meet with him.*

Carter was his usual ebullient self. He answered my questions with warmth and honesty.

How did you and Montreal owner Charles Bronfman get along?

When Bronfman called me in to see him, I thought, if anything, he was going to give me a pep talk. By no means did I ever think before the '84

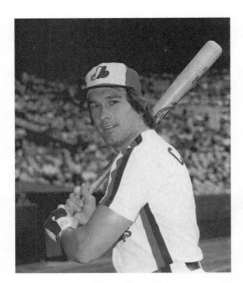

Gary Carter

season that he was going to make me feel so demoralized that I almost went into the season thinking, *My gosh, I've given my heart and soul to Montreal.*

I really felt I was giving them everything, not only on the field but off the field, and yet he was upset because of the contract I had signed.

In 1982, when I signed that seven-year extension for $14 million, at that time it was big money. Today one guy, Ken Griffey Jr., is making more in one season than I made in my entire career.

So Charles was upset with the way baseball was going, and so anyway, in 1983, I had very severe tendonitis in my elbow to the extent that Dr. Larry Coughlin flew into Chicago at the All Star break and as soon as I came out of the game, he injected me three times, and then I missed the first game back after the All Star break, and I came back and I ended up having a decent season.

If you have 17 home runs and 83 RBIs and hit .284 as a catcher, and I had 38 doubles, you'd think I was very productive, and yet Charles was upset because he didn't think I was earning my money and that I wasn't giving enough back to the city.

I went to a Berlitz course and learned how to speak French, and I got more involved in the community. I set up my opportunity to work with leukemia, with Lucan Canada, and then I transferred that into New York, but it just really amazed me that Charles felt that way.

I've talked to John McHale a little bit about this too, and he said that Charles was really adamant about the [wrong] way baseball was going. I turned out to be the scapegoat for him.

On 1984 I had one of my best years. I led the league in RBIs with 106, had 27 home runs, and almost hit .300, and yet I ended up getting traded.

We had just built a home up there. I was one of these guys who wanted to play my entire career with one organization, and that's very rare now. Most guys end up leaving an organization as a free agent or what have you.

At that point I had no idea the Expos were going to trade me. I sure did not. But when I went and met Charles before spring training, Charles basically ripped me for about two hours.

He was late to the appointment, first of all. He told me to meet him at his condominium in Palm Beach, and I was there at six, and he showed up 25 minutes later. To begin with, he showed me his place, and then he got down to the brass nuts.

"I was very disappointed in your performance this last year," he started saying. "I don't think you're earning your money."

And so forth. "You're not giving anything back. There are now jealousies on the team, and it's creating friction," he said, and it went on and on.

"Whenever you come up in key situations, I'd go to the bathroom," he said.

I mean, it was unbelievable. I walked away with my head between my legs thinking, *What have I done to get this man so upset to think I'm not giving it my all?*

I had a bad elbow. I was injured for the majority of the season, and yet I still played every game. I still caught over 150 games. I led the league in games caught six consecutive years. That's probably the reason I've had eight knee surgeries now.

But I really was flabbergasted at his approach. As we left I said to him, "Charles, I'm going to go out and have my best year for you, and if that's still not enough, then I don't know what it's going to take."

During the course of the year, I was hearing some rumblings, and then at the end of the year John McHale mentioned something to me. He had said there were rumblings, meaning the board of directors— Charles was the main board of director as far as the ownership goes, but there were others involved—they were thinking that maybe it was time to trade Gary Carter.

If you know the history of the Expos, their great players have only lasted there ten years. Tim Wallach finished his career out in Los Angeles.

Steve Rogers spent the majority of his career in Montreal, and they went to trade him, and he declined going to Houston, and then he ended up with the Angels. Andre Dawson, the same thing happened to him.

"Here is an open contract," he said. "You fill in what you want to," and he went to Chicago. Tim Raines, same thing. So there have been a lot of great players up there. Pedro Martinez was originally a Dodger, and he was in the trade that brought Carlos Perez, Mark Grudzielanek, and him there, and he became a star up there. Then they realized they couldn't keep him because of the money he was going to demand, and so he gets traded to Boston.

The bottom line: at the end of the 1984 season, I really didn't know there was that much adamancy that Charles and the rest of the board of directors felt towards me to the extent that they wanted to trade me.

After spending ten years in Montreal, I had the right to veto the trade. I said to John McHale, "I don't want to just go anywhere."

I gave him some favorites.

"If you want to trade me to the Dodgers, that's fine," I said. "I'll be going back home. If you want to trade me to Atlanta, at least that's close to home and I can be close to my home during the season." Then I said, "Maybe to the Mets," but I didn't think he'd trade me to a contending team in the same division.

On December 10, 1984, the trade was announced. I could have vetoed the trade, but I said to John, "If it's time for me to move on, then I will accept the trade."

I had a $250,000 buy-out.

"Is there going to be a problem with the no trade clause?"

"No," I said.

At the end he said, "You said it wouldn't be a problem, but the $250,000 is holding this thing up."

"John," I said, "if that be the case, then don't give me anything."

I basically wrote it off.

"I'll do this," I said. "You take away the $250,000 buy-out. All I want is that you help defer some of the losses I'm going to take on my home in Montreal."

I had just built a $500,000 house on the water, and I ended up losing over $150,000.

"We'll pay 75 percent of your loss," McHale said.

That helped out somewhat, but I went in the trade that they wanted to make, and I ended up losing what was really guaranteed to me. They felt my getting traded to New York made up for it not only for the endorsements, but also for the fact I didn't have to pay the high Canadian taxes anymore. In Montreal you pay ten percent more in provincial and federal taxes than you do in the states, even though New York hits you pretty hard.

Getting traded to the Mets was probably the best thing that could have happened, because in Montreal there was a lot of jealousy among the players who felt all I was doing was trying to make a name for myself and didn't care about anybody else, and Peter, that wasn't the case at all.

One of his problems might have been that you weren't a drinker, that you didn't fit in with the drinkers.

It might have. I just wasn't a carouser. I was a family man. I still am. I was also criticized for being too accommodating to the press. You know what, I just felt that was part of the job. Those guys were there to report on the games. A lot of guys would duck into the clubhouse or into the trainer's room to avoid the press, and I just happened to be there, and I got the nickname Camera Carter and Teeth, because I was always smiling.

Teeth. Warren Cromartie tagged me with that, because I had a good smile and I was happy to be where I was. You know what I'm saying.

It got to the point where Charles [Bronfman] was recognizing that too. I'd walk into the clubhouse, and I felt a lot of back stabbing going on, and yet, the way you turn those things to the better, you hit them with kindness, and that's what I tried to do. I killed them with kindness.

If they were bad mouthing me, I'd say, "Hey, how you doing? Great to see you." And I'd just let it go.

When I came to spring training to play for the Mets, Davey Johnson squelched it. He realized my talent and what I meant to that ballclub. I came to New York not so much for the offense, because we had an offensive ballclub, but to handle the young pitchers. I'm sure the rumblings went on spring training hearing about what I was coming from and some of the jealousies and what was going on, and you know what? I think the players found out in a hurry that, *Hey, this guy is not a bad guy.*

Davey Johnson

Davey made a comment.

"Frank Robinson was perceived the same way," he said. "Frank Robinson was a guy you loved to hate, but you loved having him on your own team."

That's the way the players then accepted me. They realized I was genuine. I wasn't a fake guy.

Everyone is always trying to find something on someone. I was the same way in Montreal, and I've been the same way my whole life. I go to card shows, and they say, "You know, you are the nicest guy that comes to these shows."

"You guys are paying to come in to see us," I say, "and I want you guys to enjoy and make it worth your while."

Why would I want to be abrupt and rude to these people because they ask for a kindness like, "Could you personalize your autograph?"

Davey made a point of it right away.

"We have something special here," Davey said, "and I think we need to go out, boys, and just play and not be concerned about all this other stuff going on. Forget about who's better than who and who is making more money. Let's play baseball."

And that's the way it went.

I thought it was a new beginning for me coming to a new ballclub that had the potential to win. In Montreal we were going in the opposite direction, because in '79 we won 95 ballgames, but the weather kept us from beating the Pirates. In 1980 we lost out by one game to the Phillies. In 1981 we got to the league championship series but lost out to the Dodgers.

Then all of a sudden there was one key trade—I'm not going to put a negative on it because it turned out to be a positive, but Larry Parrish meant a lot to that ballclub. He was an enforcer on that team, and he didn't really put himself in positions to be looked at how the segregation is on the team. He was the middleman. He was a leader. He was traded, and they brought in Al Oliver. And Al Oliver was the batting title winner. He hit .331. He hit nothing but ropes that year, had 22 home runs and led the league in RBIs with 109, and it was one of the greatest exhibitions of hitting I ever saw.

But in 1983 we didn't win. We finished third. And the next year Al really fell off, and we finished in fifth.

It was brought to my attention that fourteen of the last fifteen years I played in, the team finished third or better. I was always on a contending team, so when I came to New York, I realized I was going to be looked at as the missing ingredient, the missing part of the puzzle that was to get us to the World Series.

I tried to play that down as much as I could. I emphasized how important all the rest of the guys were. Doc Gooden was coming off a Rookie of the Year in 1984, and Darryl Strawberry was coming off Rookie of the Year in 1983, Keith Hernandez, a great first baseman, came in a trade.

There was a lot of other talent. George Foster was there. So were Mookie Wilson, Wally Bachman, and Rafael Santana, so I came there with an open mind thinking, *God, this is a great opportunity. We didn't win in Montreal, but we got a chance to win here.*

I don't know if you remember this, but before the spring training schedule started Davey allowed me to go home for a family occasion. I went home after

Dwight Gooden

practice. Northeast Airlines then cancelled my flight back to New York. Davey wouldn't have penalized me, but what I did was charter a flight from Palm Beach to make sure I got back in time. I missed the first half hour. I called him, and I said, "Davey, I'm stuck. My flight was cancelled. I had plans to be there in time."

"Don't worry about it," he said. "Just get here when you can."

He appreciated the effort.

Spring training progressed, and we could tell we had a pretty special ballclub. Opening day against the Cardinals was a bitterly cold day. Joaquin Andujar started the game for the Cardinals, and he hit me on the same elbow that bothered me in 1983. My arm went numb, and I was thinking, *I wonder if I can even continue in this game.*

After I got hit by a pitch, we knocked Andujar out, and I got a double off Greg Matthews, and that was my start as a Met. We went to extra innings, and Neil Allen, an ex-Met, was in there, and I hit the home run off him. I mean to tell you, right then and there, I endeared myself to the fans, and they chanted my name, "Gary, Gary, Gary," as they left the Shea Stadium exit.

It just made me feel so good, because I remember so many great games I had in Montreal. In one game I hit three home runs, and I barely got an encore, a curtain call. That's the difference between fans. Montreal fans are good fans, but they are not really baseball fans. They are more hockey fans. And when I came to New York, and that happened, it was like a breath of fresh air.

Gosh, this is great, I thought.

If you do well in New York and meet the needs of the fans, they welcome you, and you can really enjoy an abundant life in New York. That's happened to some of the great players who played there. These players have nothing but great things to say about how the fans can be the tenth man on the field.

That's how that all started for me, Peter. I'm just very grateful to have had those five years in New York.

I played well in that first month, and we got off to a pretty good start. In my first four years, the Mets had two seconds and two firsts. We won the World Series in '86. The Mets made it to the World Championship this year [2000], but they say there is nothing like the way that Mets team was in 1986. I have to agree.

In 1985 Dwight Gooden seemed to pitch a shutout just about every time he went out there. He was 24 and 4 with a 1.53 ERA and 268 strikeouts.

After his rookie year and his being so successful [in 1984 he was 17–9 with a 2.60 ERA and led the league with 276 strikeouts], a lot of the baseball magazines and the baseball people were saying that Dwight was on his way to the Hall of Fame. They said that because he was so dominant and so quick to adapt to big league pitching.

Doc only had two pitches. He threw 80 to 85 percent fastballs, and he threw what we called his Lord Charles, the Uncle Charlie, the big curveball. He was so dominant with that fastball that he could win games with just the fastball. That's how overpowering he was. He had a little rise to it, and he came right over the top. It was mid-90s on every pitch. He was fun to catch. He had his confidence going. If I put my glove there, he could paint the outside corner. It was just a pleasure for me to be a part of that Cy Young Award year, because every time he took the mound, he had no-hit stuff.

As for the rest of that staff, Ron Darling was maturing. Sid Fernandez was maturing. In 1986 we got Bobby Ojeda, the last piece of the puzzle as far as the pitching staff goes. Rick Aguilera was a rookie, and in relief we had Roger McDowell, Jesse Orosco, and Doug Sisk.

I tried to provide them with the leadership behind the plate to ensure their confidence that, "Hey, let me go out and call the game, and you just throw."

Doc didn't shake me off very much. If he did, it was an occasional curveball to a fastball, or vice versa. I loved that part of the game, and Peter, I have been out of the game eight years now, and I still miss it. The thing I miss most is calling the game. I know I can't do the other things. I can't run anymore. I can probably still hit. And I can still throw, but all the other things you need to do to be a complete player, I can't do anymore.

It was just fun to catch those guys. They were most of the time right around the plate. Darling could be problematic, because he liked to philosophize a little bit. That's the Ivy League mentality. Shoot, the guy is an intelligent man and good looking, and he endeared himself to New York. He had the perfect name, Ron Darling, and he was the darling of everybody, and I must say that Ronnie really matured once he learned how to master that split finger. Under the tutelage of Mel Stottlemyre, he started working on that split finger, and that became his number one pitch. He had the fastball, but it wasn't an overpowering fastball like Sid Fernandez or Doc Gooden. He had a good fastball, a good curve ball, a little slider, though not very much on the slider, but boy, when he came up with that split finger, that was his out pitch.

I really tried to get Bobby Ojeda to work inside, to throw more fastballs inside. We got him from Boston, where everyone is so reluctant to do that at Fenway Park, because you know, if the batter just hits a pop up, it's going to go out. That's what really improved Bobby Ojeda as a pitcher. He started throwing more fastballs inside, and he had a great change up, probably the best change up of anyone I ever caught.

Sid Fernandez threw 85 percent fastballs, and he threw the curveball that nobody has ever swung at. He threw this curveball, and it had a tight spin on it, and he hid it so well that there were a lot of called strikes. Sid would average about 10 strikeouts a game, and he would not top 91 miles an hour, but he had that little zip, and because he was kind of a wide body, he hid the ball so well. It's amazing, but he got a lot of called strikes on that curveball that nobody ever swung at. It was the greatest thing in the world. He'd start it outside, and they'd quit on it because they thought it was a rising fastball that would go away, and it just stuck right in.

I called Sid Dukie. Sid was from Hawaii, where Duke Kahanamoku [who made surfing popular] was from, and I'd say, "Dukie, just throw it just like you're throwing it in a basket right here."

Sid got really good with it.

The pitching staff was a fun pitching staff to catch, primarily because they didn't overwork me. When Bruce Berenyi was part of our staff in 1985, he'd throw a great game and then in other games he'd be all over the place. I'll never forget one game in St. Louis. I had on my shin guards and chest protector, and then I put another chest protector on, and I put another set of shin guards on my arms, and I said, "Okay, Double B, I'm ready for you now."

Bruce had such good stuff, but he would work me—oh my God. He'd throw balls in the dirt. I'd have to block about ten a game. Ron Darling would throw that split finger every once in a while and bounce one, but

Sid very rarely bounced them. Roger McDowell had that nasty sinker, and Jesse was pretty good with his breaking ball and fastball. It was fun stuff to catch. It really was.

In 1985 you hurt your knee so badly you had to skip the All Star game.

I tore some cartilage. I was coming off knee surgery at the end of 1984 when I had a lateral meniscus tear, which was getting caught in the joint. Yet it wasn't severe enough because it didn't break off. But what happened, I had the arthroscopic surgery and then just before the All Star break we were in Houston, and I got a base hit up the middle, and I got to first base, and I could barely run.

The next day I woke up, and I could barely walk. I could barely get out of bed. It had swelled up, and I asked the doctor, "What's the deal?"

"You might have torn some cartilage in there," he said.

I flew back to New York, and Dr. Parks took some fluid out of there and shot me up with cortisone.

"The smartest thing you can do is rest during the All Star break," he said. "It gives you three full days."

Because this happened the day before the All Star break. I was obviously disappointed. My knee was feeling good after it was drained and shot with cortisone, and I'm watching Terry Kennedy, who was filling in for me, and I was just so disappointed. I was watching the game at home. I had a glove with me, and I'm pounding the ball in my glove, and I'm just so angry that this happened.

Well, that's when it first started that I was taping my knee fulltime. Bob Sykes, the assistant trainer, locked that side in. He took the tape, and he'd cut it, and he would overlap it and pull it real tight, and it would hold that piece of cartilage that was loose in there together. I needed to alter my swing, and I stepped a little bit further away from the plate.

I had a tremendous September. I ended up being the Player of the Month in September. And I ended up having my biggest home run production in one season with 32 and ended up driving in 100, but you know what, it's amazing, because my knee bothered me, and yet I was able to get through it.

I had another cortisone shot to get me through the rest of the season, and of course we were in a pennant race, and there was no way I wanted to say, "Let's have surgery on this thing," so I waited until the end of the year, and right after we lost out to the Cardinals, Dr. Parks did the surgery on me.

There might have been some loose stuff left in there or scar tissue from the last surgery the year before. My knees bother me now after having so many surgeries, but they are so deteriorated that I just accepted it after a while. I could deal with the pain as long as it wasn't the ache. I got through it and was able to finish out the season.

Because people knew I was playing with a torn cartilage, there was more of an appreciation of what I went through. See, a uniform always camouflages injuries. I was taped from mid-calf to mid-thigh, and I had both my ankles taped from an injury I had the year before in '84, a collision I had at home plate in Houston. Tony Scott slid into me, and I thought it was a sprain, because when Dr. Cook did an x-ray on it about a year and a half ago, he said, "Did you ever fracture this ankle?"

It turned out there was a line that showed there was a fracture. It's funny because I felt my ankle was worse than it was, and I have four loose bodies in there now. Dr. Cook said, "One of these days when one of those pieces gets lodged in one of the joints, we're going to have to take those things out."

I played the rest of '84 with a fractured ankle. I played in '85 with torn cartilage in my knee, and in '86 I had some injuries too, but it kind of reminds you what Mike Piazza has gone through the last couple years. I know how beat up he's gotten. He's gone through it. But it's the position we play. It's one of those things that you have to accept.

On September 10, 1985, Darryl Strawberry scratched himself from the lineup. The players saw what you went through every game, and now Darryl, the Mets big gun, scratches himself. The players tried to talk to him. Nothing anyone could say could get him to change his mind. I understand that everyone was furious.

The biggest thing about Darryl was that everyone knew he was blessed with such tremendous talent. The word furious is pretty strong. The word disappointed is more appropriate.

Darryl Strawberry

Wally [Backman] said he was "fucking furious."

For him, yes. Wally's every other word is an f bomb. It's just that everyone was upset because Darryl meant so much to the lineup. He was an
intimidating factor at the plate. He made Keith and I better because just
where he hit in the lineup. Keith batted third, I batted fourth, and Darryl
batted fifth. If I didn't knock the runs in, he did.

Darryl was the type of guy, if you looked at his body, it was chiseled
out, and everybody would look at him, and if he dogged it in the outfield, there was disappointment, because they didn't think he was giving
it his all. If he didn't hustle after balls, if there was a lack of intensity and
desire, it was like he would mistakenly hit 35 home runs, or mistakenly
drive in over 100 runs. It was unfair. But there are certain guys who are
blessed with more talent than others, and that was where the part of seri-
ousness came into play, What if this guy really did turn it on? What kind
of stats could he put together? You think about it and say, *My God, this
guy could have been phenomenal.* It's like the years that Vladimir Guerrero
is putting together these last two years, or for that matter the kind of
career Ken Griffey Jr. has had before 30 years of age.

Darryl Strawberry very much could have had the same kind of career. But the disappointment—he would always bugger out of a couple of games here and there, and the thumb thing. We don't know what went on off the field, and now we're hearing more and more that there was a lot of that stuff going on, and it's unfortunately because what he did was take a Hall of Fame career and basically just throw it away.

Did he end up with decent stats? Yeah, you could say they were respectable for the talent he was given, but as far as what he could have accomplished if he really had had the burning desire to play? He said it was the pressures of New York and all. Bullshit. There is *no* pressure from the outside, from the media. Just play. That's all you need to do. Pressure is brought from within, and the only way you avoid that is to just go out and hustle.

I never was close to Darryl, and I'll tell you why. He felt he was a bit of an outcast. I don't know why he brought that onto himself. I've heard different interviews of him saying different things. I remember what happened in that team photo in 1989. He was so upset because he wasn't the highest paid after the year that he had in 1988. He hit over 30 home runs, but Keith and I were still higher paid than he was. Well, that's what brought on the fight. His adamancy over the contract.

Keith Hernandez was the one who was the most vocal about Darryl. He would go to the papers. And Darryl really wanted to be accepted by Keith.

Oh yeah. There was kind of a separation of leadership on that team, because of the things that Keith had been through. Everybody knew about Keith's claim to having done cocaine, especially in 1979, when he won a batting title and was co-MVP with Pops, Willie Stargell. Everyone knew it, and that was the reason Whitey Herzog traded him. And so, you are right, there was an acceptance that Darryl wanted from Keith, but Keith was smart enough not to go with that.

I tried to lead by example and not be the vocal one, but Keith was that way, and he'd come out and say some things. Keith is quick-witted, and I'm not so much in that regard. I wasn't one of those guys who was going to rip anybody. I just didn't feel it was appropriate. Guys would kid me and rip me, but for the most part the guys were pretty good with one another in the clubhouse. There wasn't too much animosity toward one another. There wasn't very much friction, and a lot of it had to do with the fact that we knew we had something special there. We were just go-out-and-play guys. Forget about all this petty bullshit that goes on.

The fans appreciated my style of play because I played hard. That's all. That's all you need to do. I wasn't blessed with the greatest talent, but I made the most out of what I had, and they appreciated all that.

Hey, this guy is going to give that extra, sliding into first base when the play is close.

You realize in the sport you have to play hurt sometimes. I know later on Darryl ended up having surgery. I don't know if it was on his thumb, but it was later. He slid in the outfield, and it turned out he had that game-keeper thumb, the same as what I had.

And 1988 was an off-year for me. I had a bad knee, and I knew I had a bad knee, and I went to Dr. Andrews in the winter of 1988, and I said, "Doc, I really think I need to get this thing cleaned out again."

"No, I think it looks pretty good," he said.

That was before MRIs. I went into the 1989 season, and I had nothing but problems during spring training, and then on May 10 I was scoring a run from third base in Cincinnati on that Astroturf, and the next day my knee blew up. I went on the disabled list. They took all these CCs of fluid out of there, shot me up with cortisone, and I went on the disabled list, came back, tried to catch BP in San Diego after the fifteen-day stint was up, and the thing blew up again.

I went to see Dr. Gambardella, who's an associate of Dr. Jobe, and I said, "If I played for the Dodgers, what would you recommend?"

"I'd have it done," he said.

I flew back to Birmingham, and Dr. Andrews did the scoping. I had eight loose bodies and two synovial cysts in there, and that tells me there is no way that could have accumulated in that short period of time.

"I misdiagnosed you," Dr. Andrews told me.

The Mets lost that pennant in '85 when with only a few games left in the season Davey gave George Foster the take sign, and George missed it, and he grounded out.

That created a problem in the dugout. Everyone was upset about that. George wanted to come through in such a big way. Those who know George—he's a different kind of guy, but you know what, he's a good guy. He really is. That was a mistake on his part. He came to New York with a lot of history of the years he had with Cincinnati, and unfortunately he didn't live up to those expectations.

The game ended when Jeff Lahti got you to fly out.

To right field. That was so disappointing, because I was so hot in the month of September. Jeff Lahti threw it, and I hit a slicer to right center. If I had hit a home run, I would have tied the game. That's what I was trying to do, and I was probably trying too hard. Rather than just try and get on base, I was trying to hit a two-run homer, and all I needed to do was just get on base. That was the reason in 1986 when I came up with two outs in the bottom of the tenth inning, I thought, *A home run is not going to do it here. Just get on base.*

At that time I just felt so grooved at the plate, and I tried to get a little bit extra, and unfortunately Lahti got it in on me, and I flew out to right field.

On July 11, 1986, you faced David Cone and the Braves. Cone had been an Expo, part of that Raines-Dawson group. You hit a three-run home run, and then Cone hit Darryl and there was almost a fight, and then you hit a grand slam. Tell me about that.

That was a special day, especially when you have seven RBIs in your first two at bats, and you're thinking, *My Gosh, is this going to be one of the world days.*

David Palmer was pitching, and I knew how he pitched. [Carter caught him when they were on the Montreal Expos.] Palmer used to throw a cutter that looked like a slider, and he used to start that pitch on the inside, and he'd get a lot of called strikes that way. He had a good curve ball. We called him Palm Ball. His name was Palmer, and he had a change-up that was a palm ball, and yet most of the time he threw that cutter.

When I hit that three-run homer to put us ahead, he then hit Darryl and both benches emptied. It ended up in a little pushing match, and then later we came back, and my grand slam was my way of paying him back for Darryl. At least I hoped that was the way Darryl looked at it. And then Palmer was out of the game, and I had a chance to hit my third homer, I forget who it was against, and I flew out deep to center, but I was in such a groove at that time.

When I hit that first home run I never showed David up. I didn't watch it or anything else, and then he just went after Darryl, and Darryl thought he was throwing at him, and maybe he was, but all in all, that's the game. That's the way it's played. That next guy has to be a little more on your toes.

On August 16, 1986, you broke your thumb. You were playing first base. How scared were you that your season was over?

First of all, I didn't want to go on the disabled list. Dr. Parks examined my thumb, and enough of the ligament was holding it that it wasn't completely torn.

I didn't have my thumb guard in playing first base, and Ozzie Smith ripped a one-hopper to me, and I landed on that thumb. I really thought I had broken it, because I had broken it back in 1976 and had two pins placed in it.

When the inning was over I went into the clubhouse, and it was hurting like crazy. I called over Steve Garland, and I said, "Steve, I think I broke my thumb."

"Let's get Dr. Parks down here," he said.

Dr. Parks came down, and he looked at it.

"Please don't put me on the disabled list," I said.

But there was a meeting of the minds, and Frank Cashen convinced everybody to cast me. I was extremely disappointed.

They didn't say it was fractured, and they didn't say the ligament was torn. They immobilized it for about ten days, then for the next five days I rehabbed so that I wouldn't lose a lot of atrophy and I could come back and play after my tenure on the disabled list was over.

I was re-instated the first part of September, but I had to have my thumb taped the rest of the year. Dr. Parks taped me to hold in my cartilage and hold my thumb together.

I played that way the rest of the season. It was Bob Sykes taking care of me once again, and boy, did I ever take care of him after each year for his taking care of me. The Mets figured that at the end of my five years they had spent so much money on tape keeping me together that maybe it would be more cost effective by letting me go. I'm kidding a little bit with that. That tape is not all that expensive. It took quite a bit to keep me in one piece, but I came back, and I had a decent September, and my breaking my thumb probably cost me the MVP that year. I ended up third.

Schmitty, Mike Schmidt, got first, and Glen Davis was second, and I finished third. I had 20 home runs and 80 RBIs by the end of August, and I ended up with 105 after coming back in September, which tied me with Rusty Staub, but the damage was done, because when the Mets went to the West Coast, it was a long trip, and they ended up 11 and 3, and John Gibbons and Ed Hearn caught during that time, and the team played so well, and so the press jumped on it and said, "This team is so good they can win with or without Carter."

And yet, other people believed that I was the MVP that year, but because I was on the disabled list for those 15 days, it probably cost me that award.

On the flight to Houston for the playoffs, things got a little rowdy.

I know the wives got a little rowdy. There was a craziness of excitement, jubilation, celebration, and I was in the back of the plane, and we were playing cards, and my wife was sitting next to me, and that was the normal thing that we did. But the flight turned out to be a disaster. There was so much damage done to the plane, eight to ten thousand dollars' worth of damage, which we paid out of our paychecks. We had to agree for the Mets to deduct that from our paychecks.

I know we had a meeting about it, and Davey was incensed over it. Frank Cashen mentioned the damage that was done, and then we had our own meeting afterward, and Davey said the best way to reconcile this whole thing is we pay for it.

I'm sucking it up here, because I was as quiet as a field mouse. I was playing cards, and we were having a good time, and I was with my wife. And really I was oblivious to what was going on.

They divided the ten thousand dollars among all the players?

Yup. We all paid. Either we paid without their taking it out of our paycheck or we gave a separate check, something like five hundred dollars. We paid for whatever the damage was.

⌐

For the players, the money was insignificant. What was important was the opportunity for the Mets to win their first World Series since 1969. Their opponent in 1986: the Boston Red Sox in what would become one of the most memorable World Series in baseball history.

CHAPTER EIGHTEEN

GARY CARTER

The Ball Goes through Buckner's Legs

You now have to play the Red Sox in the World Series.

We were picked to win the Series. We lost Game 1 1 to 0 and then we got crushed in game 2 by 9 to 3, and Dwight Evans had a big game and Boston got their heads pretty high thinking they had just beat us twice in our own ballpark, and they were going home.

I'm going to go back one on you too, and I'm going to say that after we lost the first two games in Shea, I think that the turning point in that Series, and this is where I give Davey credit, is when we were flying to Boston, he knew we were tired.

I remember Davey saying, "I know you guys are exhausted. You've come a long way, had a great season. Let's just not lose our aggressiveness and certainly where we're come from all of this. Let's don't lose what our incentive has been."

"I want none of you to come to the ballpark on the day off," he said.

That to me was the turning point, because when my wife and I got to the hotel on the off day, we took a nap, got up, and we had room service—we never left the room. My family was there too, and we never saw them. We stayed in the room the whole time. We watched a movie on TV, and slept in the next day, and I felt refreshed. I really did.

My brother then took me to the ballpark, the first time I had ever been to Fenway. My brother dropped me off. I didn't know which entrance to go in. I didn't know where the clubhouse was. I had to ask around.

But then I got into the clubhouse, and it was, "All right. We're back at it again. This is it guys." And we just came out, and I'll never forget Lenny [Dykstra] leading off the game hitting a home run off Oil Can [Boyd], and that got the spark going again. We were back at it. We crushed Oil Can, so we won Game 3 and we figure, *Ok, we're back on track and we're only one game behind them.* We know how important it is to win Game 4, cause if you fall back 3 to 1, it's almost over at that point.

So we won Game 4, and we were tied. Again, we have new life. And Game 5, really, Bruce Hurst was the best pitcher in the series. And he wins Game 5. He's won both his games.

Dwight Gooden lost the two games he pitched.
I know he didn't have his real good stuff, and I asked Doc, "Were you on drugs then?"

And he said, "No."

That next spring training, on April 1, we found out about the drugs because he took a random test that they give. Two nights before he did the cocaine, and it showed up in his urine, and he thought if one day passes, it wouldn't show up. I guess it stays in your system. So that's where he got caught in 1987.

I said to him, "You were sweating pretty profusely on some very cold nights. Were you doing it?"

He said, "No."

So I don't know what went on. I don't know what went on, Peter, and I can't really say that maybe the cold weather affected him, because I know he didn't like to pitch in the cold. But he was not that effective, and of course when you match us up,

Gary Carter

the Red Sox virtually only had two starters, with Hurst and Clemens, and if you got by them you were going to go pretty deep. With us, we had the four guys—all four of our guys finished in the top ten for the Cy Young Award balloting, but Doc, I don't know, I guess Hurst kind of just out-pitched him. Simple as that.

In game 4 of the 1986 World Series you hit a home run off Al Nipper. You hit a double, and in the eighth inning you hit a home run off Steve Crawford. The Mets won 6 to 2.

The second home run was a breaking ball that I hit not only over the Green Wall, the Monster, but it landed in the parking lot across the street. There's a parking lot on the other side, and someone scrambled and got that ball.

That was, without a doubt, a thrill. It was such a thrill to have gotten my first hit in a World Series. As a kid growing up, I was a huge fan, and even today, after playing 18 years I'm still a fan. I love the game. I played the game with great passion, and when we were growing up, we had the opportunity—back in the seventh and eighth grade—there were a lot of day games, and we would be able to bring our radios, or we would be able to watch it during PE. They'd have the games on.

I remember seeing the Mick. Mickey Mantle was my fave in just about all the World Series history, and of course Yogi Berra had the most hits in World Series history. I was just in such awe, and so when we made it to the World Series, to have been playing, and then I got a hit, and I got a double, and in Game 3 I got four RBIs off Oil Can Boyd, then I came back and had three RBIs in Game 4, and I ended up with nine RBIs and two home runs—a lot of people thought I was the MVP of the Series, and it turned out in Game 7 when Ray Knight hit the three-run homer to clinch it for us, in that same game I was 0 for 4, but I hit a ball to right field, and Wally Backman was on third and Keith was on first, and Dwight Evans came in to try to make a shoestring catch, and I knew it had fallen, but Keith didn't see that, and I got caught between first and second, and that was the difference between me hitting .276 or .310—that one hit—he was thrown out on a force play at second base.

Keith was pissed.

The umpire didn't show him whatever it was. Wally scored on that, and that was my ninth RBI. Ray Knight missed one game in its entirety, and Howard Johnson played in that one game, and Ray wasn't happy about that. He made a big stink about it too.

It was strange, because Ray was our main guy, but I think Davey just decided to change it up a little bit. It might have motivated Ray to do so well in the last couple games. He had a hard-fought at bat against Calvin Schiraldi when he flared that one over Marty Barrett's head.

When I batted in that tenth inning in Game 6 with two outs, everyone thought it was over. I was followed by Kevin Mitchell, who was in the clubhouse half undressed. Keith was in Davey's office drinking a beer. You didn't know about all that, Peter? God yes. See, Wally had led off that tenth inning and fouled out down the left field line, and Keith hit one to left center and he made the second out. Keith then beelined it down to the clubhouse and grabbed a beer and went into Davey's office. He watched it on TV. In the meantime Bob Costas and the NBC gang had the platform and all the plastic up over the Red Sox lockers, and Oil Can Boyd was already in there popping champagne. The whole nine yards.

I got to the plate, and Schiraldi fell behind in the count, and then I fouled one off. Davey gave me the hit sign 2 and 0 and I fouled it off, and the next one I lined into left field.

I just wanted to get on base. All I wanted to do was get on base, and I knew one way or another, I was going to do that. I knew a little bit about Schiraldi because he was with us the year before, and he got called up in September. I knew just that he was gutless, because of the incident that occurred when he was getting lit up in Philadelphia. That was in '85, and this was oh gosh, the middle of September, and I was catching, and we were losing 7 to 6, and I remember Schiraldi looking over to the dugout, and he wanted out of the game.

I walked out to him, got in his face, and I said to him, "Don't you ever give up. I don't care what the score of the game is. I'm out here. Everybody else is out here. Don't you ever give up."

I could see the timidness in his face, and I knew right then and there that if I was ever going to face him in a tight situation, he just wasn't

Kevin Mitchell

going to get me out. I just felt that. He was gutless. He looked like a deer, a scared puppy. And he was.

I didn't think he was capable of closing the door.

After I got my hit, I said to myself, *Hey, we got life here.* My base hit led to Kevin Mitchell's. Mitch was called out of the clubhouse to pinch hit. Mitchell was half undressed in the clubhouse when they called to him. And he comes out, and he's putting himself together, and he throws his batting glove on and goes up to the plate.

Mitch had told Schiraldi one time, "You better not try to throw me a fastball, because you'll never get me out that way." And he throws him a breaking ball, hangs it, and he hits it into left field.

Mitch got his hit, and Ray was next, and I'm giving him encouragement and all, and he battles his way and gets his hit, and I score. Mitchell goes to third, and that's when McNamara made his change—and that's when he also should have brought in Dave Stapleton as Buckner's replacement at first base.

Turns out that Bob Stanley comes in, and throws what they called a wild pitch, but it could have just as easily have been a passed ball. It did something different than what Stanley was accustomed to throwing. He threw a sinker, and it was a riser or a cutter or something like that, and it got by Rich Gedman, and just like in Game 6 in Houston, when we tied it up and went into extra innings, we had new life again, Peter.

We were tied up, and I thought, *This is God's way of saying we have another chance.* Because we were almost out of it. Everybody had basically left the ballpark. The diehards were still there, but Davey had slunched [cq] back into his seat, and everybody thought it was over.

We battled back and came on, and Mookie hit the ball that went through Buckner's legs to score Knight. I knew then, with that tremen-

dous comeback, that we were going to win Game 7. There was no holding us back then.

Davey made a double switch in the middle of Game 6.
He took Strawberry out. And Darryl was pissed about that too. Strawberry sulked, and he went into the clubhouse, didn't stay on the bench,
and as soon as the game was over, he was dressed and he was gone. He
didn't stick around after Game 6. He was gone.

He did finally hit a home run in Game 7, which was good.
I'm telling you, when all those things kind of unfolded as they did, and
us coming back the way we did in Game 6, it was meant to be. It really
was meant to be. Just the way the whole season went. We were involved
in four fights during the regular season.

Bill Robinson, our first base coach, had started one with Rick Rho-
den, because he accused him of cheating, which he did, but nevertheless
that's what happened. But it was a team where we really stood behind
one another. Keith also acknowledges being real cocky. I thought it was
a confidence. I don't think it was cocky, and we won 108 regular season
games. That hasn't been done since the Yankees won 114 and they had a
tremendous year that year. Anything over 100 wins is a great year.

It really was an awesome ballclub.

*Were you aware that Darryl was going through marital hell during the whole
of the World Series?*
No. I had heard some things that were going on, some friends saying
there was fighting going on, but I didn't know it was that severe. I didn't
know—all I remember Darryl ever saying was that Lisa, his first wife, was
a spendaholic. But I can't even imagine that, because Darryl was just as
bad. I didn't know how bad the marriage was going, or what was causing
it or maybe it was Darryl's infidelity. I don't know what it was.

*Between the fifth game and the sixth game she complained that he punched
her in the nose.*
I can't even imagine swinging at a woman. But anyway, I remember that
vaguely. I remember things happening. I didn't remember to what extent.
It's sad. It's very sad.

If it was someone else, he might have confided in the other guys. He might have gotten moral support. It seemed that Darryl would never allow himself to get close to anybody.

And that is the key word to it. You asked, "Did I ever get close to him?" He wouldn't allow me to. I would go to him, and I would share things with him, and of course with my faith and the way I professed it, I don't know if I was a threat to anyone, but I was different. I was a ballpark to hotel guy or ballpark to home guy. I wasn't one of these guys who was looking for a release or something out of the ordinary by going out to these bars or trying to pick up women. That didn't appeal to me.

I was happy at home. I can't understand Darryl coming out and saying he was burying his pain or that he did drugs because he was under so much pressure. Peter, I never could figure that out, so if there was segregation on the ballclub, it was simply because the guys wouldn't ask me, "Do you want to go out and get something to eat?"

I didn't hang around the guys very much, even the pitchers. Maybe some of the younger guys every now and then, but I didn't much.

I asked Doc this last time that we got together about the drugs that were running rampant on the team and he goes, "You would have been amazed."

"No," I said.

"Yeah," he said, "there was quite a bit of that going on." He named some names, and I was clueless. I had no idea.

People would ask me, but I never touched the stuff. I don't know what it's like. Darryl said just that. He said, "People who don't know what it's like will never be able to figure it out."

I don't know if I separated myself being that I was away from that, but the one thing I had was the respect of everyone. I played injured. I came to the ballpark each day and played hard. To them, that's all that really mattered. That's all I ever looked at too, and in Darryl's case, all I wanted him and everybody else to do was give it his all.

I looked at guys with a lot less talent who seriously would go out and play their hearts out. I'd see the way Mookie Wilson or Wally Backman or Rafael Santana played, guys who didn't have near the talent that Darryl had, and there would be days Darryl would go out there and it would look like he wasn't even trying. He'd have good games, but on other days that it would show. That's the unfortunate thing about Darryl's career.

Mookie Wilson

I really believe he could have had a very, very productive and successful career, and maybe make the Hall of Fame. To me, I think he pretty much wasted a lot because of his lack of desire, and when he said he didn't have the desire to live any more, that's heavy stuff. I can't imagine why. He said he's been in a living hell for all these years, but I never saw that. He wasn't a real happy, jovial guy, but I didn't realize he had all these problems. He said the only reason he now has a desire to turn his life around a little bit is for his kids' sake. He has five, two from his first marriage, an illegitimate one, and two others from Sharice.

According to Darryl he was abandoned by his father when he was 13, and he has a hole in his heart.

I lost my mother when I was 12. It was a void in my life also, but you have to move on. You can't blame anyone. You have to grasp ahold of your own life that's been given to you. Anyway, it's sad. It is, and I hope he can get out of it, but I just don't know. He's agreed to have the chemo done again.

Frank Cashen traded Kevin Mitchell, who I thought was incredibly talented, for Kevin McReynolds, a white bread, non-controversial kind of guy. I heard that Kevin had an angry streak.

I'm sure he did. He grew up in the San Diego area where there was a lot of drugs, and there was also gangs. He grew up with a gang. But Peter, to be honest with you, I never saw that stuff. All I saw was his talent on the field, and back then he was a lot thinner. He gained a lot of weight, and he was the National League MVP in 1989, when he hit 49 home runs that year.

I gave Kevin the nickname World, because he could do everything. Here's a guy who was a big guy, and yet he could play shortstop. He could play center. He could play left. He could play right. He could play first. The only thing he might not be able to do was catch. He was multi-talented, and I just can't even imagine what Frank Cashen must have heard or maybe he was pulling down some of the other guys, and so he felt maybe that was the reason he needed to trade him. That's all I can say.

Were you surprised when they made the trade?

Sure. I thought Kevin was in line to be the number one guy in left field. Because he had proven himself. Though he wasn't a regular, he played the whole '86 season with us and played so well. There were times he played a couple of back-to-back games.

The other player Cashen let go was Ray Knight. Cashen hadn't wanted to keep him in 1986. This time he made him a low-ball offer. Both of them were very stubborn. Knight wanted a million. Cashen offered him $800,000. He signed for $500,000 with Baltimore. Ray must have been one of those

Ray Knight

players who affected the tough-guy attitude of the club.

Ray had a great year in 1986. He was very much a part of the reason for our success, but I think that Frank was thinking that Howard Johnson was going to be the incumbent, which he eventually did become, and he did far more than Ray Knight ever thought about doing. Howard was a 30–30 guy two or three times. Howard had over 30 home runs three or four times, so Howard really did come into his own.

You know what? When Ray left the ballclub, I know he was adamant about wanting to get at least $800,000 or a million, but what he really wanted was a two-year deal. Cashen was offering one year, and he low-balled him.

Ray took a two-year deal with Baltimore with less money. He faltered there, went to Detroit, then retired. So maybe Frank saw the writing on the wall that Ray didn't have a whole lot left. It wasn't like we missed a beat with Ray gone, and so that was not the most demoralizing.

I think what hurt us was the Kevin Mitchell trade. Kevin McReynolds had great talent, but my God, he could have cared less about anything else. He'd show up just in enough time to throw his uniform on, go out and take batting practice, come in, and as soon as the game was over, by the time I had packed up all my catcher's gear and come up to the club-house, he was already dressed and ready to leave.

You know how they said that Cool Papa Bell was so fast that if you turned the light out, he'd be in bed before it went out. Kevin McReynolds was that way. Honest to God, I had never seen a guy leave the club-house as quick as him.

What was happening, the front office was breaking up the desires we had for the game. I used to love to hang around and talk baseball, but a lot of these guys couldn't wait to leave and go and do their own thing, especially on the road. They wanted to go out and do stuff, and I wanted to sit and talk baseball. All I was going to do was go back to my room and key down a little bit, and I loved those times.

Those were the best, Peter. I loved those times. I miss those times. I loved to sit with Wally and a couple others and maybe have a beer. I was not a big drinker, but they did have beer in the clubhouse. But what I am saying is that that's the time to do that. You're talking baseball, and you're learning what other guys are doing around the league. I used to follow everybody. I used to watch games on TV, and we'd come into the clubhouse, and we'd want to know what the other team was doing.

In '87 players were beginning to have desires to do other things than really concentrate on what we had. It all started with Doc Gooden having to go to rehab in '87 in April. That was a setback, and then as the season wore on, even though we finished in second, we just didn't have a real good year. We had spurts when we were good, and then spurts when we weren't so good.

Doc's going to rehab was disappointing?

It was disappointing and shocking, because I really didn't think Doc was doing that stuff. I can't even imagine he was being pulled into the group that was doing it. Peter, it was a shock to me. Of course, I was demoralized by it, because Doc was such an integral part of the ballclub, and it set the tone for '87. It really did.

The other part I don't understand. The Mets took the tests, and the Mets got the results, and the Mets blew the whistle on him. What was that all about?

I don't know. That's what Doc told me, and he thought it was out of his system, but he didn't realize the ramifications of it staying in your system for three or four days. I don't know. Maybe the Mets were trying to do something, like you were saying—why did they trade Kevin Mitchell? Why did they do some of the things that they did, where eventually they traded Roger McDowell and Lenny Dykstra. What was that? For Juan Samuel? That did nothing for us.

And I think what it was, Frank Cashen had put this club together. We finally did win in 1986. He must have recognized or noticed some of the things that were going on off the field, and he made this comment, "Teams that win cannot stand pat. You need to make at least one change."

I didn't understand it, but he did make that change with Mitchell for McReynolds in '87. But then we got David Cone, and David Cone was such a bright spot at that time. Davey Johnson said, "Just watch this guy pitch."

I caught him one spring training game, the very first time I caught him, and I thought, *What was Kansas City thinking?*

The reason they traded him, they didn't like his off-the-field shenanigans. He was pulling George Brett down, so they got rid of him. General managers see that other players have a tendency to bring other players down, and so the best way to resolve it is you trade 'em. And that's what happened with Kevin Mitchell. It was unfortunate, because he didn't last very long in San Diego. He was going back home, and he became involved in the gangs once again, and all hell was breaking loose there. But then Roger Craig took him under his wing when he got to San Francisco, and he changed things around. He became a superstar there.

I played in San Francisco in 1990, and because Kevin got the super-star status, all of a sudden there were the two sides, and that's what really upset me. We had a great ballclub. The Giants should have won in 1990. Will Clark and Matt Williams and Robbie Thompson and Jose Uribe and all these guys, and Peter, I mean to tell you, Kevin Mitchell would show up when he wanted to show up. Why? Because he was the MVP the year before.

Darryl Strawberry came back in 1987. Apparently, he had been drinking a great deal, and that his hostility had grown.

It had. We'd go on the buses, and it was like he was constantly angry. Instead of needling with humor and kidding, it was becoming more ma-licious. Guys were recognizing that more and more. I always sat up in the front of the bus. I avoided all that stuff. I wouldn't think about going to the back of the bus. To be honest with you, if Darryl said something and it was pointed towards me, Peter, it just went in one ear and out the other.

Davey Johnson was your manager with the Mets.

When Davey was with the Mets, and for the five years I had the pleasure of playing for him, he just basically let us go out and play. He got ridi-culed at times, but then when the Mets regiment traded away the talent that was there, Davey then became the scapegoat, and then there was a black cloud that hovered over him for a couple of years until he got the job with Cincinnati. He led them to a playoff, and then he got fired because of Ray Knight, and then he goes to Baltimore and does a pretty good job there, and then he gets fired there.

When he lost the job with the Mets, Cashen was bad mouthing him.

And I don't know why. I do know this about Davey, because we had talk-ed about this at one time. He wanted to be a little more hands-on, want-ing to know what was going on, the trades involved, what player he was going to be able to get and at least be involved in the decision-making.

Unfortunately for his sake that never happened, and I feel for him, because I like Davey. I thought he did a great job during my five years in

New York, and hey, we won a World Series in 1986. We should have won in 1988, but I don't think it was his fault. I look back at the turning point in that whole series, and it was Game 4 when we were up 2 to nothing, and Doc Gooden walked Mike Davis, and then allowed the two-run tying home run to Mike Scioscia, and then the Dodgers won in extra innings and that tied the series up.

We win that game, and we win the 1988 league championship series and go on to the World Series again. But I think the Mets management was disappointed because they knew what kind of great ballclub we had, and we only won one world title. I think that might have been a reason Davey got the black cloud a little bit. I don't know. I really don't know.

He won 90 games five years in a row. No one else has ever done that.

Exactly. And then he's let go and Buddy Harrelson takes over for a short period, and he's fired, and now finally they've gotten Bobby Valentine in there, and of course he's led them to the playoffs the last two years.

He's almost gotten fired.

Sure he has.

⌒

In May 2011, Carter suffered from headaches and forgetfulness. Doctors discovered a malignant tumor in his brain. He was told that the tumor was aggressive and that the cancer was inoperable. At the time, Carter was the head baseball coach of Palm Beach Atlantic University. He also was running the Gary Carter Foundation, which aided eight Title I schools in Palm Beach County for students who live in poverty. One goal of the foundation was to fund a reading program for these students.

Carter died on February 16, 2012, at the age of fifty-seven.

To be his friend was an honor.

INDEX

Note: Page numbers in *italics* refer to photographs.